179 - 4/5

14

. 1217847

SAWYER, R.

CASEMENT

13/07/84   £12.50
          .1M

Please renew/return this item by the last date shown.

So that your telephone call is charged at local rate, please call the numbers as set out below:

From Area codes | From the rest of Herts:
01923 or 0203·

Renewals: 01923 47   7

D0504698

CASEMENT

CASEMENT
The Flawed
Hero

Roger Sawyer

ROUTLEDGE & KEGAN PAUL
London, Boston, Melbourne and Henley

First published in 1984
by Routledge & Kegan Paul plc
39 Store Street, London WC1E 7DD, England

9 Park Street, Boston, Mass. 02108, USA

464 St Kilda Road, Melbourne, Victoria 3004, Australia

Broadway House, Newtown Road,
Henley-on-Thames, Oxon RG9 1EN, England

Set in VIP Sabon by Inforum Ltd, Portsmouth
and printed in Great Britain by
Hartnoll Print, Bodmin, Cornwall
© Roger Martyn Sawyer, 1984

Library of Congress Cataloging in Publication Data

Sawyer, Roger, 1931–
Casement, the flawed hero.

Bibliography: p. 178
Includes index.
1. Casement, Roger, Sir, 1864–1916. 2. Ireland—
History—1900–1921.   3. Nationalists—Ireland—Biography.
4. Consuls—Great Britain—Biography.   I. Title.
DA965.C3S29   1984   941.5082'1'0924 [B]   83–21198
British Library CIP data available

ISBN 0–7102–0013–7

To my wife, Diana
and my sons,
Charles and Rupert

CONTENTS

⎯◅○◓○►⎯

PREFACE   ix
ACKNOWLEDGMENTS   xiii

1   Antecedents   1

2   Early life   17

3   British consul   31

4   Consul on leave   42

5   Consul of Great Britain and Ireland   53

6   From consul to consul-general   65

7   The Putumayo: mission for a consul-general
    extraordinary   77

8   Commission of enquiry   87

9   The Putumayo Report   98

10 Ireland and Germany   109

11 Imprisonment and trial   121

12 Diaries and death   135

CONTENTS

APPENDICES

A   Consular functions in Casement's day   149
B   A charitable appeal issued by Consul Casement at
        Santos   156
C   G.B. Shaw to Julius Klein   158
D   Copy of a petition for clemency for Roger Casement   161
     NOTES AND REFERENCES   164
     BIBLIOGRAPHY   178
     INDEX   188

PREFACE

The purpose of the present study is to enlarge on those areas of Casement's life which have been neglected because the necessary sources have remained undiscovered. Biographical works customarily relate their subjects to family background as a matter of normal procedure, but with Casement, although his family circumstances had a special bearing on the development of his peculiar personality and the main motivation of his life – determination to help underprivileged peoples – the understandable attitude of contemporary Unionist Casements has been an inhibiting factor which has deterred research. It has, however, been found that a genealogical approach, taking into consideration Casement's own interest in his origins, especially on his mother's side of the family, can offset this deficiency. This line of investigation has been greatly facilitated by the attitude of Mallow Castle, the family seat of the Jephsons, to whom Casement's mother, Anne Jephson, was related.

In addition to guidance from the late Brigadier Maurice Denham Jephson, which served to reveal the effect of powerful familial influences on Casement, various collections of Casement's letters, all unpublished, some unseen except by their recipients, have come to light, and these serve to give a more complete impression of the man, often at crucial points in his development. Among these have been those to John Morgan which Alfred Noyes purchased just before his death. The collection shows the workings of Casement's mind just as he approached the final decision to commit himself wholly to Irish Nationalism. Another stage in the same process is shown in notes made by Alfred Noyes when confidential letters were temporarily in his possession in 1957. A further valuable letter source has been the texts of a group written to Father Nicholson, the Irish-American priest who endeavoured to enlist recruits for the Irish Brigade. Correspondence between Bernard Shaw and Julius Klein, a former newspaper reporter in Berlin, has also proved fruitful.

While newly discovered letters to friends have provided details which enable one to build up a broader picture of the application of Casement's principles of emancipation to Ireland, the personal recollections of Mrs Florence Patterson, Bulmer Hobson's sister, as expressed in correspondence over a period of six years, have made it possible to assess more fully the important influence of the organization of the *Feis* (or Irish Cultural Festival), in terms of the interaction of key figures in Ulster Nationalism. Other personal recollections came from W.C. Allison and A.E. King, who gave tape-recorded interviews in which they recalled Casement at different stages of his life and, in King's case, corrected some misapprehensions about his frame of mind during the months between capture and execution. An interview with Peter Singleton-Gates, which was also recorded, made it possible to treat the diaries as reliable primary sources, essential guides to an understanding of their author and his actions.

Much more needed to be known of Casement's activities as a consul, that is to say, in addition to his two anti-slavery investigations. In order that this may be seen against its proper background, some attempt has been made to define a consul of the late Victorian and Edwardian periods, and to assess the social milieu in which consuls of the General Service moved. Casement's performance in this field has been largely ignored, partly because of the emphasis which has been placed on the atrocity reports, but mainly because the Foreign Office files in which it is recorded have remained untouched. Researchers have confined themselves to the consuls' despatches to the Foreign Office and have ignored the Consulate to Legation files, presumably because, strictly speaking, the former should contain duplicates of much that appears in the latter. In fact, with regard to Casement's South American postings, this is not the case. While he wrote extensively to his Legation, despatches to London are, in some volumes, comparatively rare. It is also true that little or no attention has been paid to the annual reports which Casement made while at Lorenzo Marques, Santos and Pará. These, far from being mere collections of statistics, tell much of the writer's current attitudes. The majority of the papers needed to complete this part of the study have been located in the Public Record Office, London, or in the National Library of Ireland, Dublin. For an appraisal of the consul off-duty, a number of private sources, for example the Cadbury Papers which were not deposited in the National Library of Ireland, have been useful.

The present work seeks, within the traditional biographical setting, to examine with the help of genealogical detail, perusal of the diaries in manuscript (including the unpublished Letts's Desk Diary of 1911), hitherto undiscovered letters and consular despatches, the growth of Casement's concern for vulnerable groups lacking basic human rights. Part of his interest developed within the British imperial framework, which he was able to modify to suit his humanitarian aims; part involved the renunciation of Empire in increasingly virulent terms. Particularly when seen in terms of familial, religious and political influences, and even, though less obviously, on a physical level, throughout much of his life there appears an interesting parallel between his own divided loyalties and those of his nation.

ACKNOWLEDGMENTS

This study, which has been in preparation for many years, made its initial appearance in a different form as a doctoral thesis, and thanks must be expressed firstly to two members of the History Department of Southampton University. Dr Frank Colson supervised the South American part of my research and I am most grateful to him for his guidance. To Dr Edgar Feuchtwanger fell the onerous task of supervising everything else, and I thank him for all his help, advice and patience, sustained over a long period. In addition my gratitude is expressed to Miss Diana Marshallsay, University of Southampton Librarian, especially for her help with the finer points of citations.

Over the years, both before and during preparation of the thesis, much assistance came from many individuals and public bodies. Now that the time has come for me to express my appreciation, I regret that in some cases my gratitude must be posthumously extended. Among those of my helpers who died before the completion of the MS were Mrs Anne B. Casement, Miss Charlotte Casement, Mr Richard Crossman, Mr Sefton Delmer, Brigadier Maurice D. Jephson, Mr A.E. King, Mr René MacColl, Dr Herbert O. Mackey, Mr Donald McLachlan, Sir Frank Milton, Mrs Alfred Noyes, Mrs Florence Patterson and Mr Peter Singleton-Gates. And I fear that this list is unlikely to be complete; I have not been in touch with several of those whose names appear below since the early days of my enquiries.

I was very fortunate to obtain reminiscences from a number of people who remembered Casement. Some were children at the time, but others had mature contacts with him at crucial periods in his life. Those who helped me with personal information of this sort were: Mr William Charles Allison, Mr John Cadbury, Miss Charlotte Casement, Captain Roger B.N. Hicks, R.N., Miss Consuelo Keevil, Mr A.E. King, Major-General Julius Klein, Mrs Florence Patterson, Sir John Rothenstein and the Reverend Herbert Ward. And there was one other who, for the time being, must remain anonymous. Miss Casement proved to be indispensable when it came to the disentangling of genealogical knots.

Several people have been most generous in allowing me to use and quote from hitherto unpublished documents in their possession. A principal benefactor in this field has been Major-General Klein, to whom I am greatly indebted for his personal testimony and for much material originally given to him to form part of a book of his own, including Casement's letters to Father Nicholson and the Shaw statement. Mr Hugh Noyes made available a veritable treasure trove of material which he inherited from his father, Alfred Noyes, the poet; the letters to John H. Morgan form part of this collection. Mr John Cadbury, in addition to giving his personal recollections of Casement, allowed access to confidential family papers. Mr Oliver Morel, and Mrs R.C. Morel, provided useful information about the period of imprisonment in the Tower of London.

There were others who helped in numerous ways which are difficult to classify. It is probably simplest to list their names in alphabetical order and state that their assistance is none the less appreciated: Mr William H. Allen, the Reverend T.P. Bartley, Mrs Nuala Creagh (Casement's nearest relation in the Irish Republic), Mr James Dearden, Mr and Mrs G. Evans (who subsequently lived in the house which provided Casement's final lodgings in Ebury Street, London), Mrs P. Gellert, Mr Noel Harris, Sister Cecilia Kavanagh, Professor Roger McHugh, Mr Patrick MacNamee, Sir Philip Margetson, Mrs Marie Martin, Mrs W.G. Martin, the Reverend J. Murray, Mr R. O'Donohue, Mrs Eva Schofield, Mr C. Taylor and Mr William H. Williams.

Mr and Mrs J.E. King are thanked for hospitality over and above the call of duty. Their co-operation made possible the tape-recording of Mr King's father's moving recollections of the Tower imprisonment. Another whose memories are safely recorded for posterity was Mr Singleton-Gates, who opened the door to essential aspects of the Casement history for practically every investigator and was a man of conspicuous generosity.

Permission to quote from *An Anglo-Irish Miscellany* was kindly given by Commander M.C.M. Jephson, of Mallow Castle. Various organizations and public bodies deserve thanks. The most helpful independent organization, and one close to Casement's heart (and my own), was the Anti-Slavery Society, whose secretary (retired 1980), Colonel J.R.P. Montgomery, and assistant secretary, Mrs J. Alexander-Sinclair, gave moral and material support. Inevitably the most useful public archives were those of the National Library of Ireland, where the director – since retired – Dr R.J. Hayes, went out of his way to make things congenial for me, and the Public Record Office, London, where the efficient staff gave much assistance. At the Foreign and Commonwealth Office Library Mrs M.A. Cousins was a never-failing source of significant detail. Formerly secret papers were used by kind permission of the Resident Governor of HM Tower of London and much help was received from the staffs of the British Library of Political and Economic Science (London School of Economics), the British Museum, the Ministry of Defence, the National Register of Archives, the New York Police Department (Central Records Division), Rhodes House, the Society of Genealogists and the Isle of Wight County Library (Bembridge Branch), where the librarians – Mrs Mary Cullimore, Mr Alan Philips and Mr Adrian Wills – have never yet failed to conjure up the most impossibly obscure requests.

For permission to publish Shaw's views on Casement, as expressed to Julius Klein in 1934, acknowledgment is made to the Society of Authors on behalf of the Bernard Shaw Estate, the Trustees of the British Museum, the Governors and Guardians of the National Gallery of Ireland and the Royal Academy of Dramatic Art. Quotations from W.B. Yeats's poems 'The Ghost of Roger Casement' and 'Roger Casement' are made by permission of Michael B. Yeats, Anne Yeats, Macmillan London Ltd and Macmillan Publishing: copyright 1940 by Georgie Yeats, renewed 1968 by Berthe Georgie Yeats, Michael Butler Yeats and Anne Yeats (from *Collected Poems* of W.B. Yeats); and copyright 1957 by Macmillan Publishing Co., Inc. (from *The Variorum Edition of the Poems of W.B. Yeats*, edited by Peter Allt and Russell K. Alspach).

Finally, I must thank the Secretary of State for Home Affairs for granting me permission to examine the Casement Diaries.

CHAPTER 1

ANTECEDENTS

It was only fitting that a man of ambivalence should be born on the edge of Kingstown, a place which, under the Irish Free State Government, was to have its Royalist label changed to Dun Laoghaire, a name of separatist significance. And other aspects of the birth of Roger David Casement on 1 September 1864, have, with hindsight, appropriate ambiguities. Though a son of the landed gentry, he was born in a comparatively humble dwelling, by modern standards scarcely adequate for a family of six, by the standards of the Ascendancy likely to relegate its inhabitants to the category of poor relations. His father was a Protestant, his mother a Catholic; not a unique combination by any means, but there were, in the background of this particular union, factors which were to mark the last born for life, one might say for death.

By the time of Roger David's death in 1916 he had passed through many shades of ambivalence: familial, physical, religious and political, and in all of these areas, even the physical, he seemed to reflect in an unusual way the problems of identity suffered by Ireland as a whole. Indeed, the parallels between the nation and the man are so strong that it is tempting to portray his life story as an analogue of Ireland's history; that would be far too neat and tidy, but it remains true that in a remarkable number of ways Casement was Ireland in microcosm. The physical comparison is the least comfortable of the parallels to maintain, though Casement's proclivities do give an example of how the priestly tradition brought to the Irish laity a strange attitude to sexual matters and in one way, though only one way, Casement echoed the contemporary Catholic adulation of celibacy. In Ireland, even now, except among some of the young and a comparatively *avant-garde* type of Dubliner, a patriot can be celibate or heterosexual (provided he does not go as far as Parnell did); no other private inclination is open to him. In Casement's time the climate of opinion in this sphere was certainly no less oppressive, and yet, as can be seen simply by consulting his own diaries, opportunities for the sexual

1

minority were widespread. In his far from celibate practices he satisfied his yearnings with partners who, in the main, came from the lowest orders of society. Putting to one side the legal implications of their acts, their main risk was in contravening the rules of their church, his was in going against the social conventions of his class.

The religious parallel between Roger David and his chosen nation is less difficult to sustain. Just as the nation was ruled mainly by members of the Church of Ireland and its sister church, so Casement was dominated by Protestants of a Puritan tradition. The nation had, as it were, embraced its Catholicism by stealth; the man was to be secretly baptized a Catholic when on holiday in North Wales. The Catholic majority had periods of acceptance of its subservient role in the nation and Casement, in his early years, was to play to the full the part which was expected of him as a member of the Ascendancy. In politics, too, the similarities are striking: Casement was as divided as Ireland. Although there were many different schools of thought about the degree of independence, if any, which was desirable, the main division at the time of the dawn of the future separatist's political awareness was between the Home Ruler and the Unionist. When he began to serve the queen in Africa he was outwardly a true imperialist and his early career showed that he was, if anything, too orthodox to be true, despite the fact that soon after leaving school, he had shown an interest in Nationalist heroes; he seemed to find no difficulty in being both an Irishman and an imperialist, a combination which would have been normal enough were it not for the eventual development of his Irishness into something virulently anti-Empire.

In Antrim, where he spent much of his youth, there was a less definite split between Home Rulers and Unionists than might be observed in other parts of Ulster, or Ireland as a whole; the seeds of Ulster Protestant separatism were to be found in some of the great houses which, by tradition, were Unionist strongholds. It was a politically ambivalent environment and it played its part in moving the man from one side of his heritage to another. Whilst it might be argued that elsewhere in Ireland the under-privileged members of the populace were soon to mistake the social revolution which was going on in one form or another throughout much of the United Kingdom for a conflict between races, in Antrim there were factors at work which were positively pro-Irish without being necessarily anti-English. And Casement's social comings and goings were to expose him from time to time to different sides of the national dilemmas. Had he grown up in almost any other county, he would have been conditioned more specifically by a more definite climate of opinion around him. As it was, he was poised between national political alternatives during the period before he became politically aware – and he was to return to Antrim during the crucial year of his political development.

Unlike England, which had absorbed its conquerors, Ireland had resisted integration with the foe throughout the centuries, and the religion of Rome served to confirm Ireland as a nation apart; a nation in bondage, but a nation none the less. This alone would have been sufficient to give Ireland a very definite sense of identity, and a unity reinforced by persecution, but the truth of the matter was much more complex. Parts of Ireland did become anglicized in outlook, and there was always a distinct Catholic tradition of loyalty to the Crown. Also, there was much more intermarriage than is generally admitted. Above all, though, there was the cumulative effect of the number of centuries during which, for better or for worse, the fortunes of the nations were interwoven. During the latter part of this relationship, principally after the Act of Union, any Irishman of ambition who did not simply emigrate and perhaps disappear altogether in the New World, had to work his way up one of the career ladders of the United Kingdom. On his way up, although he might cherish sentimental feelings about his ancestry, if he were to succeed he had to accept the values of the race which had dominated his ancestors. Even if he were to cling with some determination to the idea that he was Irish, not English, it was much harder for his children, particularly as their schooling was almost certainly English, wherever it took place, to know precisely where they stood. And in the final reckoning, was the idea of United Kingdom citizenship such a bad one anyway? The answer to this question obviously varied from one period of history to another. What did not vary so much was that, whenever it was demonstrably true that Ireland was the exploited or neglected partner in the union, some Irishmen who had been content to accept the *status quo* began to feel uneasy about their identity.

It could be said that while many Irishmen were exposed to influences which could create divided loyalties, they did not become, like Casement, men whose later careers involved living a life in the service of a despised monarch, men whose opinions were apparently self-contradictory, and who were driven to commit an act of treason which was, at the same time, a patriotic sacrifice. The reasons for Casement's deviation from the norm lie in the one area in which he is not to be seen as Ireland in microcosm: the familial. Here is a concentration of exceptions which proves the rule. Whatever their subsequent intellectual adjustments, most Irishmen started life within the framework of a fairly straightforward family tradition; they were Catholic or Protestant, which usually, but not always, meant poor or rich; or, more rarely, they were the products of mixed marriages. Then, of course, there were the class differences, more easily discernible to English eyes on the Protestant side of the religious divide; and there were inevitable subdivisions of religion, class and occupation among all sections of the people. But with Casement the family background was uniquely arranged to mould a man especially subject to the forces of disunity. It was not

3

merely that his mother was a Catholic entering a Protestant stronghold, though bearing in mind the social level at which it occurred that might have been difficult enough. In this case the Catholic came, not from obscurity or from one of the Catholic landed families, but from a Protestant family which enjoyed the sort of illustriousness to which the Casements could only aspire.

The source of Casement's ambivalence, and he seemed to sense this himself, lay in the bringing together of two family traditions which had their superficial resemblances but were, in important ways, alien. Considered with the early death, first of his mother and then his father, Roger David's genealogy illuminates some of the ambiguities of his life. While the circumstances surrounding the loss of both parents were such as to point to a partial explanation of his sexual problems, study of his genealogy, or the contrasting genealogies of his mother and father, throws light on the different influences which led firstly to his rejection of a certain type of Protestantism associated with the repression of those of his mother's religious persuasion, eventually to his own religious conversion; and with these spiritual changes went a corresponding alteration of political conviction. It is a fruitful region for enquiry, and yet Casement's concern about his antecedents has been virtually ignored because of the difficulties presented by the genealogical evidence recorded in Burke's *Landed Gentry*. His principal aim in this field was to construct a genealogical plan which would take into account his mother's antecedents and the most profitable method of solving the problems of his origins is to follow his lead. He evidently felt that to know himself he had to know more about his forebears and it was his own probings in this area which gave rise to the most useful genealogical evidence which has so far come to light.

The best example of Casement's interest in his origins is contained in a letter which he wrote at the age of thirty-one to Miss Louisa Jephson-Norreys. All that he had to encourage him in his choice of correspondent was the knowledge that his mother's maiden name was Jephson. He had met Miss Jephson-Norreys in a hotel in Las Palmas in 1892, on his way out to the Oil Rivers Protectorate (Nigeria). They had discussed possible family connections and, three years later, when on leave from the Foreign Office, shortly before his first consular appointment, he wrote to her saying that he was 'anxious to look up' his mother's family history:[1]

I should wish to establish my mother's connections with the Jephsons so often mentioned in Irish history if possible. She died when I was quite a child and I only know she spoke of being related to Jephsons of Mallow, in my hearing, when a boy and since her death I never met with anyone whom I might make enquiry from . . .

4

if you could help me with any book or papers I should be most grateful. . . .

As far as I know my mother's father was James (or John) Jephson, and he died somewhere near Dublin from a fall from his horse when hunting about 1840. He lived in the County of Dublin – and I *think*, but here I am groping in the mists of early recollections – that he was the son of a Lorenzo Jephson of Tipperary County. One of them I believe married a Martin of County Galway – my grandfather James Jephson's mother I think was a Miss Martin.

Of course I know the account Burke gives of the Jephsons – but I am in hopes you might be able to supply me with some more extended information which would enable me to ascertain exactly the descent of my grandfather from the Jephsons who came to Ireland in Queen Elizabeth's reign. I have no doubt of his descent from them – but the occasional remarks of a long-dead mother are not sufficient warrant for my considering it sufficiently well established.

The letter suggests several lines of enquiry; it also reveals an attitude of mind. A long postscript indicates a more than superficial interest in the matter. In it he tells how he discovered that in the time of King James's Catholic parliament two Jephsons were attainted of treason under the act of 1688. They were found guilty and lost their estates for having joined the Prince of Orange. He then returns to his quest and restates it in more precise terms: what he wishes to discover is 'from what offshoot – and *when* my grandfather's branch of the Jephsons of Mallow came'. The records and historical works he has consulted mention only one separate branch, the Mounteney Jephsons, other, that is, than those members of the family who migrated to England in the early nineteenth century. But his mother's father, he believes, was 'a typical Irishman' and a man of property; in all probability, therefore, he was descended from the younger son of an early Mallow Jephson.

Casement had already made enquiries of one of the 'English' Jephsons who was in the Foreign Service with him in Africa. This man, a retired naval officer, Sir Alfred Jephson,[2] gave him no encouragement whatsoever, for what one can only assume was a personal dislike of his colleague's unwelcome familiarity. Knowledge of the Mounteney Jephsons, mentioned in the above letter, will have come, at least in part, from the meetings which he had had with A.J. Mounteney Jephson in the Congo in 1887. Casement was with the Sanford Expedition, Mounteney Jephson with Stanley's Emin Pasha Relief Expedition, and three chance meetings are recorded in Mounteney Jephson's diary.[3] On each occasion they dined together (Casement was travelling in comparative luxury) and there was plenty of opportunity for discussion: 'Casement came up in the afternoon. . . . We sat outside the tents smoking and talking till eleven o'clock.'[4]

The letter to Louisa Jephson-Norreys was written at Magherintemple, the Casement family seat, near Ballycastle, County Antrim, and the reply is not extant. A recent incumbent, Mrs Anne B. Casement,[5] commented that her late husband 'threw away everything connected with R.D.' He had 'suffered so much from R.D. publicity during World War I.'[6] Fortunately, however, Miss Jephson-Norreys enclosed a genealogical plan[7] which Casement returned and which has been preserved. It had been drawn up only the previous year by the Hon. Emily Ward, a step-daughter of Lady Bangor, to show similar links between Lady Bangor's family and the Jephson and Norreys families: accompanying correspondence suggests that it was prepared in response to a similar quest to Casement's. His letter of thanks is also extant and makes helpful allusions to the lost Jephson-Norreys reply.

Information about Dublin Jephsons raised Casement's hopes about establishing a definite line of descent. Miss Jephson-Norreys had described them as 'dissipated, reckless and brave' and encouraged by the terms of her response he admitted that he believed that his mother's father had broken his neck, 'as the result of a wager that he would jump the Grand Canal on his horse'.[8] He had substituted the idea of his grandfather being killed while hunting, as it would have been a more respectable way of coming to grief – and he added that the family property certainly went in an irresponsible way. But the Dublin line of enquiry did not bring positive results. Most Jephsons will have had a Dublin *pied-à-terre* and their temporary migrations will only have confused matters. The line of descent traced below, however, did culminate in at least one member of the appropriate branch of the family taking up permanent residence in Dublin (though not under the name Jephson) and present-day Jephsons of Mallow have 'an idea that Casement's mother . . . was a music teacher in Dublin, but chapter and verse for this has not been traced'.[9]

Enquiries addressed to (the late) Brigadier Maurice D. Jephson, family archivist and, until recently, head of the family at Mallow Castle, revealed that he had made every effort to trace the connection with Casement's mother, without success. He knew that she was not of the direct line, which is reliably authenticated since the reign of Henry VIII, and was confused by Casement's statement that his mother's father was the son of Lorenzo Jephson of County Tipperary, because these Jephsons died out in the male line in about 1770; a son-in-law, who inherited the property, changed his name from Hickie (ey)[10] to Jephson. Nevertheless, by piecing together several accounts, it is possible to develop the Hon. Emily Ward's genealogical plan (or 'Tree') to show a reliable connection with Anne Casement, née Jephson.

The relevant section of the plan is reproduced below:

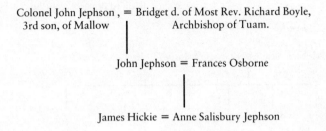

Colonel John Jephson , = Bridget d. of Most Rev. Richard Boyle,
3rd son, of Mallow   Archbishop of Tuam.

John Jephson = Frances Osborne

James Hickie = Anne Salisbury Jephson

No dates were given.

This line of Jephsons settled in Carrick-on-Suir in Carrick House, which still exists as a block of flats. Their badly kept records have provided several genealogists with problems; nevertheless there is no doubt that John Jephson (born 1650) had two sons and two daughters by Frances, née Osborne. The two sons did, in fact, die without heirs and the direct line therefore became extinct. A James Hickie married the first daughter, Anne, and they had a son, Laurence or Lorenzo Hickie, whose dates are known: 1773–1820. Laurence Hickie changed his name to Jephson[11] and married Martha, daughter of the first Lord Dunalley. In 1811 their son Lorenzo Henry was born and, although his dates would have been right, it is unlikely, on the evidence of Casement's letter, that he was Anne Jephson's father. Brigadier Jephson felt that she must have been born in the 1830s, and he was right. It therefore seems most likely that there was a second son of the union between Laurence Hickie and Martha, the James or John mentioned by Casement. If we postulate his date of birth as 1812 and allow a generation interval of roughly a quarter of a century, we arrive at a hypothetical decade of birth for Anne Jephson: the 1830s, which agrees with her known date of birth, 1834. This gives an extension of Emily Ward's genealogical plan (see page 8).

Casement continued his letter of 1 June 1895 (p. 4, above) with a remark that one of the Jephsons of Tipperary, by which he must have meant the Carrick-on-Suir branch, had, he believed, 'married a Martin of County Galway – my grandfather James Jephson's mother I think was a Miss Martin'.[12] A Dunalley country residence was, and is, in County Galway, so the 'mists of early recollections' could have concealed 'Martha' behind 'Martin'. Unfortunately a cross-check with the present Lord Dunalley, principally in an attempt to locate proof of Martha having had a second son, drew a blank: 'All our family records were burned in the "Troubles" of 1922.'[13] (Were it not for the wholesale destruction of records during the Civil War, there should have been no problem at all.) But there are other

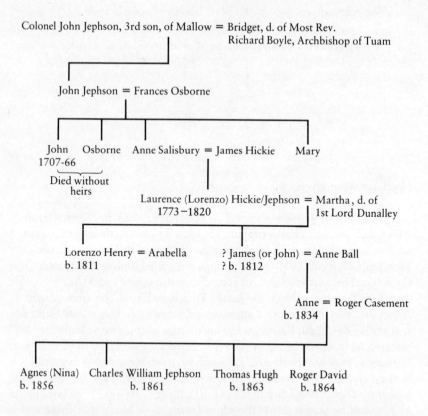

Colonel John Jephson, 3rd son, of Mallow = Bridget, d. of Most Rev.
Richard Boyle, Archbishop of Tuam

John Jephson = Frances Osborne

John   Osborne   Anne Salisbury = James Hickie   Mary
1707-66

Died without
heirs

Laurence (Lorenzo) Hickie/Jephson = Martha, d. of
1773–1820   1st Lord Dunalley

Lorenzo Henry = Arabella   ? James (or John) = Anne Ball
b. 1811   ? b. 1812

Anne = Roger Casement
b. 1834

Agnes (Nina) Charles William Jephson   Thomas Hugh   Roger David
b. 1856   b. 1861   b. 1863   b. 1864

attractions of the Laurence Hickie line of descent; the alternation between the English form of the name Laurence and the Church Latin form 'Lorenzo', carried over two generations, certainly suggests that the Hickie line was Roman Catholic, and may explain their gradual drift from the other Jephsons.

The Catholic Anne Jephson met Casement's father, also named 'Roger', in Paris, and accepted the proposal of marriage from a member of a family known to be 'Black Protestants', defined by L.G. Redmond-Howard as 'those members of the Church of Ireland and of the various dissenting churches who regard Roman Catholics as pagans and idolators, and who think that their duty in Ireland should always be the old role of Zion in captivity, of hewers of wood and drawers of water.'[14] Circumstantial evidence suggests that the marriage was motivated by love and nothing else. Roger Senior would have heard of the Jephsons; he would, however, have derived no appreciable material benefit from marrying into the Carrick-on-Suir branch of the family; nor would the discovery that Anne was a Roman Catholic have enhanced the match, except to the extent that she was forbidden fruit. It might have been difficult enough if she had come from one of the recognized Catholic families of Ireland, had been a Redmond, for instance; as it was, the implicit contradiction between her name and her faith must have generated a noticeable degree of tension when she first entered the drawing room of Magherintemple House. The strain on so young a woman will not have been lessened by the likelihood that the religious aspect of her antecedents will almost certainly have coloured her emotional attitude to her own Ascendancy origins, as well as the family of her husband.

It was only natural that Casement's main concern, when it came to tracing his ancestry, should have been to put the greater emphasis on the maternal line; he was orphaned at an impressionable age, and his relationship with the family of his father was periodically placed under strain for a number of reasons outside his control, until eventually it was severed altogether, by events very much of his own creation. Nevertheless, at least until the post-Congo period of his life, he was aware of, and often took a pride in, being a Casement. As far as his own father was concerned, that pride never left him.

Although the various editions of Burke's *Landed Gentry* and *Irish Landed Gentry* give what appears to be a thorough treatment of the Casement family, they do not mention him, his father or his grandfather.[15] Whether or not Roger Casement was aware of this, it is difficult to say. There are reasonable causes for ignorance in this area: one, the name 'Roger' is deceptively placed in the genealogy, and, two, what first hand evidence there is shows that his interest, on the paternal side (apart from that shown in his father's life and career) was directed towards his ancient origins. In his approach to genealogy he behaved as though basically interested in those elements of his antecedents which were furthest from the 'Cold North', as he called it when writing to Miss Jephson-Norreys. An entry on the fly-leaf of the 1903 diary,[16] shows his awareness of the old Norse form of the family name: Mac Asmundr. And here he was on ground which, only recently, has been shown to be reliable.

According to Burke the Casements were an old Manx family, 'having originally been of French extraction'; the name was believed to have come from 'Caissement'. A conflicting tradition of origin, distinct from that of the last invaders of Ireland, appealed to Roger Casement; Norsemen may have been comparatively savage, but they lent colour to his claim that he was descended from 'Manx Gaelic speakers all'.[17] The Casement family in general, and indeed other families of standing in the Isle of Man, preferred it to be accepted that their ancestors were Normans rather than pirates; in the quest for respectable French origins, however, only one case – the Lamothes – was satisfactorily authenticated.

The Manx period is well substantiated. Several Casements are still in

9

residence there and the most outstanding relic of a Victorian Manx Casement is the Laxey Wheel, known as 'Lady Isabella', described locally, but no longer accurately, as 'The World's Greatest Waterwheel'; this was constructed under the direction of Robert Casement (1815–92) and completed in September, 1854, ten years before Roger Casement's birth.

Testamentary entries in the Rolls Office show Casements, Caismeens and Caisments until one reaches the early seventeenth century; earlier forms of the name, Casmyn and Mac Casmund, go back as far as 1417. Roger Casement, when he signed himself 'R. Mac Asmunde', was using the form nearest to the Norse personal name Mac Asmundr, which meant 'fee of the gods'. Mundr was a dowry in reverse: a sum paid by the bridegroom for the bride. And this signature was not merely confided to his diary: the vice-consul at Rio de Janeiro had to pass on a postal item addressed to 'Mr Mac-Asmund, British Consul-General'.[18]

In the early part of the eighteenth century, in common with other Protestant families, the direct line of Casements migrated to Ulster and settled an estate in County Antrim. The first recorded Ulster Casement was Hugh, who died in 1797. Only two of his sons are recorded in Burke: George, who became a surgeon in the Royal Navy, and Roger, the first of several Ulster Casements to bear this name. At this stage the nineteenth-century custom of erecting elaborate memorial tombstones with detailed inscriptions enables one to check the extent to which Burke is accurate and complete.[19] The accuracy here is confirmed; it is the lack of completeness, understandably forced by editorial considerations, which has created difficulties. On Hugh's tombstone in Ballinderry the date agrees, his widow's death is recorded and, in addition to a useful allusion to India and a grandson, details are given of four sons. These carved details are all the more valuable as civil registration of births and deaths (and Roman Catholic marriages) did not begin until 1 January 1864; Protestant marriage registration had dated from 1 April 1845.

At two points in the genealogy a confusion of generations has occurred. Roger, Hugh's second son, married twice; firstly, Catherine Cosnahan, daughter of an Isle of Man resident, secondly, Margaret M'Quilty. This was one area of error; a more difficult confusion arose in the next generation. But, despite these genealogical hazards, it is possible to follow the line through and show that Hugh's second son, Roger, was Roger David's great grandfather; Catherine, née Cosnahan, was the great grandmother. Miss Charlotte Casement, herself descended from Roger David's great-grandfather, by his second wife, writes: 'I cannot remember which son of Roger and Catherine Cosnahan was R.D.'s grandfather . . . Roger . . . had twelve children by his first wife, some dying in infancy, and eight by his second.'[20] And only two of the twelve are listed in Burke. This was the second main area of difficulty: not only was Roger David's grandfather, Hugh, a prosperous ship-owner, hidden behind the common genealogical phrase 'with other issue', but there was another Hugh, son of George the surgeon, by his second wife, in the same generation. This Hugh appears in Burke and has been a major stumbling block for those who have tried to disentangle the line of descent. It is, however, possible to make a clear distinction between the two Hughs by means of a paper in the Public Record Office.[21] Grandfather Hugh was writing to Lieutenant-General Fitzroy Somerset in order to obtain a cornetcy in an Indian regiment for his son, Roger: 'I feel most anxious to have his commission expedited, and the more so because my cousin, General Sir William Casement, residing in Calcutta, could then forward his views considerably.' Sir William was George's second son by his first wife and could only have been referred to as a cousin by Hugh, son of Roger. Although 'cousin' is a loose term, it cannot have been used by half-brothers; there is therefore no more doubt about which Hugh was Roger David's grandfather.

In the last stanza of his poem *The Ghost of Roger Casement*, W.B. Yeats, a man of not entirely dissimilar background and ideas, wrote:

I poked about a village church
And found his family tomb
And copied out what I could read
In that religious gloom
Found many a famous man there;
But fame and virtue rot . . .

But the fame of the famous Casements, as well as being temporary, was pale compared to that of a substantial proportion of Irish landed gentry. As a close look at the family tree reveals, they did not belong to the highest stratum of the Ascendancy. Compared to the Jephsons, they were of humbler, though scarcely humble, Manx stock and had no visible aristocratic connections. However, what they lacked in lineage they endeavoured to make up for in distinctions achieved in the army, the navy, the civil service, the law and the higher levels of trade. At home, Julius Casement, MA, JP, High Sheriff, rose highest in civilian achievement; abroad, Major-General Sir William Casement, KCB marked the apex of Casement military and political achievement. But these men were exceptions; average attainment was nearer the middle rung of the chosen ladder. It was the army which inspired the dominant Casement tradition throughout the nineteenth century; as the twentieth century began the emphasis shifted to the navy. Like the Jephsons, the Casements were fundamentally Unionist, though to them it was mainly a question of tribal loyalty. The Jephsons, from their higher vantage point, were able to embrace a less narrow Unionism; their involvement was often at a parliamentary level and they found it in their hearts to pioneer such causes as Catholic emancipation.[22]

Thus two very distinct strains were united in Roger Casement and his siblings; on the one hand there was a known, if not wholly understood, link with a family which, according to an Ulster King-at-Arms, was 'entitled to forty-eight quarterings of the most illustrious families of England', which 'can boast of descent from the Royal House of Plantagenet in the legitimate line, as well as from Strongbow himself',[23] on the other, landed gentry: sometimes distinguished, often owners of an impressive number of acres, but also conditioned by aspects of their origins to a sad kind of social marginality. The label 'Black Protestant' tended to be reserved for this lower level of the Ascendancy, where there was a greater need to be clearly separated from the lower, mainly Roman Catholic, levels of the common populace.

From where the young Roger David Casement stood, however, the obvious heroes, at first, were Casements; and the principal hero, for more than the usual reasons, was his father. Roger Senior was the one Casement in whom, in later life, when so many early attitudes and convictions had been renounced, Roger David could still believe. Whilst Roger David was the last of four children, his father was an eldest son, and there were other areas in which opposites prevailed: Hugh Casement, a city-dweller in a port especially renowned for profitable shipping enterprises, was sufficiently wealthy to send his son on the Grand Tour. The experience kindled an interest in travel which contributed to later successes and failures; in the end it amounted to a rootlessness only too obviously passed on to all his children. The Grand Tour was immediately followed by a wish to pursue an army career and his father's wealth again made everything possible, without delay. A cornetcy was purchased in the Third Light Dragoons in India, at the unusually high price of £840, and the fortunate son was carried to his regiment in one of his father's own ships, the SS *John Bull*.

Fathers traditionally lay special favour on the first-born son and Hugh Casement was hardly an exception in hoping that his own son's interest would be forwarded by an influential relative. The way was paved for Roger Senior to become what is commonly supposed to be a typical son of the Empire and superficially he followed that pattern; he fought Afghans, he fought Sikhs and he became a lieutenant. Nevertheless, a change of heart did occur during his eight years in India, and events soon followed which went a long way towards justifying Roger David's opinion that his father had 'an Irishman's innate sympathy with the oppressed and enmity towards the oppressor'.[24] On 21 August 1848 he wrote to his commanding officer, Major Yerbury, asking him to submit to the commander-in-chief a request that he might retire from the army by selling his commission. He promised to pay the purchaser's passage to India, and a

Cornet Chaplin replaced him on 2 November, at the comparatively low price of £350.

In 1848 Casement was fighting Sikhs; in 1849 he was making every attempt to fight Austrians. The difference which his son, not unreasonably, chose to see, was between helping imperialism to put down patriots, and helping patriots to establish the independence of their (small) nation. The account of Casement and Kossuth has been told by Roger David in the *United Irishman*[25] and by Lajos Kossuth in his memoirs;[26] the two accounts agree, except that Kossuth believed that his saviour was a typical Englishman.

There can be little doubt that Casement Senior's Hungarian activities were motivated by altruism and some, perhaps loosely formulated, form of democratic principle; and, as he went directly from oppressing Sikhs to freeing Hungarians, an element of renunciation of the former activity in particular (an aspect of imperialism in general) is implicit in the sudden change of direction. If the term 'eccentric' means anything, his later life revealed that he was one; as is common, however, there was a measure of consistency behind the eccentric's apparently bizarre behaviour.

The background to the Austro-Hungarian (and Turkish) situation was seen by Roger David Casement in over-simplified terms; but parallels with the British–Irish (and German) relationships of sixty-five years later are tempting, and are also valid, in so far as they actually influenced the formulation of nationalist policy and illuminate the influence of the matter on the younger Casement's development as an Irish separatist. It was not a coincidence that the founder of the *United Irishman*, Arthur Griffith, had published in 1904 (the year preceding Roger David's article about his father), a series of articles about Kossuth's movement; and Hungarian policies, ranging from refusal to send representatives to the imperial parliament in Vienna to the concept of dual monarchy, subsequently had great influence on the development of Sinn Fein. What to the IRB were the nuclei of means to an end, had to Roger Casement a special personal appeal. He remembered hearing his father's first hand description of the crucial part he played in helping Kossuth to achieve Hungarian independence from Austrian rule; he had arrived at rebel headquarters and offered his help at a stage when the Hungarians had just sustained a major defeat, and was seemingly unaware of the recent outcome of events, although, when he joined them, the 5,000 remaining rebels were in Widdin, where they petitioned the Turkish Government for sanctuary. Kossuth was faced with the prospect that Austrian pressure would eventually force the Turks to hand over the Hungarians in their midst, and concluded that only British intervention would save them. It was suggested that Casement might be their courier and he agreed. He rode across Europe and took a letter from Kossuth quite literally to Palmerston's dinner table. It was a

13

feat which deserved far wider recognition than it received and it achieved its purpose. England did intervene and the rebels were saved. A small feature of Casement's deed, and one which appealed to his son, was that Kossuth had not learned his rescuer's name. Later, however, when Kossuth was travelling in America, his train was delayed and he appeared at the window for the benefit of an appreciative crowd. As the train which had caused the delay slowly passed, an arm extended from one of its windows and handed him a card. On it was printed *Mr. Roger Casement* and there was a pencilled message: 'I gave Palmerston the letter from Widdin.' Never again was there any contact between the two men, though Kossuth eventually wrote a grateful description of Casement's part in his life.[27] Having served his useful purpose, Roger Senior had retired discreetly from the scene – the calling card episode was the only sequel. Self-effacement of this sort was an aspect of his father's personality which Roger David did not emulate, except in the field of charitable donations. In courage and determination, though, he was to outshine the paternal example; indifference to personal safety became almost a hallmark of his performance in the Congo, the Putumayo and the pursuit of the Irish cause. Throughout his consular career he continued to take an interest in Kossuth, whose biography he kept on a shelf in the consulate-general in Rio de Janeiro, where its presence gave great offence to the British Minister, Sir William Haggard.

The errand of mercy had the elements of a legend – a Paul Revere legend – in it, and it was not surprising that it made its mark on the next generation. It necessarily sprang from the part of his father's life with which Roger David had had no contact and will have been none the less effective for that. The part of life which they spent together would be more difficult to idealize, without some predisposition to do so; and yet Casement, a prolific writer of indiscretions, never implied that there was any parental neglect. He was cool about Magherintemple in his 1903 diary, but one feels that such feelings only echoed those of his parents.

The chance contact with Kossuth occurred during a tour of North America, which followed soon after the Palmerstonian intervention. It was shortly after this that his perpetual restlessness took the elder Roger to Paris, where he met and married Anne Jephson. The couple went from France, via Dublin, to Magherintemple, where the bride was presented to the family of Roger's brother, John. Predictably, the stay was not unduly protracted. After a short period when Casement, presumably for financial reasons, took a commission in the North Antrim Militia, and resigned it, apparently for health reasons, they set out together on a nomadic pattern of life, which led them to various addresses about the Continent and the British Isles. Nina was born in 1856, the year in which her father became an army officer (a captain) again. There was a five-year interval and then the sons followed in closer succession: Charles (1861), Thomas (1863), Roger (1864).

The elder Roger had been a much more colourful figure than the conventionally distinguished Casements of his own time or the previous century, and as he entered into the last stage of his life the colours took on a different hue. In 1873 Anne died in childbirth and her death led to unexpected reactions on the part of her husband. The children were sent to Magherintemple House, which may have been the most practical thing to do with them. The father, however, instead of taking up his own residence there, as he had done before, under less pressing circumstances, drifted away from his children. A typescript, intended for publication in 1966, states that at this point Casement Senior took up spiritualism and began holding séances in a hotel in Ballymena.[28] Spiritualism was even less respectable than Roman Catholicism in orthodox Casement circles, and the motive for adopting such practices shortly after the death of one's wife seems plain. Although no sources are cited to substantiate the statement that Roger Senior turned seriously to spiritualism, a little supporting evidence can be found. Among the few writings of his which survive there is an essay[29] on related spiritual topics, derived largely from his Indian experiences. Then the alleged setting for these activities did exist: it was the Adair Arms Hotel, Ballymena. A man by the name of Roger Casement was soon to die in Ballymena; the entry on his death certificate simply states that the place of death was a hotel, and early editions of the Automobile Association Handbook only mention this one hotel.

The less obvious hazards of the union of the Jephson and Casement families, brought about by the marriage of Roger David's parents, did not really make their mark until Casement was well into his consular career, when it was partly the ambiguous conditions of employment in what came to be termed 'The Cinderella Service' which brought things to a head. What is more easily detectable is the extent to which both sides of the family were divided during his impressionable years. With the Casements the essential unity of the clan, which normally ensures that a wall of silence is erected when its members transgress unwritten laws, has not entirely succeeded in concealing the gulf which must have existed between Roger Senior and the rest of the family. His ideological and temperamental differences were summed up by his youngest son in 1905:[30]

Roger Casement, although an officer in the British army, was, throughout his life an ardent and sincere lover of Ireland – one who sacrificed something to his country, and never wavered in his loyalty to her National claims. . . . [He had] an overmastering love of freedom born of a close perception of the evils of Irish misrule.

The gap between Anne Jephson and the other Jephsons is less clear. As has been seen, the Carrick-on-Suir Jephsons were not in the direct line and, apart from the religious difference which may have come in with James Hickie, Anne's separation is best illustrated by the ignorance of Mallow Castle about where exactly she fitted into the family. What is clear, however, is that her sudden death magnified the significance of her isolation and placed all the Casement children in a position of uncertainty. When that happened, the youngest one was neither young enough to avoid the shock of his first bereavement, and the difficult period which followed it, nor old enough to be able to escape the disruption of the adolescent years which were immediately preceded by the death of his father.

CHAPTER 2

EARLY LIFE

At the time of his mother's death, the youngest child, Roger, was nine. Finding himself in the physically more spacious, but emotionally less free, environment of Magherintemple House, it cannot have been of much practical comfort to him that the father he admired chose to reside twenty-seven miles away. It was not long before arrangements were made for him to board at the Church of Ireland Diocesan School at Ballymena (now Ballymena Academy) and the death of his father in the immediate locality must have cast a cloud over his early days there. Roger David was nearly thirteen years of age when this occurred and, his father having by this time exhausted almost all his funds, the children found themselves wards in Chancery, dependent on Uncle John at Magherintemple and the sympathy of other relations.

Anne Casement's influence during Roger David's initial nine years, though scarcely chronicled at all, was to be crucial in more senses than the obvious one of the emotional deprivation caused by her early death (aged thirty-nine). Apart from the links with what was, in his early colonial days, a tantalizingly attractive heritage, she made him different in a subtle and intangible way by the secret Catholic baptism which she arranged during a holiday without her husband in North Wales. The ceremony was performed by a Jesuit priest in Rhyl and the degree of secrecy was unusual in the extreme. Although it was not surprising that Roger David, who was not quite four, was unaware of what had happened it was most unlikely that one or two of the other children would fail to detect the purpose of the ritual; and it seemed inevitable that they should discuss it among themselves. Throughout nearly half a century Roger Casement spoke of himself as a Protestant, and yet, not very far beneath the surface, there were unconscious leanings towards the church of the great mass of the Irish people. It would be easy to dismiss them as springing from his Nationalist inclinations, but there was more to it than that, and the reverse may even have been true. He was, in an unusual sense, aware of a connection with

Rome. That this is not a fanciful idea is shown by his recalling, when in the condemned cell at Pentonville, actual physical details of the ceremony.[1]

While visiting Casement during his period of imprisonment, Gertrude Bannister, his cousin, jotted down his various needs and messages in a small personal note-book which has survived.[2] Among the entries appears the following: 'Baptized by Father Poole S.J. R.T.C. & N. all baptized at St Asaph. 5th August 1868. Conditional baptism.' A check with the baptismal register at St Mary's, Rhyl, however, shows that only the boys were present.[3] As Nina (her real name was Agnes) was twelve years of age, her absence would have greatly helped to prevent the boys from discovering what was going on; and it is always possible that she was baptized separately.

The effect on Casement of unconscious awareness of Catholicity is difficult to assess. It was certainly one area of several in which his loyalties were divided, and it gave rise to modes of behaviour which influenced the impression which he made on others: his habit of placing a crucifix above his bed when visiting friends is recorded below (page 63), and again, though supposedly very much a Protestant by upbringing and education, he chose never to attend services of any sort, if they were avoidable. Roman Catholic tendencies, conscious or unconscious, were reinforced by the division of the children which occurred, initially under their Uncle John's supervision, after they had become full orphans. Although there was a certain amount of passing around, the eldest and youngest, Nina and Roger, stayed for the most part with Anne Jephson's sister, Grace. Her husband was Edward Bannister, who looked after the West African interests of a Liverpool trading company and later preceded Casement in two West African appointments, though in the more modest capacity of vice-consul; and, moreover, he was to anticipate some of his foster son's Congo findings.

There was an interesting parallel between the principal foster parentage and the true parentage, in so far as Edward Bannister, a Protestant, had, like Roger Casement Senior, married a Jephson of the Catholic line. She was now the dominant, and final, maternal influence on Roger, as far as blood relationship was concerned, and she, like her late sister Anne, ostensibly reared as Protestant her unofficially adopted children, and her own children: Gertrude, Elizabeth and Edward. However, though Grace Bannister became, at least nominally, a Protestant, there is an oral tradition that quiet Catholic influences were at work and Gertrude, as well as Roger, was later to embrace fully the Roman Catholic faith.

Nina proved too old to accept the new domestic environment and her subsequent history was a series of difficult relationships, including a failed marriage. At this stage Roger had the advantage, albeit a temporary one, and life at the Bannisters' house in Liverpool, had it been more prolonged

18

and without interruption, could have saved him from much of the insta-
bility of later years; he was immediately idolized by his cousins, especially
Gertrude, and this was the mainstay of his contentment. Within an
emotionally congenial suburban setting his outwardly Protestant upbringing continued and the apex of his Anglican development was reached
when, a few months before his seventeenth birthday, he was confirmed at
the local parish church, St Anne's, Stanley. But he never wholly reconciled
himself to this step and his furtive link with the church of his mother was
stronger than one might reasonably expect from the simple fact of the
secret baptism; at times it lay dormant within him; occasionally, and well
before the exceptional pressures which might well have precipitated his
official acceptance into the Roman Catholic Church at Pentonville, it
would rise to the surface and he would say, when writing to friends: 'I am
more Catholic than anything else,'[4] or he would proclaim it publicly, as
when, in 1911, a letter of his was published over the signature 'A Catholic
Reader'.[5] Although, during this early period when he was cared for by his
Jephson aunt, he was already showing interest in the Irish cause, and is said
to have covered the walls of his attic retreat with political cartoons from
the *Weekly Freeman*,[6] it would not be safe to assume that his underlying
Catholic sentiment was merely a nationalistic convenience, a wish to
identify his own faith with that of the majority of those whose cause he
eventually embraced. He was only too aware of a dramatic Protestant
tradition of rebellion, which he might more easily have exploited had he
been so inclined (he actually succumbed to this temptation in America in
1914, when he found it an embarrassing advantage to be a Protestant and
made full political use of his nominal religious status, not without a sense
of shame).

What may be termed the Catholic part of Roger's nature was not
invisible during the time of his service to the Crown, but did not place him
at any significant disadvantage. During his adolescence, however, it can
have played a part in establishing the beginnings of a gulf which came to
exist between his views and traditional Casement attitudes which eman-
ated from the family seat at Magherintemple. But too much should not be
read into his immediate departure from County Antrim, once he had left
school; breaking away from the restraints of early environment is only
natural for an adolescent, particularly when the immediate surroundings
are insular in more than one respect. On the other hand, in Casement's
case, particularly as he was still only fifteen when the break actually
occurred, the reverse interpretation of the facts has to be considered. Was
he simply looking for a home, rather than rejecting one?

Hitherto his time in the Bannister household had been limited to
school holidays. Now (1880) the bond which had developed was sufficient
to enable him to take up permanent residence there. After a short period

the two sides of his family combined their efforts to put him on a ladder not very far removed from the world of his paternal grandfather, Hugh. John Casement, of Magherintemple, held a directorship of the Elder Dempster Shipping Company and Alfred Jones, head of the firm, was a family friend of the Bannisters. A clerkship was soon forthcoming and Roger David appeared to have embarked on a secure career in the tradition of those other Casements who had done well in trade. He did not, however, take kindly to the drudgery of junior office work, nor to being his employer's protégé, and, but for his Uncle John's intervention, the appointment would have ended in dismissal. The incident which led to the crisis was a seemingly trivial one, refusal to run an insignificant errand for Alfred Jones, but it showed that blind respect for authority could not be counted upon, and served to bring everything to a head. The solution was to send Casement overseas with one of the company's ships, and in 1883 he became purser on board the SS *Bonny* which traded with West Africa.

Relationships with Casement's next, and more immediate, superior, were little happier. Captain H.G. Harrison, of the SS *Bonny* had nothing good to say of him when interviewed by the press four days after his former purser's arrest in Kerry.[7] But although the pursership was terminated in 1884, it was by no means wasted experience; it initiated his generalized love of Africa, which later gave rise to his more specific concern for oppressed peoples, black or white. After his three round trips with the SS *Bonny* he went out again in 1884, this time in the service of the International Association, whose aim it was to civilize the Congo under the chairmanship of Leopold II. Originally known as the African International Association, this collection of national committees was soon floundering for lack of a common sense of purpose. At this point Leopold, who had failed to interest his country in colonialism, intervened personally, with a considerable financial commitment, and the surviving body, renamed the Congo International Association, became his direct responsibility. Stanley, who, after his feats of exploration, had wished to develop the area for British interests, but had received no effective encouragement, eventually, and not without some misgivings, agreed to perform the same service for Leopold; he assumed charge of organization and administration of the territories. It will have been Stanley's reputation and, to a greater degree, instinctive love of Africa which brought Casement into the employ of the man he would blame, twenty years later, for being responsible for cruel exploitation of natives.

Casement was to become one of the most knowledgeable men of his age on the subject of Africa. At twenty he had paid three brief visits and then taken up full-time employment there. Frequently he found himself one of the youngest to fill responsible posts, and this remained true during his consular career. However, in the light of later events his present position was a not altogether satisfactory one; the uncertainties of Leo-pold's International Association, which had been seen to go into decline under its first constitution, and had only started its new lease of life in 1883, gave him a superficial resemblance to the adventurers of the Putumayo whom he was to meet in 1910. He soon had worries about the Belgian nature of the 'International' enterprise[8] and made half-hearted attempts to dissociate himself from the régime; these were at first ineffec-tive because he was so drawn to the work and the country. Had he not broken away altogether in 1891 he would soon have found himself in the situation of an accessory before the fact. From the family standpoint he was already in an uncertain position: as an adventurer in a non-British enterprise that could not be seen to be gilt-edged, his exploits will not have been wholly approved of by Magherintemple. The young Casement was already revealing some of his father's restlessness and unconventionality.

In 1886 Henry Shelton Sanford, an American diplomat who had been appointed United States Minister to Belgium in 1861, founded the Sanford Expedition, which was awarded the only trading concession on the upper Congo, other than the Free State's own agencies. Sanford, an exceptionally wealthy man, enjoyed a special position in Belgium, where his courtesy title was 'General'; he had been a delegate to the Brussels Conference of 1876 which created the African International Association and became a member of the association's executive committee; in 1884 he had been instrumental in bringing about recognition of the Congo Free State by the United States. The main consideration which led to the setting up of the expedition under Sanford's direction was financial; it was believed that American money was needed in order that a survey might be made of the areas still unknown to white men. Casement, who agreed to join, did so on the understanding that the work was in line with the declared aims of the association: development for the benefit of the indigenous population. One of the fascinations of Africa for him was the constant need to solve communication problems and these were his principal concern during the early part of his employment with Sanford. The work was to lead to a life-long belief in the virtue of travel as a means to improving relations between peoples, and, fortuitously, it brought about one of his rare contacts with the family of his mother.

A portrait of Casement at this time (1887), and an insight into the style of expedition which Sanford supported is given by A.J. Mounteney Jephson:[9]

Casement of the Sanford Expedition came up and camped by me. We bathed and he gave me a very good dinner – he is travelling most comfortably and has a large tent and plenty of servants. It was delightful sitting down to a *real* dinner at a *real* table with a table

21

cloth and dinner napkins and plenty to eat with Burgundy to drink and cocoa and cigarettes after dinner – and this in the middle of the wilds – it will be a long time before I pass such a pleasant evening again.

Three days later there was another meeting:[10]

At about 12 o'clock I came upon Casement again, he was camping for breakfast beside a cool clear stream. I stopped and had breakfast with him – how I tucked into his oatmeal cakes!

As mentioned on page 5 above, they met again on 19 April. Jephson, who was conveying the dismantled sections of the steel boat, the *Advance*, at the rear of Stanley's expedition, was held up by a stream in flood and, when Casement arrived during the afternoon, he was quite unable to cross with his heavy loads and pitched camp on the adjacent ground. This circumstance probably saved Jephson's life. They camped together for three days until a crossing was possible. On 21 April, when Jephson awoke, he was far from well. Nevertheless he managed to transport Casement's party and baggage to the other side, and eventually his own people. By the time he himself had crossed, Casement's party had moved on. Under a particularly intense sun Jephson dismantled the boat and, feeling too ill to keep up, sent his men on ahead to Stanley's camp. He made slow progress following them on his own and it was fortunate for him that, on staggering into an apparently deserted village, he found Casement settling down to another breakfast. Jephson was completely exhausted and Casement was his salvation. Casement at once decided to postpone the march until the cooler hours of the day and in the meantime gave Jephson ten grains of quinine. He had his own bed made up and the patient stayed in it until a hammock was prepared so that he could be carried to Stanley's camp. Four men were detailed to carry him there and on arrival he was barely conscious.

The Jephson diary account, contrasting as it does Sanford luxury with Stanley austerity, shows Casement as almost a caricature of the English explorer and gentleman, a family representative of whom Magherintemple would have been proud. In one sense it is misleading; jungle exploration came naturally to him, as it did to many a humbler Irishman and, some years later, when his entourage was reduced to two bull dogs and a Loanda boy, his progress was equally nonchalant; Sanford trappings were enjoyable, but not essential. Conrad's 1903 description of him emerging after months in the 'unspeakable wilderness' . . . 'as though he had been for a stroll in the park',[11] can be accepted without too much allowance for poetic licence. The ability to survive unscathed long periods of isolation was happily matched during the early Congo years with a corresponding ability to form firm lasting friendships. His friends were his colleagues: Edward Glave, W.G. Parminter and Alfred Parminter, Frederick Puleston and, closest of all until the diaries were circulated, Herbert Ward. Such men left memoirs,[12] some of which contained glowing tributes to Casement's integrity and capability. The African environment removed the tensions which had marred his relationships with his Liverpool colleagues; it was, for a time, as though he had broken away from the constraints of his origins.

It was not long before Casement began to realize that the Sanford Expedition had commercial aims that had little to do with freeing the natives from their primitive ways. Despite a firm belief in the benefits of travel, which was to become a feature of his general attitude to life, his early acquaintance with railway construction did not fire him with zeal, partly because he thought that a line from Matadi to Stanley Pool should not be a priority, and partly because the laziness of the natives came as a shock. Nevertheless the survey was completed under his direction towards the end of 1887 and, being temporarily unemployed, he was recruited as a lay missionary the Rev. W. Holman Bentley. This lasted for a few months and in 1888, according to his own testimony, he 'left the Sanford expedition to go elephant-shooting'.[13]

Casement's next activity was the one which most nearly compromised him in the eyes of Leopold's defenders in 1904. It was not hard to persuade him to return to the railway and take charge of its construction. But now he was in that position of privilege where he could see and be responsible for the relationship between the Europeans and the natives, and that more dangerous relationship between chosen natives and subordinate labourers; at the same time he was, in effect, paid by Leopold. As he was to recollect when inspecting another such project in Brazil:[14]

> I took part once in the work of constructing a railway in Africa
> under far harder conditions than anything the Madeira–Mamoré
> people have to face – the Congo Railway from Matadi to Stanley
> Pool, passing through, probably, the most unhealthy region on the
> face of the globe. This line could never have been constructed had
> the Congo Government not actively intervened in the work.

It was the intervention of the government which, though crucial to the success of such an operation, eventually led Casement to leave the Congo. He had, he later wrote, 'no wish to continue in what was clearly becoming a Belgian enterprise'.[15] The statement was made soon after the publication of his Congo Report and is generally regarded as expressing disapproval at least partly on humanitarian grounds. The railway construction and rubber-gathering enterprises were, however, so distinct, in time, place and, above all, method, that this would be a wrong interpretation, even though it would not have displeased its author. For grounds of disapproval one had only to remember the philanthropic spirit in which the state had been established, but at this stage in his career it was not long before Casement was to find himself, as he put it, 'on the high road to becoming a regular Imperialist Jingo'.[16] He left the Congo with reservations about the Belgians and immediately entered British government service.

At this point one may enquire into the extent to which the alleged adolescent nationalist propensities, of which some mention has been made, had any real substance. Testimony to the effect that Casement was a conscious separatist from the dawn of his youthful political awareness is principally derived from witnesses who, for reasons which admittedly demand sympathy, had come to despise England. Nina's American account[17] reflected her own sadly mismanaged life and revulsion at the use made of the diaries in her presence by Alfred Noyes; Gertrude Parry's narrative[18] was distorted by grief and her personal sufferings at the hand of British officialdom, prior to the trial and in the arrangements for the disposal of the body after the execution. For the most part both accounts can be accepted as factually sound, but very different interpretations can be made of the facts. There are three main conditions to be balanced: affection for Ireland, dislike of England or the political link with England and, the possible outcome of these: separatist conviction. The first condition is not direct evidence for the existence of the second, despite common assumptions to this effect.

Confusion of the quite distinct phenomena of separatism and love of country, a variant of the more common confusion of republicanism with nationalism, can be illustrated by possible interpretations of Casement's part in 'buy-Irish' campaigns, which have been a feature of Irish economic affairs from time to time. The firm which equipped him for his African excursions, W.J. Allison and Company, still exists and a director of the firm, William Charles Allison, at the age of eighty-two described at length[19] his impression of Casement over a period of twelve years. It transpired that early in his long association with Allisons, he had demanded that all his supplies must be of Irish manufacture; the only known example of discord between him and the firm arose when he was supplied with English matches, and Allison had to point out that no matches were manufactured in Ireland. Insistence on the provision of Irish manufactured goods (a principle sometimes advocated in print at the head of his letters) is, however, no answer to the second part of the imputation made at the state trial that the prisoner's hatred of England was 'as malignant in quality as it was sudden in origin'; the Aberdeens at Dublin Castle and lord lieutenants before them had bought Irish and supported buy-Irish campaigns, as had Horace Plunkett, whilst remaining a staunch Unionist. Even papering one's walls with journals which in their early issues sought to restore the balance between two halves of what might have been a respectable political equation need not be assumed, with Gertrude Parry, to be the action of a rebel; it can as easily be seen to be the natural behaviour of a young man wishing to see Ireland assume its rightful place as an equal partner in the Union. So far the only perceptible steps taken away from the conventional path of the 'Black Protestant' were his tacit refusal to be a Protestant at all and his selection of heroes of an unorthodox stamp, beginning, understandably enough, with his father.

Casement's own conclusion in 1907 that, up to and including his Boer War service, he was conforming to what might be loosely termed an imperial norm, is a frank, if vague, assessment of his early career. He was a high-minded pioneer and there was plenty of scope in his experience for British imperial advancement to be the genuine vehicle of humanitarianism: a circumstance which he still found to be true (a less welcome truth, but truth none the less), as the end of his consular career approached. Only towards the end of his life did he remark abruptly of his Nigerian service 'the protecting power ultimately became the annexing power'.[20] His activities there, and the activities of his associates, led innocently, almost inevitably, to the acquisition of the territory for the Crown, and this process had Casement's full approval.

Nigeria was then known as the Oil Rivers Protectorate and 'I entered the Service there, not in a consular capacity, but in a branch of the public service that was administered by the Foreign Office through consuls and vice-consuls.'[21] On 31 July 1892 he was appointed a member of the staff of the Survey Department and, whilst still only twenty-eight, became assistant director-general of customs at Old Calabar. The director-general, Vice-Consul T.A. Wall, was senior deputy commissioner of the Protectorate and, as a result, Casement was sometimes 'acting' rather than 'assistant'. These functions helped to give him a good 'apprenticeship', as he later described it, for his entry to the Consular Service. His next three years were spent in the Protectorate and his duties were varied and exciting. The commissioner who administered the territory was Consul-General Sir Claude MacDonald. He was usually fulsome when it came to tributes to his subordinates and his references to Casement were no exception: 'it would be difficult to find any one in every way more suited to the work of exploration.'[22]

The commissioner had been prompted to pay this particular compliment because its subject had just completed three exploratory expeditions into the interior of the Calabar district. Accounts of two of the journeys were received in time to be incorporated in the commissioner's report to the Earl of Kimberley, dated 19 August 1894,[23] and are precursors of their author's consular reports. Sadly the literary conventions of government service current at the time rob them of stylistic quality, and style was one of

25

the major characteristics of the outstanding consuls. However, although disappointing in this respect, the reports more than compensate for this deficiency as far as content is concerned. The first journey had as its aim the opening up of a route from Itu, on the Cross river, to the Opobo river and in this, in purely physical terms, it failed. In March 1894, accompanied by forty-three natives (no white companion), he set off into country where at first the reception was marked by 'a certain surliness and dislike to the presence of a white man',[24] and the first night was spent at the house of a friend of one of his guides. On the second day, at about 9.00 am, the party entered the large village of Ibiaku, where a hostile crowd became threatening: dancing and shouting 'and clashing swords and matchets in our faces'.[25] A swarm of bees was let loose upon the visitors and, as matters worsened, Casement attempted to make the customary gifts of tobacco and cloth to the leaders of the mob. When he gave the order to his unarmed party to move on a full scale attack began, during which most of his baggage and some carriers were captured. King Urofia of the Inokun people, who resided in the next village, then arrived and, although his presence at first only aggravated matters, he was ultimately instrumental in saving Casement. A woman, a friend of the party's host of the previous night, took Casement by the hand, led him through his attackers and persuaded the king's warriors to support the white man. This they did with enthusiasm and for the rest of the day 'prisoners, goats, and many of my loads were brought back with shouts of triumph to Urofia's yard, and laid down before me.'[26]

A series of palavers now took place, over a period of more than two weeks, about the advisability of proceeding any further in the direction of the Opobo river. At first it seemed that the interested parties would permit the expedition to continue, but a particularly savage cannibal chief, the King of Anang, was reluctant to allow it and when it became evident that negotiations would go on at least until July Casement decided to return to Itu without further delay. He arrived at Calabar on 27 March, the journey from Itu being accomplished by steam-launch.

As a first full record of Casement's official behaviour in the service of the Crown, the report reveals him to be brave, diplomatic and usefully observant. The long period of palavers was not unprofitable; much information relevant to a consul's commercial responsibilities was noted. Local agricultural and trading traditions were observed, as were pagan customs and religious rites. It was plain that both the main tribes of the area were cannibalistic and that slavery was an accepted part of the social structure. When a king died, many slaves were killed; some were eaten, others buried with their masters. Casement believed, and later events proved him right, that his journey had not been wasted. Although he had not traversed the area himself, he had, in terms of native diplomacy,

26

succeeded in opening up the route for those who would follow.

It was imperialism in the raw and Casement had experiences which might have turned the heads of lesser men. He was always regarded with awe, and this was continually brought home to him: one chief asked him for a medicine to provide eternal life. His physical survival was itself remarkable: 'On all occasions I pointed out how great was the "big Consul's" reliance on their good faith; and as evidence of his belief in their friendly feelings how he had sent me quite unarmed among them,'[27] words which Sir Claude MacDonald must have enjoyed reading. He concluded that the local Inokun would 'welcome the presence of any official with power to open to them the markets of their neighbours, now closed, and strong enough to enable them to use the paths and trade routes now barred by the hostility of other branches of their own race'. Then followed the cautionary statement: 'No good could result from endeavouring to force these changes.'[28] This was still the voice of the protecting power, rather than the annexing power.

The second journey, described by the commissioner as 'partially successful',[29] began on 16 April and on this occasion another white man, Arthur Bourchier, accompanied Casement. The area to be opened up by this expedition lay between Esene on the Opobo river and Ikorasan on the Kwo Ibo river. They set off from the vice-consulate at Old Calabar and travelled overnight by canoe to Esene, where they asked the local chief to provide them with guides to take them to Kwo Ibo. Again distrust of the reaction of neighbouring tribes proved a stumbling block. The white men therefore went off on their own initiative, sounded out one chief who might have proved hostile and, having won his confidence, returned to Esene to find a change of attitude. On 23 April they were able to proceed, with the Esene chief's brother and eleven other Esene men as guides and carriers, together with their own three Timanis and Krooboy servants.

The expedition as a whole proved to be a series of near skirmishes; there was much evasive running from place to place, as the natives reacted to the sound of drums, the sudden appearance of men in hideous masks and the shrill noise of 'the peculiar cry that proclaims a fight'.[30] Cloth and tobacco averted one chief's armed attack at the last possible moment and, as was customary, similar gifts were made at the other villages and towns. When the end of the Esene tribal territory was reached, further progress was dependent on the friendly disposition of the Chief of the Akpania. Here the white men found it expedient to accept, as cheerfully as possible, the imprints of many hands dipped in the blood of a goat beheaded in their presence and endured having morsels of the sacrifice placed in their mouths by the chief's unwashed hands. They found, however, that the prospect of white intervention in their area was something for which the chief's old mother had prayed all her life, and the chief himself decided to be their guide through the extremely hostile territory which lay between his own land and the Kwo Ibo.

On this occasion the explorers succeeded in reaching their destination, with much help from their blood-brothers, but the expedition was deemed to be only partially successful because of the refusal of all guides and bearers to return by land through the region that had in theory been opened up to the white men. A steamship, the *Linthorpe*, chanced to be up river and Casement chartered it in order that he might convey Chief Akpania and his men, with the Esenes, back to Opobo. They arrived on 29 April and Casement's report, complete with notes on the physical geography of the district and criticism of Admiralty charts and Intelligence Division maps, was despatched to Sir Claude MacDonald on 2 May.

The administrative development of the Protectorate at this time was very much in the hands of the Consular Service, of which Casement was not a member, though he operated from vice-consulates and was inclined to act for vice-consuls; under the commissioner and consul-general were six deputy commissioners and vice-consuls and sixteen consular agents, of whom eleven held consular rank. Both the Customs Department and the Post Office were organized and supervised by vice-consuls. Casement moved away from the comparatively narrow confines of the Customs Department into realms of wider responsibility; his title became general service officer. He was clearly the sort of person the Consular Service required and, not having sat the appropriate exams, could be seen to be a fit object for patronage. Now his third expedition served to consolidate his reputation as an efficient pioneer in this sphere of imperial expansion. From apparent failure to partial success, he went on to accomplish a completely successful expedition; leaving Old Calabar and taking a route parallel to the Cross river, he opened up the country which lay to the east of it and gained access to its upper waters, which were hitherto cut off during the dry season. The commissioner noted that 'the tribes ... welcomed him all along the journey.'[31]

His letters during this period show that Casement's life-long concern with the anti-slavery movement had dawned. The Consular Service, with its old tradition of following local custom even in this difficult matter, did not worry him. He was still sufficiently level-headed to accept his commissioner's conclusion that there would be 'a greater cruelty to the slaves themselves were the latter to receive their freedom forthwith'[32] and to wait for external influences gradually to bring about the withering away of the institution. What outraged him and was the spur to most anti-slavers, was the concomitant torture and putting to death of so many unfortunates; the deep-rooted savage conventions of primitive slavery which could only be alleviated by the civilizing force of the benevolent Great Power which he represented. He expressed his feelings on the matter to Sir Claude Mac-

Donald, both in general terms[33] and specifically about murders of slaves for ritual burial purposes.[34] The consequence of his intervention served to reinforce his commitment to the British Government as the proper vehicle for reform; there was a show of force which stamped out the practice in the area he had personally opened up. But progress in this field was hampered whilst Great Britain's territorial authority in Nigeria derived from the rights which had been obtained by the National African Company (granted a charter as the Royal Niger Company in 1886). Not until 1900 were the rights of the company transferred to the British Government and in 1901, when company rule had been finally superseded by Whitehall, slavery was declared to be illegal, six years after the commissioner had advised against summary abolition.

While on leave at Magherintemple in June 1895, after nearly three years in the Oil Rivers Protectorate, Casement wrote the letters to Mallow Castle mentioned above (pp. 4–8) and made incidental references to the progress of his career. He was, at this time, conforming to the Casement family ideal: serving his queen in a far-off land; exploring in order to extend the benefits of benevolent British rule to a people who needed its protection. The Jephson family had done, and were doing, similar things and he was emboldened to explore his maternal ancestry. After the publication of his reports in February he had become quite well known to those interested in African exploration and he told Miss Jephson-Norreys[35] how busy he was 'writing up some account of my recent journeys in Africa for the British Association Meeting in the Autumn', though international events were to prevent this project from ever being completed. He added that he expected 'to go to Uganda on a Foreign Office mission next – if I am lucky.'

At home, while Casement had been pioneering elsewhere for the Crown, Gladstone had been labouring to carry the second Home Rule Bill through parliament, and whilst the Grand Old Man's dogged devotion to this cause proved futile in the end, it had the effect of keeping Irish Nationalism in constitutional channels. If Casement had time on his expeditions to spare a thought for his home country, it was unlikely that contemporary political events would eclipse his concern for the fortunes of suffering African natives. He was fully stretched while exploring new territory and there was little time for self-examination – for casting doubt on motivation or beliefs which his formal upbringing had hardly encouraged him to question. The heavy physical and emotional demands of exploration, or simply survival, postponed the doubts. Like the Irish majority of the time, his unconscious yearnings for fulfilment, more sentimental than separatist, were sublimated. For a few more years he was to love Ireland's traditional enemy as much as he loved Ireland.

One may also enquire how the other potentially dangerous aspect of

Casement's personal ambivalence was developing at this stage: his illegal sexual bias. In the absence of diaries, it is difficult to tell. Bearing in mind the detailed information one has about his practices only a few years later, one is inclined to attach perhaps undue significance to 'phallus-like mounds of earth painted black and red'[36] seen in a town called Oiritu. Their relevance to the purposes of the expedition is, to say the least, tenuous. But undoubtedly the comment would go unnoticed in any other author. Judging by subsequent private descriptions of expeditions among naked tribes, the explorer was able to gain much visual gratification from his experiences. The peculiar circumstances of his childhood, particularly the early severing of the bond between him and his mother, and the unfortunate family tensions and separations which followed, initiated, in a classic way, the search for alternative sources of affection. But there is very little written evidence of deviant inclinations prior to this date, and certainly no evidence of actual practices until 1903.

The Ugandan possibility pleased Casement. The need for his services there had arisen because other European interests were beginning to impinge on the activities of the British South Africa Company in a region which, like the Oil Rivers Protectorate, had much potential as an imperial acquisition and he had proved himself to have the requisite qualities for achieving British goals. But his mood was changeable (Magherintemple never agreed with him for long) and, nine days later, he was writing of 'the dismal surroundings of Africa' in the context of 'despondent fits' blamed on '*Liver* – the great fetish of tropical life'.[37] Then a change of government led to a change of direction for him and with the sense of urgency his enthusiasm seemed to return. His last extant letter to Mallow Castle came from 50, Jermyn Street, St James's, S.W.: 'I got orders from the Foreign Office last night to hold myself in readiness to go very soon. . . . The resignation of the Ministry has caused this alteration and hurry in my plans – and I *may* have to sail for the Cape in a week or ten days.'[38] The new Conservative administration feared that a greater threat to British interests was to be found in the Transvaal. What is sometimes termed a 'listening post' needed a strong British official without delay. Lorenzo Marques on Delagoa Bay in Portuguese East Africa was a neutral port on the edge of the Transvaal, linked to Pretoria by rail; were Casement to be consul there, he would, theoretically, be in a position to discover what arms were passing through the port and might glean other information. He was not the sort of person to confine himself to a narrow interpretation of consular responsibility. Although the question of examinations was discussed, 'My examination was dispensed with, and I was sent out without any examination at all to Delagoa Bay in 1895.'[39]

CHAPTER 3

BRITISH CONSUL

The waiving of Casement's consular examination was an act of enlightened patronage, justified by his excellent record in the Civil Service and the need to get him into the post with a minimum of delay. It was not, however, patronage in the traditional sense; he was sounded out about taking examinations, but said he would need time to prepare himself. As he eventually realized, he was not singled out on social grounds. He was not on a sufficiently high level for all doors to open to him; expediency was one factor which helped to open this particular door; soon his powers of conversation would open others.

A consideration of the Consular Service and what it required of its members during the late Victorian and Edwardian periods is given in Appendix A. Consuls often complained that their duties were ill-defined and that there was nowhere to turn for guidance. In fact, they had a twofold task: to protect British subjects and to further British interests; and, among other aids, to help them carry out their duties, they had the various editions of *General Instructions for H.M.'s Consular Officers*. These were printed by the Foreign Office and were both detailed and enlightened, striking a nice balance between direction and discretion; and yet, Foreign Office officials in London frequently had cause to complain that consuls never seemed to consult them. The truth of the matter was that consular dissatisfaction, at any rate in the General Service, had other causes, including: uncongenial climate, inadequate provision of official accommodation, unsatisfactory promotion arrangements and, most significant of all, a feeling of inferiority, particularly in the social sphere, derived from being, according to the Foreign Office code, almost a diplomat, but not quite.

After so promising a career in the Oil Rivers Service, the circumstances in which Casement took up his first consular post were distinctly disillusioning. Until that moment the British Government had seemed to be an appreciative employer; when he entered his first consulate he found

31

that the outgoing consul had sold the entire contents: 'I took over a roof and bare walls. . . . I had absolutely nothing with which to discharge my public functions.'[1] Part of the blame attached to his predecessor who, as convention demanded, offered to sell to the new consul, but, when the prices were found to be too high, sold literally everything to other purchasers. Nevertheless the root cause was the way in which consular emoluments were organized; the office allowance supplemented the salary and there were no restrictions as to its use. Other than the consulate itself (and even this could not always be relied upon),[2] nothing belonged to the government. Beds, desks, stationery and secretarial staff: nothing was guaranteed. Casement's first physical contact with the harsh realities of a consular career was to sleep on the floor for three nights.

More disillusionment was to follow, when the exciting prospect of uncovering the activities of gun-runners at first yielded nothing of any real consequence. After the Oil Rivers expeditions, which had demanded stamina, initiative and bravery, the highly inefficient Portuguese port was a disappointment. And yet, although single-handed, the consul soon established an office which maintained wide-ranging services of a high standard. One reason for this was Casement's love of things clerical, and his wish to write extensively on all matters. He had literary aspirations and, though he is generally adjudged to have been mainly (but not always) useless as a poet, and his printed works, other than those published by HMSO, are unimpressive, he had a style which breathed life into despatches and official reports, a very real advantage in the career on which he had embarked.

An important part of the consul's duty 'to further British interests' was the preparation of an annual report, and Casement's first, on the trade and commerce of Lorenzo Marques for the year 1896, although not comparable with his later achievements, was a creditable performance, and set precedents for those of the same authorship which were to follow.[3] For some of the customs statistics, he admitted that he was indebted to the *Cape Gazette* and he drew attention to those items which had a special significance in the light of unrest in neighbouring territories. The trade of Lorenzo Marques, he stressed repeatedly, was almost entirely 'an import transit trade to the Transvaal' and the value of imports during 1896 was 43 per cent higher than the previous year. He noted that the total value of government imports to the Transvaal during 1895 was £812,170, of which £629,842 was dynamite and £121,396 was arms and ammunition. Moreover, whereas in 1895 '(Not Government)' ammunition amounting to £7,113 was imported, in 1896 this increased to £22,387. As the *Cape Gazette* was available to all, the need for discreet enquiries on the consul's part did not seem to be very great.

The tone of the report was distinctly loyalist; fear of German, French and other competitors was keenly felt in commercial matters as diverse as shipping and cement. What worried him was the British unwillingness to adapt goods to suit the importer's needs, or even to advertise in the vernacular; while German advertisements in Portuguese abounded, he himself had received a journal 'dealing with a most important branch of British industry' written in Spanish (it was addressed to 'Lorenzo Marques, Portugal'). English cement came in frail barrels, German in strong iron drums. Butter was a considerable import, although unpopular because it was tinned, 'it is certain neither Ireland nor England contributed anything, unless perhaps the labels.' And already one has a suggestion that, although the author is speaking with the voice of the United Kingdom, he is conscious that he speaks for two partners in a union; has a dual responsibility. One's impression is immediately reinforced as one reads a complaint that the 'open pastures of Munster and Leinster' were not capturing the market by using earthenware containers instead of tins. Is Ireland's loss more keenly felt?

There was some self-consciousness in what was a first annual report and more than a hint of self-importance; 'Suggestions may be made by a British Consul; their execution, if worthy of execution, lies only with the British manufacturer and trader.' And there followed a rebuke for those who wasted two months by writing to him, instead of buying a copy of the last annual report, which sold for less than the cost of a stamp. Uncharacteristically the main body of the report (excluding seven pages of annexed tables) was only eighteen pages long and it also differed from its successors in having in parts a more flowery style, as when the author was contrasting the Zulu 'on the long grass hill-sides . . . amply clothed in naught beyond the sunshine and shadow of a summer's day' with the same individual in Johannesburg on 'his Sunday-off', 'donning on that happy day shirting, abundant collars, and fancy trousering'. British manufacturers were urged to study this local tendency, particularly as, 'until higher wants can be called into being', native cash should be spent on 'jackets and trousers' rather than 'gin and rum'. Outwardly Casement was not yet adopting an attitude to the black man very different from that which was commonly expressed in the literature of his time.

The period in Lorenzo Marques was marred by a sense of anti-climax and by the beginnings of ill-health, the lot of many expatriates in Africa at the time. The comparatively young veteran of several African adventures was no longer the exception; extra leave, and extension of leave, caused by malaria and general debilitation, brought the first consular appointment to a close. At the end of 1897 he left the post for the last time. Although co-operative in the matter of heeding medical certificates, the Foreign Office was not very imaginative in reallocating missions. From other points of view, however, the step from Portuguese East to Portuguese West made sense and, putting aside the South African experiences, which were forced upon the Foreign Office, there is a logical development in Casement's five appointments in Portuguese, or formerly Portuguese, territories, spoiled only by his refusal to stay in Lisbon. The Congo was initially an appendage of his Portuguese West African sphere of duty.

The move to St Paul de Loanda brought a great deal more responsibility in theory, but no significant action. 'I was really three consuls,'[4] by which he meant that he had to see to British interests in the Congo and French Congo, in addition to Portuguese West Africa. Though he was prone to exaggerate the trust placed in him, it was true that he held three separate commissions from the queen and exequaturs from the French, Belgian and Portuguese authorities. The triple appointment could be accepted as a compliment and, coming just before his most pronounced period of imperial fervour, can be seen to have entrenched him, for the time being, in the older traditions of Magherintemple. Like his father's Indian service, this part of his career was orthodox and betrayed little evidence of any tendency to depart from conventional Casement lines of development.

The high point of what verged on a fanatical devotion to queen and country came with the South African War. And yet, paradoxically, it was one of the more colourful events of this time, the raising by Major John MacBride of an Irish Brigade to fight for the Boers, and the attempt to allow volunteer prisoners into this body, which was to have the most influence on Casement's political planning and practical behaviour when he came to the final phase of his activities as an emancipator. The deterioration of relationships between the Uitlanders and the government of President Kruger brought about renewed fear that, despite the official neutrality of Portugal, arms were still being shipped to the Transvaal via Lorenzo Marques (with the connivance of the port authorities) and it was immediately apparent that a reliable official should carry out a discreet inspection. Because of 'my previous experience at Delagoa Bay' the natural choice was Casement and the next six months saw him on 'special service'[5] enthusiastically engaged in defeating the Boers.

The South African War occupied Casement from January to July 1900. After some enquiries, he concluded that no illicit arms were being allowed through by the Portuguese. Then, as if frustrated by this negative result, he proposed, and volunteered to take part in, an extraordinary commando operation which the Foreign Office allowed him to put before the military leadership in Cape Town. The aim was to cut off possible gun running by capturing or destroying a bridge on the Netherlands Railway line between Lorenzo Marques and Pretoria. In April the plan was approved and 540 men in two contingents, one accompanied by Casement, set off in May, only to be recalled by Sir Alfred Milner, who had had somewhat belated second thoughts about the overall effectiveness of the scheme. The originator of the operation was once again disillusioned, this time whilst actually translating his loyalist ideals into physical performance. His next leave began in July and general deterioration of health led to two extensions of it, amounting to three months in all. Any misgivings which might have begun to germinate were for the time being sublimated by his receipt of the queen's South African medal. He spent his time in London, C. Antrim (at Magherintemple) and Paris. Then, before he returned to West Africa to resume his consular duties, he paid a carefully arranged visit to Brussels.

The impracticability of the threefold responsibilities of the St Paul de Loanda consulate had led to a suggestion by Casement, shortly before his return to Lorenzo Marques, that the consulate be split in two;[6] the old consulate, to which the Congo State and the French Congo were comparatively recent additions, should confine itself to Portuguese West Africa and a new consulate should be established within the Congo State. On his return from South Africa, that suggestion was implemented and he was to set up the new consulate in the Congo State at Kinchasa, a site within easy reach of his other responsibility, the French Congo. This new development would bring him into direct contact with an area from which were coming many reports and rumours, no longer eclipsed by South African events, of the enslavement and torture of native rubber-gatherers. There had been a steadily increasing flow of accusations against Leopold's régime, one of the earliest of which had come from Edward Bannister, Casement's uncle and unofficial stepfather, who, as vice-consul in Loanda in 1892, had had the Congo as his special responsibility. Bannister's complaints were reinforced by the experiences of Edward Glave, a friend and fellow member of the Sanford Expedition, and those of Consul Alfred Parminter, another friend who succeeded Casement at Lorenzo Marques. All this information was now put before Casement by Sir Martin Gosselin, new head of the Foreign Office's African Department, and it was because the new post carried responsibility for the French Congo that a journalist and anti-slavery campaigner, E.D. Morel, French by birth, had an almost immediate influence on the activities of the Boma consulate (Kinchasa was rejected in favour of the seat of the Free State administration). Morel, who like the consul had been an employee of the Elder Dempster Company, was to become one of Casement's heroes and, through a mutual friend, John Holt, was also able to exert pressure on Gosselin.

Before departing for Boma, Casement was encouraged to visit Constantine Phipps, British Minister in Brussels, in order to prepare himself for what was likely to be a delicate appointment. His visit was made known to the court and an invitation to luncheon with King Leopold awaited him. This proved to be the social preliminary to a 'diplomatic' meeting between the two men, which took place the next day; for an hour and a half, Leopold attempted to discredit the atrocity stories appearing in the press. The main outcome of the largely one-sided discussion was a determination on Casement's part to see for himself.

Although it might be thought that the reason for sending Casement to Brussels and arranging the audience with the king was to educate the consul for his new post, such thorough preparation was unusual in the Service and it is reasonable to look for other motives. The atrocity stories which had, naturally, upset the Belgians were to be disputed even after a Belgian commission vindicated Casement in 1905.[7] As late as 1926, Edgar Wallace who, as a reporter, had been sent out by Alfred Harmsworth in 1907, wrote: 'There was missionary support for these stories, but, beyond question, there was bad blood between the British missionaries and the Belgian officials . . . I saw no evidence of atrocities which were not four-teen years old.'[8] Several powers either coveted the potential riches of the region or resented the clever, oblique way in which, as it appeared to them, Belgium, through the shrewdness of her monarch, had gradually circum-vented the decisions of the 1884–5 Conference of Berlin, which had guaranteed the independence of the territories which came to be known as the Congo Free State. Among the specific guarantees were freedom of navigation on the Congo and its tributaries, free trade rights for all nations and prohibition of trade monopolies. The natives were to become civilized and slavery was to be abolished.

Rival powers which had been diverted or delayed by the agreement reached at Berlin were the French who were to the north and west of the prescribed region, the British and Germans to the east, and the Portuguese to the south. As a nation, prior to Leopold II's accession, Belgium had been reluctant to engage in the hazards of colonization, and the colonial powers might understandably have disregarded her as a contender for the acquisi-tion of an area so central and so rich in natural resources. But the wishes of King Leopold did not accord with those of his people and he had so engineered things that, from 1885 until 1908 the Congo Free State was virtually his private property. Even when the Belgians had undergone a modification of attitude, they found it difficult to obtain sovereignty when, after much international and internal pressure, he agreed in 1907 to relinquish his personal control. It was as a result of a combination of rumours and forceful disclosures, notably those made by Great Britain (based on Casement's report), the United States of America, Italy and Belgium herself, that public opinion among Belgian electors grew hostile to Leopold in 1906. Faced with a general election and the possibility of a critical parliament in that year, Leopold announced that he wished to see the Congo annexed to Belgium, under Belgian, not his own, control. After the election he went back on his supposed intention of ceding his sovereign rights, but by that time public opinion was too strong for him; the Belgian parliament ratified the change of sovereignty in 1908. Belgium was to retain her control until the end of the colonial era.

The early entries of the 1903 diary[9] made while its author travelled to Africa and amused himself at Funchal and Las Palmas, show him to have spent much time socializing and to have been more distressed than most when news reached him of the suicide of Sir Hector Macdonald, a soldier who had had a distinguished career in India and South Africa, and who had been summoned to face charges of homosexuality. His reaction to the tragedy had prompted some to regard the diary entry[10] as evidence that elsewhere the text was subsequently tampered with in order to discredit him: with some compassion he recorded his belief in the need for medical rather than judicial treatment for such sufferers. Taken as part of a wholly genuine document, the passage is an early example of the abruptness with which he could stand back from his own activities; the emotional and intellectual approach was completely at odds with the spirit in which he entered into his liaisons, and one is shown with some force how the man's mind was suspended between two worlds. This diary which, like those of 1910 and 1911,[11] embraces the period of his atrocity investigations, also gives evidence of his occasional feelings of social inadequacy. It appears sometimes as though the great cause which, largely on the basis of hearsay evidence, he is to champion, is unconsciously embarked upon to purge this feeling and elevate him into the stratum to which Casements nearly belonged: to make him more of a Jephson. Such a conclusion would be an unwarranted simplification and would do less than justice to the man's bravery and the sincerity which certainly came as he entered further into what was to become the one dominant and consistent theme of his public life. Nevertheless, faced with the catalogue of the titled people with whom he comes into contact (excluding the Lords Lansdowne and Percy, and others with whom the association is purely official) and the obvious reassurance he gains from gambling and dining with them, one wonders about sources of initial motivation. 'Lunched with Hon. A. Bailey',[12] 'Laura Lady Wilton there',[13] 'Introduced to . . . Lady Edgecume (sic)',[14] 'To Casino met Duke of Montrose,[15] played with Lady Edgecume', 'Duke of Montrose there. Charming again',[16] 'met Sir McDonel';[17] sometimes the titled persons are mentioned for no other reason than that they share the same public room. There is an obsessive air about it all; while such entries would be commonplace enough with some diarists, they do not ring true in the context of Casement's very private writings.

Another aspect of insecurity, more emotional than social, though the two can seldom be separated, runs through the entire diary: his concern about the health of his dog, John. Day after day, when he is hearing testimony of the most bestial sufferings of helpless natives, a disproportionate amount of his daily reminiscences is devoted to the decline or improving health of this animal, its misdemeanours and his occasional impatience with it: 'broke my stick over him'.[18] A charitable, though not altogether convincing, interpretation is that the dog helped to take his mind off the otherwise unbearable horrors of which he was hearing.

Casement was now entering the scene of dramatic disclosure and often equally convincing Belgian refutation, charge and counter charge, but he did so with little trepidation. On arrival, as one who was becoming increasingly familiar with the fine balance which had to be achieved between consular obligations and restrictions, he started by concerning himself, wherever possible, with offences against British subjects; thus his diary for 20 May records:[19] 'Wired F.O. (2 wires) about . . . Ill treatment of Br. Subjects out here,' and again, the following week, 'Finishing F.O. Africa 8 on the Hardship inflicted on Br. Subjects.'[20] Such precautions were not, however, as necessary as when later, he was to investigate alleged Peruvian outrages. The Congo was theoretically, in certain respects, an international zone. There was one flaw in the way his investigations were going, however; he was hearing for himself more than he was seeing for himself – a fact that the Belgians were quick to seize upon, and the diary, had it been available to them, would have supported this part of the Belgian case against him. There are many instances: 'Called on Miss de Hailes at her hospital. . . . She complains of State Exactions bitterly upon the people,'[21] 'saw Basingili and heard the dreadful story of their ill-treatment',[22] 'Interviewed Frank Etova and drew out a long story from him of recent "indecents" of State',[23] 'Mr and Mrs Stapleton are convinced the rule of the State has swept off the population wholesale',[24] 'At 10 a.m. [a man ?–indecipherable] came to say 5 people from Bikoro side with hands cut off had come as far as Nyanga intending to show me – but hearing there I was leaving at daylight they stayed. Sent out canoe tell them come on.'[25] But the entry for the next day records: 'They went near Nyanga y'day but found the people with their hands cut off had gone back hearing I had gone.'[26] A month later he was noting, again on the basis of hearsay evidence, that atrocities were not confined to Leopold's territory: 'Shocking stories of the mutilation & illtreatment of natives in French Congo.'[27]

Although he was only too ready to believe that hands were cut off as a punishment for insufficient delivery of wild rubber, and that this was part of a 'system' for which the Belgian administration was mainly responsible, from his previous extensive acquaintance with the locality he was able to see with his own eyes that the claim that much of the region had been seriously depopulated was true. Almost immediately after setting off on his journey of investigation he wrote: 'The country a desert, no natives left.'[28] Then, at Lukolela, 'population dreadfully decreased – only 93 people left out of many hundreds.'[29] Travelling at first by 'B.M.S. Canoe'[30] and then by a specially chartered steamer, he was able to make a close and independent inspection of the shore settlements. At Ikoko he observed, 'has perhaps 600 people – once 4,000 or 5,000'.[31] His diary yields little evidence of first hand acquaintance with the alleged cause of depopulation, physical cruelty; what there is is summarized in two entries: '16 men women & children tied up from a village Mboye close to the town. . . . The men were put in the prison, the children let go at my intervention.'[32] Then, a week later, 'In evg. Bompoli came with wounded boy – hand off. Awful story.'[33] The latter entry referred to the Epondo case, on the basis of which the Belgians came near to discrediting the whole of Casement's report.

While Casement, having proudly recorded that he had hoisted his consular flag on his steamer, persevered in his cause, equally enthusiastic Belgian apologists were at work. The result of their industry was an anonymous publication entitled *The Truth about the Civilisation in Congoland*[34] which contained, as Part I, a collection of testimonials carefully extracted from the writings of various authors whose verdict was judged to be likely to carry weight with world opinion. After an introductory 'Letter from the King-Sovereign of the Congo Free State to the State agents' the anthology gave extracts from a varied selection of men, including HM Consul Pickersgill, Sir Harry Johnston, Sir Henry Stanley, Casement's old missionary acquaintance, the Rev. Holman Bentley and several other missionaries. Judiciously selected quotations either maintained that the atrocities did not occur or admitted that they did occur because the Belgian administration had not yet had time to eradicate the barbarous traditions of the savage population. Of necessity it was from among those who were practising the bestial tribal traditions that the first generation of native officials had been recruited. Was it really so remarkable that in the first decades of the introduction of civilized ethics there were many cases of reversion to savagery? Considering the vast area in which little more than two thousand Europeans lived, it was not surprising that officers found it difficult to discipline raw recruits. Nevertheless, the Belgians were making good strides towards civilizing the savage; atrocities became less frequent as Belgian influence was extended. Part II was subtitled: 'Answers to the attacks of Messrs Murphy, Sjöblom, Sheppard, Morrisson, Parminter, Burrows, Canisius, etc., etc.' Casement, whose opinion had not yet been published, was not a lone voice crying in the wilderness. He proved, however, to be the most effective voice.

The great disadvantage of the White Paper which appeared in February 1904[35] was that it did not name names. Code letters were used for people and places and in the one instance in which the Belgians were able to identify the victim and the alleged perpetrator of the crime, they were able to bring forward a plausible refutation. A second White Paper, containing 'a preliminary reply to Mr Casement's Report' appeared in June 1904.[36] The Belgian reply gave general explanations for an admitted decline in population, attributing it to sleeping-sickness, smallpox, difficulties of replenishing the stock of slaves under the present administration and ease of migration. It then turned its attention to the Epondo case, which they had been able to investigate fully as Casement had taken accused and accuser to the authorities at Coquilhatville and, in the course of his investigations, the acting public prosecutor had discovered that the natives had plotted the whole affair in order to avoid work (the obligation of natives to work was tacitly accepted by both sides as part of the civilizing process). Epondo had been bitten by a wild boar and gangrene had set in, resulting in the loss of a hand. But Casement was quick to notice that an adjacent bullet wound had not been explained. Also, the intimidating circumstances in which Epondo retracted his statement deprived the Belgian defence of some of its strength. Nearly half the Belgian reply was devoted to the case, whereas Casement's treatment of it amounted to two and a quarter pages out of nearly sixty.

The international repercussions of Casement's report were not as clear-cut as might have been expected. In the absence of specific accusations, other than the Epondo case, the United States press was, at first, inclined to accept Leopold's refutation at its face value. The publicity served a useful purpose, however, by attracting the attention of persons with missionary connections in the Congo and this led to the report being put before the Senate. Once this step had been taken, it was only natural that the United States should come round to Lord Lansdowne's view that Leopold should be encouraged to set up a commission of enquiry. The king, making one of his few tactical errors, had mentioned the need for judicial investigation as the reason for his wishing to obtain a copy of the uncensored version of the report. Now he had to make the best of his own suggestion.

Soon the Italian Assembly was demanding an investigation. Italian officers had been serving as mercenaries in the Congo Free State and this involvement might well have been enough to keep the Congo out of their headlines, had a lieutenant not chosen to kill himself rather than face trial for alleged atrocities. Even so, the issue remained confused because for a time it seemed that both sides were prepared to use false testimony. Leopold had influential friends, such as Henry Wellington Wack, a New York lawyer, who were prepared to distort the record in order to defend the vested interests of the Free State; eventually Wack was denounced in the American press, but not until he had achieved a propaganda coup with *The Story of the Congo Free State*,[37] an impressive volume with the air of authority about it. A still greater achievement in the war of words was the compromising of Morel by Antonio Benedetti. Formerly an employee of the Free State, Benedetti offered to write atrocity stories on receipt of suitable payment; he then presented the contract to his Belgian employers as evidence of Morel's willingness to bribe him. As the months went by it became clear that confusion in the minds of the thinking public would only be dissipated by a Belgian report which substantially agreed with the consul's findings. Then, and only then, might the cruel system of native exploitation be ended, and the European powers take warning that they must tread more carefully in future.

It was a period of much heart-searching for Casement. The humanitarian cause which he had espoused seemed to be being undermined, and he felt that his personal integrity was no longer taken for granted. One implication of the replies of Belgians and other friends of the Congo régime was that he was the dupe of English rubber interests, and though it was unlikely that contemporary public opinion thought any less of him, the slanders stuck well enough for them to be remembered, and at least partially accepted, by British agencies when, years later, his treasonable acts had brought him low. A major source of resentment at the time was the Foreign Office's refusal to support him by publishing a selection of the contents of its Congo atrocity file. Such a revelation would have added great strength to his case, but would have opened Great Britain to the charge of inexcusable inaction over a long period. Disillusionment came to the fore again and one symptom of it was the feeling that his superiors would be a lot happier if he were to resign.

There is no doubt that the Foreign Office did not wish to see the last of a man who, though touchy and long-winded, was showing what great things a positive interpretation of consular responsibility could achieve. On the contrary, it had earmarked him for promotion and, in August 1903, he had received congratulations from Underwood, vice-consul at Boma, on his appointment to Lisbon, a coveted post which was to be regarded as a just reward for good service. What the Foreign Office had not bargained for, however, was a major change which was occurring in his beliefs and priorities. During the period of the preparation of the report, its publication and the reactions which it set in motion, he had been living at a number of addresses in Great Britain and Ireland and had undergone various stresses and strains, some, but not all, of which were connected with the Congo. Part of the difficulty came from his being pulled in too many directions at once; his brothers and sister were a constant emotional and financial burden to him; he was heavily involved in the Congo Reform Association; and there was another factor which played its part in unsettling him: the suddenness of his fame. It threw him off his balance and led to a certain amount of tension between him and some of his Foreign Office superiors, notably Sir Eric Barrington. But other, more fundamental, influences had begun to make their mark on him.

CHAPTER 4

CONSUL ON LEAVE

The influences which exerted special pressures upon Casement during 1904–6 had two main geographical locations: London and the area which is traditionally known as the Glens of Antrim. Except when his means allowed somewhat extravagant holidays, usually in the interests of physical recuperation, it was normally to these two centres that he returned when on leave. In London, although some lodgings proved more congenial than others, they were all, to use one of his favourite adjectives, a little 'seedy', and he never enjoyed a wholly satisfactory *pied-à-terre*. In Antrim, until 1914, one door was always open to him as of right: Magherintemple. The uncertainties and ambiguities of his early years had brought about a confused attitude to the family seat. The practical effect of this was that he was repeatedly drawn there, but, once arrived, soon sought alternative company and accommodation. His diary entries for the end of 1903[1] provide a good example of his pattern of behaviour. On 22 December he left London to spend Christmas with the family and, after some sexual indulgences in Dublin, made his way by train, with an overnight stay in Belfast, to Ballycastle, where he arrived on Christmas Eve: 'No one to meet me. Cold and bleak. I will not go there again. . . . House changed but *not* improved at all – on the contrary.'[2] Christmas Day was no better: 'Miserable day';[3] nor St Stephen's Day: 'Miserable place to stay in this.'[4] On 27 December the adjective was used for the third time and he recorded that all except himself went to church. On 28 December he had had as much as he could stand and went off to meet his sister Nina in Portrush; there followed a hectic and happy social round which included a call at the Ascendancy house of Rose Young, a friend of his youth and an ardent Nationalist.

Since the Treaty of 1921 and the closing of ranks which followed it, there has been a temptation to oversimplify the social and political background of the parts of Ulster in which Casement lived or moved. The division between staunch loyalists of Protestant persuasion and Roman

Catholic agitators, though it has statistical support, glosses over many important exceptions and counter currents. Stereotypes, built in the image of Craig or Collins, conceal the diversity of conviction held by individuals whose origins and environment appeared to be firmly on one side or the other of the main issue. While the dark clouds of Home Rule gathered over their heads, the Protestant majority were, it is true, opposed to a weakening of the links with Westminster and the Crown; they found themselves faced with the prospect of a reversal of fortune: from being the privileged representatives of the United Kingdom they might become the persecuted minority of a Catholic state. But within the Province there were many other shades of opinion and Casement, lured to Magherintemple by filial instinct, quickly turned his back on its cold comfort and made his way to more congenial surroundings. Although the evolution of his separatist convictions was, overall, a long drawn out process, beginning with the circumstances of his parentage and early development, he was about to be exposed to pressures which would accelerate his transition from one who had a largely sentimental attachment to Ireland and its less fortunate citizens to a Nationalist who became wholly committed to the Republican cause. There was to be an intermediate stage, when he could be loosely termed a Home Ruler, but this finally gave way to the extreme separatist position.

It was easy for Casement to make the first steps without breaking the ties with his own class; some of the great families of Ulster managed to divide over the basic political issue without the division interfering with family friendships. The Youngs of Galgorm Castle, Ballymena, were one such family; traditionally Unionist, they had produced Rose and another daughter, Charlotte, whose views lay somewhere between the two extremes. They had provided an alternative home for the Casement children after the death of Roger Senior and the relationship was strong until the end ('Love to R.Y. and to Charlotte'[5] was sent from the Tower). Other rebellious folk who were his social or cultural equals, and in whose company he moved more and more freely, were friends of the Youngs, such as Ada McNeill, one of the McNeills of Cushendun. Ada McNeill moved in circles which included members of the Society of Friends and because of this it was at her house that Casement first met Bulmer Hobson.

The McNeills of Cushendun provide another example of an Ascendancy house which, despite a deep gulf of political conviction, remained otherwise united. The only child of an eldest son, Ada McNeill (known to her friends by the Irish form of her name: 'Ide') owned the whole of the Cushendun estate in her youth and showed great hospitality to those concerned with a resurrection of whatever was thought to be best in Ireland. While she moved further towards the principles of Sinn Fein, her first cousin, Ronald (subsequently the first Lord Cushendun), became a promiment Unionist. However, the only outward sign of the split was that when Carson came to stay, Ada McNeill was difficult to locate. Early in her association with Casement she fell in love with him; when she went over to England for his trial, it was in her cousin's London house that she stayed.

It might well be thought that as much of the cultural and political activity, the latter including much verbal rebelliousness, was at a drawing-room conversation level, it was open to the charge of dilettantism. Doubtless there were some whose interest was superficial, but the practical output of week-end house parties and the like, was ultimately of major significance in the resurgence of Ireland in several fields. Part of the reason for this was to be found in the social bond between the politically and culturally non-conformist members of the Ascendancy houses and their easy links with kindred spirits in London. A key figure in the bringing together of interesting minds was Miss Margaret Dobbs, of Castle Dobbs, whose cultural activities led to the festival to which both Casement and Bulmer Hobson were invited. Another important figure, one who, by marriage and career, forged links with London salons, was a principal writer for Bulmer Hobson's weekly paper *The Republic*, Robert Lynd. His subsequent fame as a journalist and essayist, and his marriage to Sylvia Dryhurst, brought her mother, a leading London hostess, into the separatist cause. She became sufficiently close to Casement for the mere mention of her name to bring tears to his eyes when he was confined in the Tower.

Much of the stimuli which elevated the activities of the educated classes, and bridged the gap between their religious and political extremes, was derived from what came to be known as the Irish Literary Renaissance. This, under the guidance of Standish O'Grady,[6] had its beginnings during the late 1870s. O'Grady, who had discovered the Celtic nature of his nation's history on the bookshelves of a country house in 1872, initiated the creation of an Irish national literature in the English language; 'The spirit was Celtic, if the form was English.'[7] Though in the more rigid interpretation of Revival method, the basic grammatical and metrical form was Gaelic; only the vocabulary was English. After the turn of the century, when the Revival was at its height and the greatest works of what had become known as 'Anglo-Irish Literature' were appearing, serious divisions appeared in the ranks of authors and critics; culturally and politically it could be argued that the only truly Irish literature must be expressed in Gaelic. The rise of the Language Movement had been a necessary precursor to the Literary Revival in order that the heroic period of Irish history could provide sources for the new writers, but for some a new work was degraded if it were not expressed in the native language. Again, the term 'Anglo-Irish Literature' had connotations which led to the prejudging of literary merit. That the early writers had substituted a sense of nationality for aggressive Nationalism did not endear them to the purely politically motivated Gaelic writers who came with the rise of Sinn Fein.

Latent troubles of this nature were less obvious as the Literary Renaissance gathered momentum during the 1880s, its body of new literature greatly enhanced by the poetic works of W.B. Yeats. On his leaves, Casement found himself influenced by the differing aesthetic viewpoints which found expression in the country houses of the Antrim glens. A friendship developed between him and an old friend of the Hobsons, Alice Milligan, whose works now form part of the canon of the Revival, and Casement himself contributed in his own way to both sides of the subsequent dispute. At the age of eighteen, while staying at Portglenone House, he had written a very different sort of poem, containing the lines:[8]

> And if a Home Ruler should be such a fool or
> Ass as to come with his preachin' up here –
> He'd get a back hander from Bob Alexander
> Would lave him a black eye for many a year.

Maturity brought about a radical change of style and sentiment:[9]

> Since treason triumphed when O'Neill was
>   forced to foreign flight,
> The ancient people felt the heel of Scotch
>   usurper's might;
> The barren hills of Ulster held a race proscribed
>   and banned
> Who from their lofty refuge viewed their own
>   so fertile land.

Here Nationalist motivation is clothed in the method of the Anglo–Irish writer and such a poem could well have alienated both main schools of thought; as it was published posthumously, it offended no one.

From time to time Casement attempted to learn Gaelic, but could only pay English lip service to the austere convictions eventually expressed by the political Gaelic revivalists. Again, had it been published in his lifetime, *The Irish Language*, from which the following extract is taken, could only have fallen unconvincingly from the lips of a man who was Anglo-Irish in two senses of the term:[10]

> It is gone from the hill and the glen –
>   The strong speech of our sires;
> It is sunk in the mire and the fen
>   Of our nameless desires:

45

We have bartered the speech of the Gael
For a tongue that would pay,
And we stand with the lips of us pale
And all bloodless to-day;

There came something of a climax in this sort of verse writing and in more serious works with the approach of the centenary of the 1798 Rebellion. This was celebrated throughout Ireland and no doubt influenced the founding of the Irish Dramatic Movement in 1899, but in Antrim it led to the development of a wider spectrum of Gaelic cultural activity. Bulmer Hobson's sister, in her ninety-eighth year, remembered how Constance Oldham came from Dublin in 1898 and preached the need for a festival, modelled on the Welsh *Eisteddfod* which had been revived in 1798. The Irish word for such an event was *Feis*, which is today loosely translated as 'festival', but to students of Gaelic, or Gaelic ways, the word 'assembly' would have been a happier translation; like their Welsh equivalents, the *Feiseanna* had roots in their distant past, the earliest having met at Tara in the sixth century. 'It was a tradition among the greater chiefs, or those who sought a commanding leadership, to gather together the learned men of the whole country in national festivals of all Ireland.'[11] Aware of the wider scope which the idea of the *Feis* gave them, Dublin Gaelic enthusiasts had, in 1897, founded the *Feis-ceoil* for the encouragement of native music.

In Antrim, where the Protestant nationalists, still largely in lower case, tended to have the extra enthusiasm of converts to an unexpected heritage, the concept of the *Feis* broadened considerably, so that it could include arts and crafts, traditional games, spinning and weaving, old agricultural talents and much Gaelic music, dancing and poetry. In some ways it was inevitably diluted by such diversification, but the obvious advantage over a purely literary gathering was its appeal to all classes of the community at large. Another factor contributed to the breadth of the appeal: the Antrim movement was able to draw support from the Gaelic League which, founded by Douglas Hyde and Eoin MacNeill in 1893, was still sufficiently non-political to be accepted without many misgivings by Unionists and Home Rulers alike. Practical arrangements did not get going until Casement returned from the Congo, completed his report and, for the first six months of 1904, devoted the major part of his attention to Irish affairs. He became heavily involved in both the organization and execution of the inaugural Cushendall *Feis*, which took place in June. Arranging the event brought together a number of people who, because of their connections, were able to ensure the success of the *Feis* within its own terms of reference, but in the long run it was the friendships which came about because of the enterprise which proved to be more significant to the spread of separatist conviction.

46

Sir Horace Plunkett, the pioneer of the Irish agricultural co-operative movement, came over from London to open what in many ways outwardly resembled an agricultural show. Ada McNeill, on whose home ground the *Feis* was staged, was secretary of the organizing committee and some two thousand people attended, many drawn from the semi-literate Catholic population whose Irish awareness derived from the oral traditions rekindled by the 1798 centenary; anxious that the humbler Irish should not be deprived of the means to attend, Casement himself chartered a boat to bring across the Rathlin islanders. Bulmer Hobson and Casement were the guests of Ada McNeill at Cushendun House and they saw much of Margaret Dobbs and Alice Milligan, both of whom were Gaelic scholars. Another of the organizers was Francis Bigger, Belfast antiquarian and separatist sympathizer, with whom Casement formed a strong relationship. Other than the friendship with Hobson, however, the most important of Casement's liaisons which prospered at the *Feis* was with Alice Stopford Green.

The initial contact between Casement and Mrs Green came about as a result of repeated advice from a mutual friend, Richard Edward Dennett, an agitator for Congo reform since 1886, that Casement should enlist Mrs Green's support in the difficult early days of the Congo Reform Association. Morel, who knew Dennett, also advised Casement to approach her, and he eventually wrote a long, rambling letter, in which he said that 'we must have so much in common in our love for Ireland that I need not go to Africa to seek an introduction to you.'[12] The letter betrays at least as much concern for Irish problems as those of Africa; he knew, from those who spoke of her, and from her writings, that she was 'a patriotic Irishwoman' and he sensed that he was addressing a kindred spirit.

They had come to hold similar views by virtue of remarkably similar personal histories. Alice Stopford had been born in 1849 into a house which, in religious terms, was as narrow as Magherintemple. Her father was the Church of Ireland Archdeacon of Meath and her upbringing was Puritan in the Irish Protestant sense of the term. She sought consolation from the bleakness of her environment in intellectual pursuits and, when her father died in 1874 and the family migrated to London, less than three years elapsed before she was married to one of the most celebrated historians of the day, John Richard Green. Since 1869, however, Green had suffered from tuberculosis and the couple had barely six years together before he died. During this time they worked closely together on a history of England[13] and, when Green died in March 1883, it was left to his widow to conclude his final work.[14] The next few years saw the appearance of Mrs Green as an historian in her own right and her London house became one of the 'salons' which influenced some of the more radical thinkers and talkers of the day.

In simple terms the relationship between the intellectual woman of fifty-four and the man of action of forty was based on a common heritage repudiated in favour of an alternative culture, with which their connection was oblique; each had suffered bereavement and the scars could be seen in their sometimes cynical approach to life. While Mrs Green did not introduce Casement to separatism, she was the catalyst. He wrote to her constantly, as a son might write to his mother, seeking approval of his actions, and seeking forgiveness for doubtful acts, such as the acceptance of a knighthood. They were complementary to one another, in that she saw rebellion in terms of the genesis of ideas (her most rebellious act was to co-operate in the production of an anti-enlistment leaflet)[15] while to Casement, although words were important, and he had a talent for them, all was pointless unless translated into action. They did not become aware of this divergence until the German venture. The summit of Mrs Green's personal contribution to the separatist cause was the publication of *The Making of Ireland and its Undoing*, and Casement fully approved of it; when she heard of his imitation of Wolfe Tone, she became hysterical.

With the arrival of Alice Green at the *Feis*, there had come about a conjunction of several sources of influence which were to lead to the crystallization of Casement's commitment. Although the organizers were in the main Protestant believers in a resurgence of Ireland, not all were to develop their ideas to the extent that they became full Republicans; and a number of individuals found that separation, when it came, was not quite what they had foreseen when they set out along the path of cultural renaissance. Casement was himself at this time pulled in more than one direction; one of the influences which might have diverted him from his eventual belief in nothing less than complete severance of links with the United Kingdom was Richhill Castle, then the house of a close friend of *Feis* organizer, Francis Bigger, Colonel R.G.J.J. Berry.

During the years of Casement's fame as an emancipator of persecuted primitive races, he often used Richhill Castle as what he called 'my sanctuary'.[16] He could even do this when his career required him to be in London; at that time a Foreign Office week-end was much longer than it is today and he was known to go to the extent of travelling from London to Richhill for three week-ends in succession. The friendship spanned twenty years, during part of which time the two men saw much of each other in South America, where the consul and Major Berry, as he then was, travelled long distances together and talked endlessly of Ireland. Despite his friendship with Bigger, which derived much of its impetus from a common interest in archaeology, and the increasingly Nationalist and sometimes anti-English argument of Casement, Berry remained Unionist in conviction. At times his very opposition helped to forge his friend's ideas; but other aspects of life and friendship served to delay the process.[17]

They had in common a love of Ulster, and interest in farming, folklore and orchids, the latter inspired by an expedition which they made together in Brazil. At times Casement was in very poor health and Mrs Berry once nursed him through what her son Desmond believes to have been a nervous breakdown, possibly exacerbated by awareness of the increasingly false position in which, as an employee of the Crown, he was placing himself. For years the relationship survived the tribulations of the growing political gulf; Casement remained a favourite guest, especially popular with the children, to whom he always brought generous gifts and with whom he would spend many hours as a rather special uncle with a gift for story-telling and playing exciting games.

After the *Feis*, Casement went, with much reluctance, to take up his Lisbon post, but could not bring himself to stay longer than two months. He was soon back in Ireland, supposedly unwell, though obviously suffering more in mind than body. It irritated the Foreign Office that he should fail to appreciate the favour that the Service had attempted to bestow upon him, although his employers can have had no intimation, as yet, that a division of loyalties was at the root of his uncertainties. For the whole of 1905 and half of 1906 he was seconded without pay and might well have continued his unimpeded progress towards the Sinn Fein philosophy had it not been for two events, one totally unexpected, which disorientated him. The first of these was the award of a CMG, announced in the king's Birthday Honours List. There followed anxious conferences with friends about the propriety of one who regarded himself as a Home Ruler accepting such a thing. It was purely an acknowledgment of Congo achievements, but it came when its recipient was becoming more inclined to see the source of such honours as one of the sources of Ireland's ills. Bulmer Hobson thought he should accept it; he himself thought otherwise. In the end he compromised and, in so doing, gave a fair commentary on the state of his mind at the time: he became a CMG, but he would not accept the insignia from the hands of King Edward. He wrote from Richhill Castle, declining to attend at Buckingham Palace; later, more diplomatically, he proffered illness as a reason for non-attendance and was sent the insignia by post. The episode was to have an interesting postscript: in February, 1915, when he had strayed a long way from the paths of St Michael and St George, he concluded an open letter to Sir Edward Grey by divesting himself of this and all other honours which it was possible to cast off; when the insignia were returned it was found that the package had never been opened.

Four months after the CMG announcement the findings of the Belgian Commission of Enquiry were published and, although the wording had been cleverly toned down by Leopold, there was no doubt that Casement's report was entirely vindicated. The psychological effect of this

very different event was to draw him back to the British vehicle of emancipation and, for the time being, restore the African natives to pride of
place in his activities. He had been greatly depressed by the way that his
muted report had appeared to be so easily discredited in the eyes of a wide
readership (and had laid part of the blame for this on the squeamishness of
the Foreign Office); now his depression lifted; it seemed to him that a slur
on his honour had been removed, and the Belgian admissions would give
the Congo Reform Association, which he and Morel had established, the
added impetus which it needed.

It would be difficult to confine his Congo investigations within the
terms of a narrow definition of consular functions. What he had achieved,
despite his initial concern with British subjects, was scarcely 'protective',
nor was it clearly seen to be the 'furthering of British interests', over and
above those of other European powers. It was the outward looking side of
consular work, seldom seen by the average consul, and far removed from
the superficially trivial, and often merely clerical, aspects of a consul's
duties which awaited him in his three South American posts. He had
helped to show how the strength and reputation of the British Consular
Service could be used in ways which were not wholly motivated by
national considerations. One measure of his success was that he was to be
called upon to bring the authority of the Service to bear upon a second
humanitarian matter within the same decade; he had set an important
precedent, which reflected credit on himself and the Service generally.

As a public figure now, Casement was going from strength to strength
and the force of his career, despite an apparent slowing down during the
early part of his time in South America, was to absorb some of the energy
which, later on, would be channelled into the Irish cause. However,
looking at the next few years purely from the point of view of consular
leaves, and putting to one side the stream of letters from Mrs Green
addressed to the consulates, one sees that another factor, namely conflicting personal loyalties, also had the effect of delay and diversion from the
taking of a more direct route to Republicanism. There were Unionist
friends in Ireland and there were strong personal attachments in England
with which his sense of loyalty had to contend. The English country house
which exerted the greatest pressures on the embryonic separatist, and
often only served to confuse him, was The Savoy, Denham, Buckinghamshire, where his friends Richard and May Morten lived. There he saw
English traditional hospitality at its best, and was free to extend that
hospitality to others of his own circle; a fine old moated manor house
within half an hour's train journey of central London contained a room
which he could always regard as his. The Moses Room, decorated with
scenes from the life of Moses, painted by a recusant priest, was the nearest
thing to a place of his own which he had in England; it was an appropriate

setting for one who was more Catholic than he knew, and he spent much time in it, writing reports for the Foreign Office and a large number of letters, many of which are still extant and bear his friends' address.

While considering the journey towards a total political commitment one becomes aware that, apart from the wider influences of the anti-slavery movement, and their bearing on the comparatively narrow quest for Irish National Independence, there was a distinctly Celtic factor at work, wider in implication than Irish Republicanism. One of the country house guests whom Casement met – probably not at The Savoy – and to whom, in his long and involved brief to counsel,[18] he gave the credit for bringing him to the moment of realization, was one of the early Scottish Nationalists, the Hon. Louisa Elizabeth Farquharson of Invercauld Castle. The parallel of her origins with Irish Protestant Ascendancy rebels was striking; four years older than her recruit, she became Chief of the Gaelic Society of London in 1908. Then there was also, though this was much more ephemeral, a Welsh dimension in the evolution of his thought. It has already been seen that the *Feiseanna* owed much to the *Eisteddfodau* and there were many loyal Irishmen and Ulstermen to whom, as with most Welsh people, cultural aspirations were the beginning and the end of a renaissance. But a frequent visitor to Richard Morten's house was a sympathetic Welshman who inspired sufficient confidence for Casement to develop and confide in him his most radical hopes. He was John Hartman Morgan, the son of a Congregational minister from the Rhondda, who rose to be adviser to the American War Crimes Commission at Nuremberg. From his mother, the daughter of Felix Wethli, he drew an interest in German affairs and was research scholar of the University of London at Berlin in 1903 and 1904. He and Casement first met (probably at Joseph Conrad's Sussex house) in 1904; the friendship grew in the hospitable environment provided by the Mortens. Apart from the help which he gave (without fee) to the defence at the state trial, Morgan's earlier relationship with Casement has been largely overlooked. Letters which illuminate this area of his life did not appear until after his death in 1955. Auctioned at Sotheby's on 15 July 1957, they were bought by Alfred Noyes, whose book on Casement had already been published on 15 April of that year. Noyes died less than a year after the purchase and the key to the cabinet in which the letters were kept was mislaid by his widow; the letters next became available in 1979.

F.E. Smith's declaration at the trial that the prisoner's hatred of his country was 'as malignant in quality as it was sudden in origin',[19] modified in his reminiscences to 'his interest in his native country was of recent origin'[20] had the effect of tilting scholarship too much in the direction of an early Republican decision. The truth was not so simple; while the seeds of the treasonable acts are to be found in his ancestry, his early inclinations towards separatism were spasmodic affairs and there was much drawing back from the brink. An indication of this hesitancy is given by the anonymity of his contributions to journals sympathetic to the concept of devolution; at first he is 'X', and only a chosen few can identify the author; then the circle widens a little and he becomes 'Shan Van Vocht': 'The Poor Old Woman', a popular representation of Ireland, used by his friend Alice Milligan for the name of her own journal, and made most powerful in Yeats's 'Cathleen-ni-Houlihan' in 1904. At these points in his development the die is not yet cast, and only when his own signature appears does the possibility of turning back become less feasible.

The shift of emphasis which occurred between the part of Casement's consular career which took place in Africa and the important part which was still to come was soon to be nicely summarized by the letterhead which the consul had specially printed for official use in Santos; 'British Consulate' became 'Consulate of Great Britain and Ireland'. It was not just a matter of Casement the clerk having a joke at the expense of the Foreign Office. It reflected with some accuracy the present state of his political evolution: he was still a servant of the United Kingdom; the time had not yet come for the British connection to be severed altogether.

CHAPTER 5

CONSUL OF GREAT BRITAIN AND IRELAND

Apart from his abortive two months in Lisbon, Casement had had no active consular employment for well over two years, and no pay for eighteen months. Now, in the latter part of 1906, the Foreign Office coaxed him out of his premature retirement and, still consistent in their predilection for Portuguese posts for him, offered Santos, and he accepted it. The conditions and surroundings of a South American consul were completely alien to anything he had experienced in Africa; therefore, before considering this part of Casement's performance as a public official, some consideration should be given to the social milieu in which he found himself and the social environment within which consuls in general were expected to move.

The social position of the consul in Victorian times and, to a slightly lesser degree, in Edwardian times, was an ambiguous one. As is well known, in the nineteenth century social strata and the financial levels of society were closely correlated and, as until 1919 the minimum private income required to allow one to follow a diplomatic career was £400 pa, a more precise and practical line was drawn than is commonly found in the English class system. Those who fell below the mark and became consuls might have been expected, as was customary in England, to know and accept their place in society. But for the consul there was a complication; he might happily accept that he wore silver where the diplomat wore gold, he might be unworried by his seven-gun salute, and he might forgive the St James's Club for only admitting the true diplomats, were it not for the change in his social status which occurred – or seemed to occur – when he accepted certain overseas postings. Despite the squalid conditions of many a British consulate, it was often an easy matter for the General Service consul abroad to assume the social, if not political, status of a diplomat. It is true that certain European clubs were closed to him, but in Africa and both the Americas he could generally be expected to be treated as an English gentleman.

Finding himself on a higher social level abroad than he was accorded in his own country, the career consul might have been expected to make the best of things and accept the consolations of life overseas; unfortunately, precisely because of the prejudices against him in Great Britain – he was, after all, reputed to be in some way dabbling 'in trade' – his salary was often insufficient to permit entertaining on an adequate scale. There was a way round this, and it was permitted by the terms of his appointment: he could (as has been seen) divert the office allowance into his own pocket. This, naturally, lowered the standard of his professional services (if they may be so termed) and went some way to explain the poor physical state of many consulates.

From Canning's time consuls had urged that if they were to be sources of commercial intelligence they had to enter fully into the social round of their district, and yet in some (not all) postings this could only be achieved by cutting back in office efficiency. Inefficiency led to repercussions at the Foreign Office, which served further to strain relations and give the Service a bad name. It was just one of the vicious circles. An entertainments allowance was the answer, but orthodox Foreign Office opinion was that consuls, unlike diplomats, were not expected to entertain, although on-the-spot conditions could make entertaining imperative.

The attitude that the consul was a lesser species was expressed in a letter from Sir Hughe Knatchbull-Hugessen to Sir Alexander Cadogan, in which the author amplified the minority report signed by the diplomatic members of the 1938 Departmental Committee:[1]

> Though we should be far from suggesting that personality, 'address', and *savoir-faire* are not of great importance in the Consular Service, it is in the Diplomatic Service that these rather intangible qualities are most essential. A diplomatic officer must be . . . able to deal as an equal with foreign colleagues, Cabinet Ministers, Prime Ministers and Heads of State; to hold his own with Sovereigns and other royalties and to fraternise with the governing class . . . all suspicions of an inferiority complex must be absent from his make-up.

Clearly it would not have suited Sir Hughe Knatchbull-Hugessen's case to have recalled Roger Casement's easy association with such personages, particularly as the chip on Casement's shoulder was a common ingredient of Foreign Office gossip.

It is, however, possible to lay too much emphasis on the consul's socially marginal position; on his being nearly a diplomatic gentleman, but not quite. One should accept that low morale came from other causes. A common cause was simply the inability of Victorians and Edwardians to adapt to new climatic conditions. Then there was disease. Consul Cowper, one of Casement's predecessors in Santos, emphasized this in his annual report of 1880;[2] 'When they [the rains] hold up it is simply assassination to the olfactory organs, and death begins to walk long-legged through the population.' This had practical consequences, too, which will have had a depressing effect: 'Usually the dampness of Santos is so great that the impression is that of a constant vapour bath; it ruins clothing, and turns writing into blotting paper.' Language was another problem. Consuls were seldom good linguists, and yet Casement inherited a vice-consul who could neither write nor speak English. Money, as has been seen, was an ever present source of grievance; but, above all, there was a feeling of abandonment, a feeling that in this 'aggregation of posts' circumstances effectively ruled out the development of the *esprit de corps* that was so badly needed. The poor relation syndrome was a factor, but it was one of many.

In some ways a consul's situation was like that of a Church of England parson in the period between the wars. There were good livings, but the majority were scattered throughout the country in their island parishes. Stipends were generally inadequate, but the office and sometimes the vicarage accorded a status in the local community which was beyond worldly means. A basic difference was that in the clergyman's scale of values poverty was a virtue and he always had his Bible. The consul had the same attitude to money as his diplomatic superior, and he consistently declined to accept that his consular instructions were embodied in a sacred book.

In Africa the supervising legation or embassy might be as far away as Lisbon; therefore the consul, who usually reported direct to the Foreign Office, could achieve something approaching the political status of an ambassador, and his social position within the expatriate community, or the society at large, might not be as delicate as in (ex-colonial) independent states such as those of South America. Although Casement's three South American appointments were all Brazilian and all ports, the social environment within which he found himself was varied. The variation in social milieu was not merely geographic, as the distance from Santos to Pará might suggest, it was significantly altered by his promotion to consul-general and the shifting of his domicile to the capital city. In some ways a consul-generalship was socially more ambivalent than the status of consul; the constrast between the consulate-general in Rio de Janeiro (rooms over a cookshop) and the legation at Petropolis was dramatic and the situation was probably only aggravated by the thin line of gold braid edging the predominantly silver embroidery of the uniform and the addition of two guns to the salute. Such things carried more than reasonable weight with Casement, whose personal ambiguity had started with the union of his Roman Catholic mother with his Ulster 'Black Protestant' father, and whose political, religious and social development had always been subject to the uncertainties which pre-dated his mother's own birth within the Catholic (untitled) line of the famous Ascendancy house of Jephson.

The acceptance of coffee as the chief national crop led to a shift of economic power from north-east Brazil to south-east Brazil,[3] and eventually, over a period of some forty years, to the rise of Santos. The economic change of emphasis, with other factors, meant that, even during the period in which the abolition of slavery was anticipated, São Paulo became increasingly bound up with the institution. Drought, disease and famine in the sugar districts of the north led to quick slave sales and the São Paulo coffee planters were the buyers, so that as late as February 1885, Acting Consul Hampshire wrote: 'The cultivation [of coffee] is almost entirely carried on by slaves, and nothing is being done to substitute free for slave labour,'[4] and Consul Cowper commented in 1889 that the Province had contained over 100,000 slaves when the law of abolition was promulgated.[5] By the time of Casement's arrival, not very long afterwards, the ex-slaves were simply accepted as part of the normal labouring class. This comparatively enlightened attitude was not shown, however, where mixed blood was concerned; and sadly, Casement, whose genuine respect and affection for the negro and the amerindian was an example to his generation, shared this prejudice of the day and expressed his feelings about 'hybrid' races with considerable vehemence.

The inauspicious beginning of his South American career recalled the mishaps of his arrival at Lorenzo Marques. On 16 October 1906 he wrote, as was customary, informing the President of the State of São Paulo of his appointment and requesting an audience. There was no reply and, some weeks later, his attention was drawn to a paragraph in the *Estado de São Paulo* reporting the contents of his letter. While having luncheon in Santos on 12 December at 1.30 pm he chanced to see an announcement in the same newspaper that *Vice*-consul Casement was to be received by the president in São Paulo (49 miles away) at 2.00 pm on the same day. As copies of the newspaper did not reach Santos until 10.00 am on the day of issue and the first train to São Paulo departed at 1.50 pm, to arrive at 4.25 pm, one can sympathize with the consul in his predicament. There was a typical flurry of despatches from him: in the end he – untypically – decided that he should take no action and attribute the unfortunate episode to 'local custom'.

Having performed the necessary rituals of assuming a new post – reporting arrival, sending a list of fee stamps received and specimen signature (all to the Foreign Office) – Casement immediately made himself known to the legation and applied himself to the consular duties defined above as 'protective'. His predecessor, Francis Mark, had handed the consulate over to Acting British Consul Thomas Thornton, a coffee merchant, who had seen fit to notify the Foreign Office, in May 1906,[6] that he thought 'it somewhat of a disgrace that a British consulate should be in such a condition', and had offered to spend some money on it if the Foreign Office would guarantee him a definite period of tenure. His offer was not well received and when, in October 1906,[7] he reported that he had handed over property and archives to Consul Casement, CMG the minutes revealed the Foreign Office attitude to him: '? Thank for services.' (Initialled by Chauncy Cartwright and Cecil Francis Dormer.) 'I don't think we need thank. He probably made something by it.' (Initialled by Rowland Sperling.)

Thornton had not exaggerated; Mark had allowed things to sink to a very low state and had eventually to arrange for a wire-netting frame to be installed to prevent hostile sailors from throwing things at him. Casement's immediate worries were twofold: the state of the archives and that Mark had been ignorant of consular instructions with regard to *Lex Loci* marriages. The problem for Casement was how to make his point without actually harming Mark, and the oblique method which he adopted can be variously interpreted as cowardly, sly or diplomatic. A letter,[8] written three days after he had taken over the consulate, was addressed to Sperling at the Foreign Office and gave his true feelings in the matter of the archives; Mark was a disgrace, though the disgraceful state of affairs was partly caused by lack of Foreign Office policy in this field. This letter had 'Cancelled R.C.' written neatly on page one and was enclosed within a 'PRIVATE' letter (dated 20 October) to Sperling, saying that Mark was a good man, popular in Santos, justifying the enclosure and also justifying its cancellation. In other words, the consul wanted his original letter read, but did not want to take the consequences of having written it; the Foreign Office saw through his ruse and took no action.

Casement's concern for archives was not a passing whim, prompted by the inheritance of a post in a poor state of repair, it is a recurrent theme throughout his despatches. A compulsive letter and diary writer – he sometimes had three diaries running simultaneously – it was a matter close to his heart, as is implied by the large percentage of Foreign Office and legation records extant in his hand. He was concerned with the recording of matters of great import: one of his diaries was offered and used in evidence given to the Select Committee investigating the Putumayo atrocities in 1913;[9] and he was concerned, perhaps disproportionately, with the small details of clerical matters: cost of stationery and difficulty of obtaining envelopes of the right size, particularly when new regulations came out saying that sheets must not be folded. Trivial matters at first sight, but very much to the point if office efficiency was to be improved. In Casement's view the Foreign Office should have assumed responsibility for the supply of uniform stationery throughout the consular service (an opinion which, if translated into fact, would have prevented him from introducing his new letterhead, and illustrates, in a small way, the beginnings of his ability to face two ways on an issue). The peak of his feeling in this matter was reached when, on transfer to Pará, he took over a consulate 'without a bottle of ink, a pen or a sheet of paper'.[10]

Contrary to the popularly received view of Casement's dramatic fall from grace, the evidence points to excessive zeal in the clerical area as an early source of irritation. Thus, apropos another letter to Sperling about stationery, one finds the minute, dated 8 March 1907, signed L.M. (Louis Mallet), 'he will always be a source of trouble.'[11] The wish for good clerical standards, coupled with a similar desire to change the arrangement whereby consuls bore a responsibility to pay clerks out of their own office allowances, led to much haggling over expenses and, by the time he had taken over the consulate-general at Rio, the issue had engendered unfair reaction, viz. W. Chauncy Cartwright's minute of 15 November 1909: 'The salaries of the Chief Clerk and the Second Clerk are very high, but Mr Casement seems to leave a great deal to the Chief Clerk which he might do himself.' As the author of many eleven-page despatches on issues great and small, Casement was often guilty of shouldering too much of the secretarial work; never too little.

The *Lex Loci* marriage matter reflected an aspect of Casement the archivist. While sorting out the muddle of the Santos consular records he discovered that Mark had illegally solemnized more than one marriage in breach of paragraph 18 of Chapter XXI of the general instructions,[12] the operative words being 'the Consular marriage alone can be registered at the Consulate.' Mark's error was to allow the ceremony to be performed in São Paulo, to which town Mark was not accredited and where the local vice-consul was not a marriage officer. At first Casement cited two cases, one 'marriage' which took place in 1897, and another in 1902. These examples he used in his Foreign Office despatch, received 7 January 1907.[13] To the legation at Petropolis he sent (on 6 December 1906)[14] eight foolscap pages of explanation and eight additional pages giving details of many marriages which he claimed to be invalid.

His worry was that numerous children had been born and their legal status was now called in question. Carried away with the argument he explained how, although Mark had had rooms over a music shop in São Paulo, they were 'essentially his private chambers and could not be termed the 'British Consul's residence', an irrelevant observation as the marriage he was citing had taken place in the private residence of one Percy Lupton. In any case, he went on, Mark only went there 'from Saturday to Monday, and on public holidays when the Consulate was officially closed'. In another instance a marriage ceremony had been performed by Alan S. Hawksworth, the English chaplain, at the bride's stepfather's house, in breach of another part of paragraph 18 (Chapter XXI), which stipulated 'in a church or chapel'. This, therefore, was not *Lex Loci*.

Here, plainly, was a case of an unusual consul leaning too heavily on his consular instructions. Testily the Foreign Office took the common sense view and simply ruled that the marriages were valid. Their attitude was echoed a few years later when the Law Lords ruled that Casement himself was the king's liege wherever he was. Another example of his tendency to lose his sense of proportion was reflected in a letter to the Foreign Office, dated 12 April 1907,[15] from which his superiors learned that when issuing a passport he had charged 2/6 instead of 5/-, and affixed a stamp for 2/6; there were no passport forms, so he had used a sheet of foolscap. What should he do? The enquiry may, of course, have had an ulterior motive; it certainly shows the trivial nature of aspects of an official position which might also demand political acumen.

Shortly after Casement's arrival in Santos, William Haggard took up office as the new British Minister in Petropolis and Casement immediately addressed a loyal, rather fulsome, letter to him, expressing the wish that he would soon visit the British Community of Santos. This was soon followed by a more routine consular despatch (seven foolscap pages) complaining that the Royal Mail Steamship officers were no longer being allowed to send consular bags direct to the consulate. The customs officer insisted that they went via the post office instead. The crisis was soon smoothed over.

Throughout his period at Santos it became more and more evident that Casement was not the, at best, inactive, at worst, disloyal public official – only to shine later when revealing the iniquities of a British registered company in the Upper Amazon basin. His sins are those of excessive commitment, rather than sins of omission. Firstly he showed himself as the keen archivist and clerk; next he was to protect the good name of England in a generous and unusually positive way which might be described as being over and above the call of duty.

There had appeared in the local paper a strongly worded protest about the large number of drunken vagabonds, German and English, who roamed the streets of São Paulo and Santos and made themselves a public nuisance. The new consul was quick to accept responsibility for the distressed seamen among them, but there was still a substantial residue who were technically ineligible for assistance and Casement found the situation disturbing. The solution, as he saw it, was to be found in General Consular Instructions (1893), Chapter XVI – Relief of Distressed British Subjects, where paragraph 4 obliged him to show 'that every effort has been made by recourse to local charitable agencies or other available sources.' This, to him, provided a way of overcoming the limitation imposed by paragraph 1: 'Such relief . . . should be refused to persons who make a profession of begging.' Casement knew from his experience in

Africa that the Foreign Office was a fickle employer when it came to reimbursing a consul for helping a pauper out of his own pocket, and there was no 'charitable agency' in São Paulo on which he could draw. He therefore launched an appeal to raise a fund, couching his circular in patriotic terms: 'I think that as British subjects we cannot view with complete unconcern the degradation and demoralisation to which many of our fellow countrymen expose themselves in the streets of a Brazilian city.'

The circular letter[16] went out with a sheet headed 'SUBSCRIPTION LIST. Amounts Already Subscribed or Promised: Roger Casement, C.M.G. . . . 100$000' (£50 at the current rate of exchange). It was circulated to the principal British residents of the district and the first recorded donation to be received was 500$000 from a personal friend, John Keevil, on behalf of the London and River Plate Bank. The appeal circular was dated 12 December 1906 and by 17 January 1907 the consul was able to report to the Foreign Office that 2.050$000 had been subscribed 'and promises have been received from other quarters.'

In his short period at Santos Casement showed positive interest in other 'protective' causes and began to formulate minor campaigns for consular reform. His opinions on honorary consular officials were already beginning to conflict with the Walrond Committee of 1903,[17] that 'unpaid Consuls, in some cases foreigners, are doing most useful service.' This may be contrasted with: 'Useless to instruct V. Consul at Paranagua',[18] referring to Senhor Gomes, the Honorary British official who could speak no English, and from whom replies were never received. But the issue was much more serious than was at first realized and Casement's opinions were to find their most telling expression when the vested interests of honorary consuls came into conflict with their own 'protective' responsibilities in the Upper Amazon basin.

Late 1906 and early 1907 saw the carrying out of typical consular chores, of which a brief selection is given to illustrate the lot of a South American consul of the period. Colville Barclay, the British Minister (before Haggard) to whom Casement had acknowledged 'Commission and Exequatur' sent a despatch to all consuls on the subject of their duty to report the movement of foreign warships and the inadequacy of the documents which were used for this purpose; subsequent correspondence emphasized that it was a specific function to obtain photographs of foreign war-vessels. This matter having been attended to, there was the death of distressed seaman Joseph Waugh, on whose relief the consul had expended 50$800. Then William Aldred, in England, encouraged by his MP, sought to find Thomas Aldred, last heard of in the state of São Paulo. Thomas Aldred was found. And Senhor Gomes was 'for some time now absent from his post and . . . thought to be in Rio de Janeiro',[19] a circumstance which led not merely to his dismissal, but to the abolition of the post. A 'Private' letter[20] to Haggard shows that the inspector of customs in Santos, 'an ignorant, ill-mannered boor', brought a charge of attempted smuggling against the captain of the sailing ship *Dawn* when, apparently, he was merely obeying the pilot; the fine of 500$000 was eventually waived, after a petition to the Ministro da Fazenda by the local shipping agent. And throughout the period the consulate devoted much of its time to the steady stream of distressed British seamen.

Part of the other main division of a consul's functions – the furtherance of British interests – lay, as has been seen, in the preparation of the annual report. In length, as might be expected, the Santos report[21] does not disappoint, though many of its forty pages are devoted to tables lifted, in the customary way, from the *Brazilian Review*. If one is concerned with the amount of work put into it, it compares very favourably with the efforts of his contemporaries and his predecessors. At this time it was not unknown for a consul to limit his remarks to little more than a page, complaining that there was nothing to say, except that local conditions were difficult to endure. Again, convention allowed a brief essay: general introduction, followed by a few relevant topics and then a few pages of tables, showing details of imports and exports and the shipping companies used, from whatever sources were available. Casement did not keep to the minimum: he gave a thoughtful analysis of the British position and took the trouble to intersperse his tables of trade figures at appropriate points and relate them to the text.

The report as a whole is a thorough piece of work which, by any standard, could be said to serve British interests. There is, though, more to it than might meet the eye. After an innocent enough reference, on page 35, to possible openings for Irish ham and bacon dealers, Casement goes on to reveal that there is a protest motive at work in what he has to say. Under the heading 'Irish Trade' on page 36 he points out that all goods coming from Great Britain and Ireland are lumped together in Brazilian Customs returns as 'Ingleze' – this makes it quite impossible for a statistical report to take Ireland into account and, by implication, the annual report from HBM Consul for Great Britain and Ireland is not serving one of the kingdoms. Guinness alone, by virtue of its famous brand name, was immune from statistical prejudice, and the consul reported that it was increasingly imported 'owing partly to the recommendation of the medical faculty'.[22]

The serious belief behind the amended wording at the top of Santos consular headed paper was to be explained at some length, nine years later, when Casement addressed Irish prisoners in a German prisoner-of-war camp:[23]

The King you agreed to serve is, in law, King of Great Britain and Ireland. There is no such person as the King of England in law. How have these Sovereigns discharged their duty to their Irish subjects? For remember these obligations are mutual.

The dual-monarchy principle had had respectable antecedents in Hungary, a country in whose affairs Casement's father had played a small yet significant part, and was influencing Arthur Griffith, P.S. O'Hegarty and Casement's friend, Bulmer Hobson, in their creation of the political philosophy of Sinn Fein. That the principle was already taking root in Casement's mind may be evidenced by the peremptory tone of a letter now bound (by the PRO) within a diatribe of 20 October 1906[24] on the subject of archives. In it he stated that he understood that a circular had been sent to all consuls early in 1906 instructing them 'to make special reference to imports from Ireland into their consular district in their Annual Reports'. He could not find the circular in question in the muddle of papers he had inherited and asked for a copy.

The evidence for Casement's attitude to the Brazilians during his Santos period is contained in his letters to friends and, if for no other reason than that it is contradictory, is distinctly misleading. Most letter writers are guilty of distorting their views to some extent, to come to terms with the views of the recipients; with Casement it was a chronic failing, which serves as a guide to the degree of his ambivalence: to Sir Edward Grey in March 1907 – 'people are kind and obliging';[25] to Gertrude Bannister in April 1907 – 'Brazil and the Brazilians are vile. I can't bear them – mud-coloured swine!'[26] One of the characteristics of Brazilian society which he (consistently) found irritating was the way in which they aped Parisians. Contemporary photographic evidence supports his impression that over-extravagant Parisian modes of dress were worn in the 'wrong' place at 'wrong' times. The Brazilians were not alone in their unconvincing attempts to follow French fashions, but Casement's response showed that in this particular form of intolerance he was more English than the English.

If, in this matter, the evidence of letters is an unreliable guide to Casement's true thoughts, one must turn to the actual behaviour of the man to see how, in fact, he reacted to the social environment of Santos. In so far as the Casement biographers have accorded space to the Santos year, they have largely based their accounts on his letters to Mrs Green. She now regarded him as one of her protégés, and he, increasingly, cast her in the role of mentor; their correspondence, and what he wrote to Gertrude Bannister, gives the impression of a frustrated rebel, living a lonely life, isolated both from the Brazilians and the expatriate community. In fact, like his famous predecessor in the post, Richard Burton, he took up residence as far from his place of work as his salary would allow and became a respected member of the English colony; that he lived in the 'settlement', as it was called, and was part of it, has been overlooked.

The 'settlement' was in Guarujá on the healthy, seaward, side of the island of Santo Amaro, which partly sheltered the entrance to Santos harbour. The island boasted an old Portuguese fort in good repair and, with its thirty miles of sea beaches, colonial style houses and good hotels, was wholly unlike the bustling community of Santos which was a good forty minutes away. Here social life was in the traditional English overseas style and Casement seldom stepped outside it. There is reference in a Foreign Office despatch to 'service having been performed at the Consul's private residence ten miles from Guaryá (sic)',[27] but for the most part he lived at the leading hotel or stayed with his friend, John Keevil, manager of the London and River Plate Bank.

Much has been made of acceleration of rebelliousness at this stage in Casement's career. The 'small, rather snobbish, English colony', as Consuelo Keevil (daughter of John) later described it,[28] merely regarded him as eccentric – never a great sin in English eyes – and he remained a firm friend of the Keevils until the day he was executed. His host, of Puritan stock, noted that his first act on arrival was always to hang a crucifix above his bed (an action not typical of Ulster Protestants) and he was known to talk about Ireland to excess – the only extant photograph of him at this time shows him reading *Some Recollections of an Irish R.M.* on the Keevils' verandah. Invited to dinner, he might come in correct dinner jacket and tie, but with old brown trousers and gym shoes. Such behaviour excited much talk, but little resentment.

The only *faux pas* of the Santos period which really did cause offence actually occurred when Casement stayed with English friends in Rio de Janeiro. Put together with comments[29] made later by Ernest Hambloch, Casement's vice-consul during his consul-generalship, it may account partly for the contrast between the comparatively friendly social life which he enjoyed in Santos and the ugly rumours which circulated about him in Rio. It happened that when two Irish stowaways – young illiterate peasant boys – who had boarded a Royal Mail Line ship at Southampton, were discovered and put ashore at Santos for the consul to dispose of them, John Keevil took one as a gardener and Casement took the other as a valet, dressing him in navy jacket, 'yachting cap' and white trousers to suit his new station in life. The disagreeable incident occurred when Casement discovered that his servant had been given a folding canvas bed in the servants' quarters; enraged, he had the boy removed to his own room and gave him his own bed. The hostess was predictably furious and did not keep the details of the incident to herself.[30]

Casement was granted two months leave 'on urgent private affairs'[31] (nature unspecified) from 1 July and returned to his former landlady, a Miss Cox, in Earls Court. Thence he soon departed for Magherintemple. His leave, though brief, had its share of such incidents as can influence the course of a man's political development. Among these was a Belfast labour dispute which led to troops opening fire on strikers, killing three and injuring many. Letters[32] to Gertrude Bannister show the deep impression which this tragic event made on her cousin. The atmosphere of the Irish College, at Cloghaneely, his next port of call, probably intensified this feeling. The Irish cultural revival was still of real importance to him and he went to the college in an attempt to learn the Irish language. From the narrowly British standpoint, it was unfortunate that it was during this leave that the Foreign Office should mishandle the circumstances of his next appointment. Ever since his Congo achievements it had been felt that he deserved promotion, despite his ungracious response to the opportunities of Lisbon. Now he was offered the consulgeneralship of Haiti and San Domingo, again a much sought after post, and one which would not normally go to a man of forty-three. Casement accepted readily, only to be asked to step down in favour of a Boer War veteran. This he did, not without bitterness, and convinced himself in the process that he accepted the alternative, Pará, merely as a stepping stone to resignation from the Service.

CHAPTER 6

FROM CONSUL TO CONSUL-GENERAL

Pará (Brazilian name Belem) had had British consular representation since the first decade of the nineteenth century; the first records of the archives are dated 1810, the year in which the original treaties of 1642 and 1654, defining the rights and jurisdiction of British Consular Officers in the Portuguese dominions, were renewed and amplified by the Treaty of 19 February, signed at Rio de Janeiro. The consulate had, however, fallen on difficult times and Casement found himself faced with a genuinely disgraceful situation. It was not merely a repetition of Santos, where Casement's meticulous dependence on instructions cast a slur on his predecessor. Here consul Rhind had taken to drink and let everything degenerate.[1] 'I arrived after a decrepit consul who could not work and had to be carried away.'[2]

Rhind had taken a house which was wholly unsuitable as a consulate: 'It suited him because he was in bed the whole time and unable to move.'[3] Casement arrived in February 1908, and promptly made arrangements to move the consulate to the building of the London and Brazilian Bank, an event which occurred on 7 April. An advertisement appeared in the local press announcing the new address, which was in the Rua 15 de Novembro, in the centre of the business part of the city. Having made the change, Casement notified the Legation that he had done so. Although the move was definitely in the interests of the efficient working of the consular service, after three months the bank was having second thoughts about the effect on their business of the stream of undesirables which the consulate attracted; Head Office exerted pressures on the Pará manager to 'get rid of the consul',[4] but by that time the end of Casement's residence in Pará was in sight.

Altering the location of the consulate was one thing, but sorting out its contents was another. Before his eventual transfer to Rio de Janeiro, Casement sent the Foreign Office a detailed description of the state of the archives as he had found them. Seven foolscap pages outlined the basic problem.[5] As was the general practice, distinct dossiers were kept for 'Foreign Office' and 'Legation', but 'Separate and Secret' were mixed indiscriminately with ordinary correspondence, and entered on the common register. Mixed with both dossiers were loose bundles of old unclassified correspondence. Casement had found the 'so-called archives . . . in three wooden cases, loosely nailed, on the ground in an open outhouse in the backyard of the dwelling in which the consulate was then established'. They were 'worm-eaten, spoiled by damp, cockroaches and dirt so as to be almost illegible'. The outhouse was accessible day and night to 'servants and their friends'.

Although the despatch ends with a plea for financial support in order to enlist clerical assistance, most of it shows concern for a genuinely needed reform in Foreign Office practice. Casement pointed out that the keeping of a common register for ordinary and confidential matters was the rule at Santos – also with unsatisfactory consequences – and was the accepted procedure at all the African postings with which he had been acquainted. The argument really formed part of his anti-acting/honorary consul thesis. When the consulate was left in the charge of a local resident, that man should not have access to everything. He pressed the Foreign Office at least to provide a second safe for 'Separate and Secret' documents and to see that acting consuls never received the keys of this safe. Aware that his outspokenness might offend, he crossed out some of his more forceful sentences, making sure nevertheless that their contents could not fail to be read.

While heavily involved in moving the consulate to new premises and improving the state of the records, Casement did not neglect his day-to-day 'protective' responsibilities. Three typed foolscap pages dated 17 March 1908[6] show him investigating the case of Mary Hislop, a minor, daughter of James Hislop, son-in-law of Thomas Greaves, who *may* have been a naturalized Brazilian. Miss Hislop's parents were British by birth, but she was born in Brazil. Now all were dead except Mary; three Brazilian liquidators had been appointed and creditors were being paid about £4,500 out of an inheritance of between £10,000 and £20,000. What steps should a British consul take to protect the lady? The answer from the Legation was that Mary Hislop was a British subject within British dominions, but could not demand protection in Brazil. The consul was instructed that although he could take no official steps, he might exert discreet private influence. Casement hastened to fulfil the spirit of the ruling and, at least during his tenure of office, Mary Hislop (resident in England) received remittances from the estate.

A wish for consular reform which found favour with Casement's superiors was his conviction that a consul's duty necessitated much travel, partly to inspect the vice-consulates, partly to see the district first hand and gauge the opportunities which existed for the promotion of British commercial interests. Accordingly Casement, without waiting for official sanction from the secretary of state, set off on his first Amazonian expedition on 22 April. His report[7] (six typed foolscap pages) was entitled by the Legation 'Madeira–Mamoré Railway. Reports on. Voyage up Madeira R'.

Casement was well-qualified to report on the construction of railways through disease-ridden jungle, having taken part in a similar undertaking in the Congo. The aim was to construct this aid to the development of the Amazonian Basin within a period of four years and he was quick to diagnose the causes of likely failure: labour problems and ill-health. The environment was clearly unsuitable for white or Chinese labour and already expensive importations from Cuba had either gone down with malaria or resigned and mixed in with the local vagrant population of Santo Antonio. Despite the conclusions of his Congo Report, he felt that in this type of project Belgian methods had been right; the secret of success lay in the Brazilian Government making a federal investment to the extent of providing a well-disciplined police force. Given a strict régime the right sort of labour would stand up to the physical conditions and do the job:

> The 'darkie', and I mean the pure article, not the nigger, mongrel or half-caste of Brazil, but the pure-blooded, vigorous native African is the only type of humanity that can successfully grapple with hard work, hot sun and Malaria at the same time.

The report was well received and led to Milne Cheetham (*chargé d'affaires* at Petropolis during Haggard's illness) recommending to the Foreign Office that other consuls follow Mr Casement's example and move around their districts to gain first-hand impressions.

While at Pará, Casement was to furnish two more reports: the annual report and another in response to a request from the Governor of Jamaica, Sir Sydney Olivier. The governor had asked for consular reports on the health conditions of all the Brazilian ports and received some alarming statistics from Pará. In the first six months of 1908 there had been 111 deaths from yellow fever, five from smallpox and two from bubonic plague. Nothing was being done about yellow fever because, Casement believed, the Brazilians were largely immune from it. The physical site of Pará, only just above the high water mark on the Tocantins river, made drainage difficult and sanitation was on a soak-away basis. However, hope lay in the possibility of a London concern taking up a municipal concession for drainage into the tidal estuary. Casement hoped that the current development of the harbour facilities would lead to some badly needed land reclamation which might ease housing congestion, another factor which contributed to the city's poor health record.[8]

.Casement's three Pará reports and the activity which went into their production constituted the bulk of his work in the 'furtherance of British interests' part of consular responsibility. The annual report 'for the year 1907 and previous years'[9] ranks among the more lucid, comprehensive and genuinely useful contributions which the Board of Trade received. Here the statistical information is integrated with analysis to an unusual degree. Of the 62 pages, some 52 are from the pen of Casement himself, the remaining comment and tables are confined to the annex from Manaos and were written by Vice-Consul Fletcher. Unfortunately, as a Board of Trade witness admitted before the MacDonnell Commission,[10] a certain amount of censorship sometimes occurred before a consul's remarks appeared in print and some of Casement's more pungent comments were toned down.

The district for which the consulate was responsible included three entire Brazilian states: Maranhaõ, Grand Pará and Amazonas, the last-named being the largest state in Brazil. This vast area obviously obliged a consul to travel and Casement made use of the knowledge which he had gained whilst on the Madeira expedition. He had also done some reading and used such sources as the naturalist Bates to help him construct an authoritative geographical and sociological summary of the situation as he found it, its opportunities and potential dangers. Naturally he was familiar with the contents of the preceding British report, but also gave his attention to French consular information. Inevitably some space was given to an outline of the history of the district; the major part, however, is concerned with a wide-ranging consideration of Brazilian products, seen in the context of world markets and internal economics. Fresh from Santos, Casement was well-placed for meaningful comparisons. He did not restrict himself to rubber, cocoa and Brazil nuts; much emphasis is given to latent sources of wealth, e.g. timber.

Under the heading 'Pará health statistics' Casement covered similar ground to that used in his report for the Governor of Jamaica and if one wanted to locate a recurrent theme in the report as a whole it would be found within the passages drawing attention to what are today called 'Third World' problems. Deriving support from his Congo experiences he gave thought to the basic food problems and recommended the use of banana flour as a wheat substitute for baking – an idea to be exploited some sixty years later. In his rubber account he emphasized that although the plantations of Asia were as yet only producing 3 per cent of world output, the future belonged to them. But he also pinpointed less obvious human problems within the rubber environment. The statistics did not conceal from him that where there was rubber gathering there was practically no schooling, and yet the same was not true in backward areas where otherwise similar populations depended for their livelihood on, say, fishing.

Three other aspects of the report might profitably be singled out for comment. Firstly, there is a return to the plight of the Irish portion of British imports: 'All are equally entered in Brazil as "made in England" '; this time specific goods are considered, in addition to Guinness: whisky, poplin, lace and linen. Allied to this topic is the concern of the recent student of Irish for the rapid decline of the local language, the *Lingua Geral*: 'The Tupi-Guarani language was formerly spoken from the Amazon to the Paraguay . . . Its extinction today, and in a few brief years, in a region once its stronghold is not without interest to the philologist.' And then there is Casement's special interest in travel, which finds expression in several contexts. He was much impressed by the journey from London to Lima, via Pará and the Amazon undertaken in the spring of 1908 by George Booth (of the Booth Steamship Company) and his wife Margaret.[11] By steamer, canoe and mule they ascended the Amazon, crossed the Andes and were in Lima in less than two months, apparently with little difficulty. This part of the report recommends the development of a tourist industry for the hardy and shows Casement rejoicing that there are some others who share his confidence about the areas traditionally thought inaccessible to the white man. That improved communications were of great benefit to mankind was becoming a deeply held conviction.

Although the Pará report exceeded the standard of his Santos report in presenting a much more comprehensive survey of the district, it came under attack in the local press because its author had 'merely pointed out that the term "Estate" which means something definite to European minds is misapplied to these non-demarcated and always uncultivated wilds whence the chief supplies of the rubber are drawn.'[12] It was in this section of the report that the Foreign Office toned down the language: 'I termed the whole game of rubber exploitation "vegetable filibustering" in my report, but the F.O. funked that and struck out some of my most truthful remarks.'[13]

Pará was, as may be seen, a period of conscientious hard work, and yet it was carried out by a none-too-healthy consul. During his time there, and some eighteen months before *Truth* magazine forced the issue upon the world, he notified the Legation of allegations in the press about atrocities in the Putumayo. Although he specifically mentioned Julio Arana as the man whose company had reduced the Indians to slavery, the area of the alleged atrocities was disputed territory (principally claimed by Ecuador, Colombia and, most forcefully, Peru), and he, like the Legation, thought that certain Brazilian elements 'would like a chance of carving a fresh "Acré territory" out of Peruvian soil'.[14] 'These telegrams in the local press are greatly exaggerated I fancy . . . much of it may not be true. I fancy there

is a certain amount of *wish* among local Brazilians to find fault with Peru.'
His letter was simply filed as 'account of frontier incident'.

The social environment of Pará was different from that of São Paulo.
Santos had had the only sizeable docks in Brazil – those of Rio de Janeiro
did not follow until several years later – and had therefore been simply a
place of commerce. Pará, like Manaos at the height of the rubber boom,
had cultural pretensions as well. Here it was not possible for Casement to
insulate himself from Brazilian society and at first he found the cultural
amenities attractive. Unfortunately he also found them expensive, because
of the rate of exchange. Moreover he had suffered again from the Consular
Service tradition that incoming consuls were expected to buy the furnish-
ings of the consulate from their predecessors and eventually sell them to
their successors when they departed. Soon the theatre was not the asset it
had seemed. When he fell ill, with gastritis, he found that a trip to
Barbados to recuperate cost him less than if he had stayed at his post.

Again letters reveal contradictory attitudes to the local people. In
March 1908, Lord Dufferin received the consul's vivid description of some
of them:[15]

> hideous cross-breeds – of Negro-Portuguese with, up here in the
> Amazon, a very large admixture of native blood. Altogether the
> resultant human compost is the nastiest form of black-pudding you
> have ever sat down to . . . the 'Brazilian' is the most arrogant,
> insolent and pig-headed brute in the world I should think.

However, what reads today as racialism of a particularly nasty type,
amounted then to little more than socially acceptable casual gossip.
Though among Brazilians themselves, of the educated class, this was not
the case; serious views were held about undesirable elements in the racial
mix, and if Euclides da Cunha[16] is to be believed, many would happily have
witnessed the extinction of these elements. In May Casement was writing
to the Legation about 'good-natured and cheerful' people . . . 'amiable,
gentle and . . . caressing in their manner with much passive goodness of
disposition . . . lively and vivacious'.[17] Plainly the former personal expression of distaste for Brazilians was not regarded as a disqualification from
serving the Crown among such persons and later that same year the author
was promoted to be HM consul-general at Rio de Janeiro.

The last months at Pará were very unhealthy ones for Casement. His
stay in Barbados had achieved nothing. In November he went on leave,
breaking his journey for a week in Lisbon. Thence Liverpool and across to
Ulster, to stay with his old friends, the Berrys at Richhill Castle. Then came
the offer of the consul-generalship and his immediate acceptance of it. He
had been toying with the idea of employment with the Mozambique
Company, but had no hesitation whatever in accepting promotion within

the Service he sometimes affected to despise. His acceptance, which is at first surprising is, on reflection, in keeping with the divided personality which is beginning to emerge. It is really no more difficult to comprehend than the two-sided expression of his attitude to Brazilians. In the same year he had threatened resignation again,[18] and spoken of the Consular Service as 'only jobbery and corruption';[19] now he was one of its most senior officials.

On 22 March 1909, he sent the customary despatch to the Foreign Office announcing that he had taken charge of the Rio consulate-general. His leave had been extended to allow additional convalescence from his previous tour of duty, but he still felt far from fit. The situation which he inherited had some similarities with his other South American posts, though there were some advantages as far as archives and clerical methods were concerned. For the actual state of the consulate-general one is not merely dependent upon Casement's despatches or Hambloch's subjective account as in February 1909, it had been inspected by Milne Cheetham, whose thorough report generated favourable reaction in the Foreign Office.[20]

While the relevant chapter in Hambloch's memoirs is subtitled 'The Consulate over a Cookshop' and enlarges upon the odorous aspect of this, Cheetham more coolly reports that it is 'on the second floor, and access is by two flights of a dark and narrow staircase, which is a drawback'. It was in the centre of the city near the Custom House, which meant that it was noisy; on the other hand it was convenient to most likely clients. The state of the archives must have been a relief to the new consul-general: Cheetham recorded that they were 'now properly kept'. Generally speaking, from 1895 all was well, everything had been carefully collected and bound. And, as if in answer to a specific request from the new incumbent, there were two safes. Cheetham, Hambloch and Casement seem to have been of one mind that the happy state of affairs was attributable to the efficiency of the middle-aged failed businessman C.G. Pullen, who was in the best tradition of chief clerks.

In 1909, Rio de Janeiro was Brazil's largest commercial city, as well as being federal capital, and Cheetham expected business opportunities to increase. While generally disposed to praise the running of the consulate-general, there is, however, a hint in the report of the strained relations between consulate-general and Legation which had arisen during the time of Casement's predecessor, Arthur Chapman. Tension appeared to arise from a very trivial beginning, but there was soon a clash between the very different personalities of Chapman and Haggard. The incident which led to a heated exchange of correspondence occurred at a dinner party when a message from the Legation was given to Vice-Consul Campbell about coffee reports. Campbell passed this on to the consul-general who, because there was no written confirmation, did not take it seriously. Embarrassment had been caused because Chapman's full and wide-ranging reports had been going direct to the Foreign Office and had, as far as one can judge, completely eclipsed those from the Legation. At one point Foreign Office instructions and consular instructions appeared to be in conflict and the argument focused on the interpretation of General Consular Instruction 7(b):[21]

> Despatches of interest should be forwarded by Consuls-General and Consuls, under flying seal, through Her Majesty's Diplomatic representative, except in cases where rapidity of communication is of importance; in such cases they should be sent direct and copies should be sent to the Diplomatic representative.

The difficulty had arisen because of the phrase 'where rapidity of communication is of importance'; it might have been smoothed over, were it not for the dissimilar natures of the two main antagonists. It certainly led to Casement's inheriting a very sensitive relationship.

Cheetham's report was written after Chapman had departed, and criticized him for not playing a sufficient part in the social round: 'He lived a too retired life, and did not take quite the position in the colony which would have been the most useful.' Here Casement was well-qualified, by temperament and inclination, to assume just the role required of him. By this time, however, his outspokenness on the shortcomings of England had made him unable to offset the fault of his predecessor; though happy to occupy the centre of the stage, his opinions had consolidated and he was no longer able to curb his tongue – any thoughts of him as a peacemaker with the senior British voice at Petropolis proved short-lived. He had communicated easily with Cheetham, but relations with Haggard were cool.

Casement had some knowledge of Portuguese, an accomplishment in short supply in the consulate-general of Chapman's time,[22] and he was again able to shine in quite complex 'protective' duties, even those which were technically outside the scope of his responsibilities. Such a case (and one which also taxed his ability to speak French) was that of the elopement of Mademoiselle Lecocq (aged seventeen) with her married uncle Robert Lecocq (aged fifty-five). Casement had been approached by relatives in Rio de Janeiro and had received a letter from the girl's father asking his help in locating the uncle and niece when they arrived in Brazil and dissuading them from continuing their association. 'I was aware that no offence in law was sustainable and that my action must be confined to persuasion on the one hand and, to some extent, to reprobation on the other hand.'[23] Accordingly he secretly arranged with the chief of police for the couple to be 'invited' to visit the consulate-general. The chief of police interpreted 'invited' as 'compelled' and arrested the pair as they disembarked from their steamer. Casement received his telegram just as he sat down to a farewell dinner to the Japanese Minister in Petropolis. Somewhat alarmed, he immediately demanded their release and arranged to return to Rio on the 9.30 am train the following morning (a Sunday). Full melodramatic details of what occurred are contained in the Foreign Office records; throughout the Monday a 'Conseil de famille' gathered at the consulate-general and eventually an agreement was reached whereby the girl was to live in the care of a married cousin, and the uncle and 'abductor' gave his word that no contact would be made for a 'cooling-off' period of two months. The final Foreign Office comment was that Casement should be congratulated on his 'tact and good judgement' in handling the matter.

As well as showing the sort of extracurricular supervision sometimes required of consuls, the correspondence incidentally throws light on the sort of hours which they and their staff worked. Cheetham's report stipulates that 'Business hours in general are from 9 a.m. – 5 p.m. . . . . . shipping being attended to after hours when necessary.' The police delivered the Lecocq couple to the consulate in the evening of the Saturday, when they found Pullen, the chief clerk, still working there (Casement had left for Petropolis at 4.00 pm). It was then up to Pullen to arrange respectable accommodation for the week-end and personally to escort Mademoiselle Lecocq to her relatives.

As consul-general Casement found even more of his time taken up with the vexed question of vice-consuls. Were they worth the trouble? Were they actually harmful? – 'unpaid honorary Vice Consuls treat their duties, after a brief period, with neglect if not contempt.'[24] He had to see to the appointment of L.H. Atkinson as first British vice-consul at Cuyubá, 4000 miles from Rio, and made use of a newspaper article (by special correspondent 'O Paiz' of Rio) in order to illustrate the remoteness of the region from British interests. In Casement's précis the contemporary Indian situation is described: the Bororo Indians are imprisoned for entering the town naked; the missionaries attract them; the police and populace take them and lock them up in the prison or the barracks. Then the death of Vice-Consul Youle at Victoria created a vacancy which could be filled by the old boy of Ballymena Academy, Brian Barry: 'a native born subject of his Majesty, having been born at Castle Blaney in Monaghan, Ireland, in 1854'.[25] Barry was appointed acting vice-consul, and then the appointment was confirmed. At that point he changed his mind and therefore Casement recommended the abolition of the post. The Foreign Office agreed to the closure, but, on hearing that this was the outcome, Barry asked if he might withdraw his resignation. Casement and the Foreign Office complied with this request. As if by way of compensation, Corumba vice-consulate was closed.

'Protective' duties of the Rio period may be briefly indicated. On 18 June 1909, Casement started to enquire why the property of a Canadian British subject, James Albert Hewitt, murdered in 1907, was 'not yet handed over to Conste Genl'.[26] In certain matters of principle the case resembled another which it overlapped in time; another native of Canada, Thomas O'Meara, had drowned at Rio and Casement tried to assist the mother to locate objects of sentimental value; the Brazilian authorities had sold the personal effects and levied 'sellos e custos'.[27] And there were two further matters involving points of law: on 13 August Casement reported the case of an unseaworthy vessel being made subject to survey by a consul before being given clearance by the captain of the port – the Marine Department of the Board of Trade ruled that only a naval court could order a survey; the consul could convene the court.[28] In the other case the Leopoldina Syndicate tried to persuade HM consul-general to accept power of attorney in order to receive proceeds of an action pending against the government of Brazil and the Banco do Brazil.[29] This Consular instructions forbade. And in the midst of these duties Casement rose to more cultural matters with a long typed letter[30] to the Foreign Office about the Botocudo Indians; he enclosed photographs by a German photographer which he thought should be donated to the Royal Anthropological Institute. The Foreign Office agreed.

The Rio period was, in some ways, a repetition of the Santos experience, in the sense that Casement soon found ways of escaping from the aspects of Brazilian urban life which he found objectionable. Although his first reaction was negative; 'no friends; no social life or pleasant friendly intercourse',[31] he soon mellowed a little and conceded that rural Brazil (which he found beautiful) had virtues of simplicity which Rio, in its pathetic imitation of Paris, lacked. Excursions into the hinterland provided one escape, excursions to the diplomatic colony of Petropolis – a socially and physically elevated (in its mountain setting) version of Guarujá – provided another.

Hambloch quotes Casement as saying: 'A consul's real functions are diplomatic.'[32] In Hambloch's opinion this observation explained Casement's hostile attitude to the British community in Rio; it was a commercial community and therefore Casement looked down on it. This opinion is not necessarily invalidated by Casement's near absorption within the English colony in Santos – a more completely commercial environment than Rio – because one should take into account the possible effect on Casement of promotion to consul-general. The unsatisfactory prospects of promotion available to consuls had long been a source of grievance, and his achievement of consul-generalship at the age of forty-four was a rare feat. The instant lure of Petropolis, referred to by Hambloch, is supported by detailed claims for travel expenses now filed in Foreign Office records.[33]

Petropolis attracted Casement for a variety of reasons. It was not merely the home of the British Legation; the Diplomatic Corps of all the nations represented in Brazil gathered there and the place, founded by the Emperor Don Pedro, was still the haven of many of the old court families. Certainly there was no higher social level in Brazil and Casement's new view of his consular role, together with his undoubted charm as a conversationalist, gave him the confidence and qualifications for admission to society.

A friendship which began at this period was with the German consul-general, Baron von Nordenflycht. The evidence is thin, but Hambloch later concluded that the 'wooing' of Casement which occurred when he spent a holiday in Germany in May 1912 (at any rate an official car was placed at his disposal) was the result of indiscreet anti-British outbursts made at the Nordenflychts' at this time. As anti-British outbursts were now frequent in his letters to known Irish Nationalists and their sympathizers, it seems logical, particularly in the light of Casement's subsequent political writings, which made Ireland the gateway to Lebensraum,[34] that Casement should look upon the Nordenflycht house as a place where he might expect a sympathetic hearing. There seems little reason to doubt Hambloch's assertion that the Nordenflychts themselves told him of the consul-general's 'anti-English sentiments'.

The British community was also the Irish community and much of Casement's socializing was in the company of a wholly loyal (to the United Kingdom) old boy of Casement's old school, now Ballymena Academy. Casement grew to despise his school for teaching him nothing about Ireland: 'I don't think the word was ever mentioned';[35] this made no difference to the joy with which he greeted Brian Barry and the pains which he took (in another somewhat English enterprise) to see that his old school-fellow became vice-consul at Victoria. However, Hambloch describes how, later, Casement swept orange flowers (and their vases) from a table at Barry's house during a cocktail party, and, at a similar occasion given by the general manager of the Leopoldina Railway, Knox Little, delivered an anti-British speech. The cumulative effect of such behaviour in the close-knit social enclave must have made a mockery of Casement's social obligations as a 'diplomat'. It may help to explain the haste with which he departed on leave; on the other hand his diary[36] suggests that he had a pressing engagement of a sexual nature in Buenos Aires. This sort of liaison, as mentioned above, was whispered about in Rio. His leave began on 1 March 1910 and he would never set foot in the federal capital again.

Casement's career as a public official within the limits of the conventional mould was now over. Although he did not know it, the next annual report from Rio de Janeiro was to come from the pen of Acting Consul-General Hambloch and the bulk of his own remaining official writings was to constitute the major part of a Blue Book. Looking at the extensive evidence available in consular despatches to the Foreign Office and, more especially, in consulate-legation records, it is reasonable to conclude that, in Santos and Pará, he was a conscientious and efficient civil servant both within the area of official duties specifically detailed for him by the rules and in the wider world of social responsibility. In much of his work he was prepared to step beyond the narrow limitations of the letter of the regulations and interpret his instructions with common sense and humanity. In short, he was an exceptionally good consul; the one flaw in the early days of his South American experience – unless a consul may be held responsible for his private correspondence – was his inclination to become obsessed with clerical minutiae.

When it came to consul-generalship things changed. It is, of course, arguable that a good consul-general was doomed to failure in any case, because of the inbuilt situation, particularly with a weak Legation, or one which had a history of tense relationships with the consulate. Down in Rio one could see what was going on; up in Petropolis the realities of life could pass you by. Casement was not the first Rio consul-general to fall out with his minister, but there were additional factors which helped to disillusion him, among them the mishandling of the Haiti and San Domingo appointment, which had soured him; and, moreover, his growing involvement with aspects of Irish separatism, when on leave, was sublimating what was left of the idealism that formerly had entered British imperial channels. It is also difficult to escape the paradoxical view that he saw his proper position as being in Petropolis; that being a consul had been bearable because the role had less ambiguity than a consul-generalship. The delicate social and political relationship between an Edwardian consul-general and his minister required a very different temperament from the one that had had such ambivalent beginnings. Personal friendship could still cut across this trend; nevertheless, after Pará it is difficult to escape the conclusion that a change of heart was making itself manifest within the social sphere of duty, thus making him, at best, ineffective as far as 'furthering British interests' was concerned. He remained, however, a reliable public official in his 'protective' role until relieved of these duties in order to make his investigation of alleged atrocities in the Putumayo: an undertaking which may be variously interpreted as 'protective' or 'furthering British interests', but which went beyond narrowly national limitations.

CHAPTER 7

THE PUTUMAYO: MISSION FOR A CONSUL-GENERAL EXTRAORDINARY

⟫∘⊙∘⟪

To understand the circumstances which led to the publication of Casement's Putumayo Report of 1912[1] and the subsequent House of Commons Select Committee Report of 1913[2] it is necessary to examine the development of the rubber-gathering industry in the territory actively claimed by Peru and Colombia during the latter part of the nineteenth century, and this will involve consideration of local traditions with regard to the Indian population of the forest regions.

The relevant territory – some 12,000 square miles – which lies mainly within a triangle bounded by two tributaries of the river Putumayo, the Cara-Paraná and the Caquetá, has its eastern extremity about 400 miles upstream from the Putumayo's junction with the Amazon. In the early part of the nineteenth century the area, supporting a large population of Indians, was the object of much slave-raiding which helped to reinforce the traditional system of peonage which had developed in Peru and neighbouring states. Slave-raids were spasmodic and difficulty of the terrain, coupled with the ferocity of some (a minority) of the tribes, armed with poisoned blow-darts, made the forest regions unattractive to any but adventurers. Little-known explorers passed through the Putumayo in 1827[3] and 1851[4] and not very long afterwards Colombians in search of wild rubber made their way in a south-easterly direction down the indisputedly Colombian tributaries of the Caquetá river (known as the Japura in Brazil) to the energetically disputed tributaries of the Putumayo river, where they set up small estates. The attraction was an inferior kind of rubber known as 'sernambi' and it is unlikely that it would ever have been marketed had it not been for the supply of virtually free labour which the forest provided.

The Putumayo was part of the much larger area of Loreto which was from time to time the subject of friction between Ecuador, Peru, Colombia and Brazil. However, in 1852, before the beginning of the rubber exploitation period, Peru had ceded to Brazil the large eastern section which included the lower reaches of the Putumayo river, and although Ecuador continued to be shown as the owner of the region on many maps, including the one in Casement's Pará consulate, the principal disputants claiming sovereignty over the district defined above, during the years of the rubber boom, were Colombia and Peru. Colombia claimed sovereignty as far south as the Napo river; Peru was *de facto* ruler by virtue of occupation of most of the territory and maintenance of what law and order there was, largely through the offices of powerful commercial interests. A thinly scattered militia served to confirm Peruvian ownership of most of Loreto.

After the early nineteenth-century slave-raids had taken their toll an estimated 50,000 Indians remained in the Putumayo, and 40,000 of these were claimed to be employees of the rubber company which Casement investigated. They were basically of four tribes: the Boras, the Andokes, the Ocainas and the Huitotos, and varied in degree of inherent aggression from the warlike Boras to the timid Huitotos who numbered about three-quarters of the labour force. The Huitotos lived in the central part of the Putumayo, between the Cara-Paraná and Igara-Paraná and the Peruvian or Colombian 'caucheros' initially induced them to collect rubber by making advance payments to them of simple articles of European origin and steadily building up the time-honoured system of debt-bondage.

Although slavery, as such, was illegal in Peru it was generally accepted that the Indian population stood either within the laws of peonage or outside the law altogether. Indeed, Reginald Enock in his testimony to the Select Committee[5] went so far as to say that in Spanish terminology forest Indians were classified as animals. The dialogue which developed between the chairman of the Select Committee and Reginald Enock led to the conclusion that a distinction must be made between the comparatively mild system of peonage, by which the labour of a man in debt could be bought or sold, and an altogether crueller system termed *Correrias*. Peonage was widespread in the mountain area and was embodied in the legal system: a fugitive debtor would be recaptured by the Peruvian authorities and returned to his master. *Correrias*, which was the subject of complaints in *El Comercio*, a principal Lima newspaper, in 1905 and 1906, was the slave-raiding system of the lowland forest areas and made full use of expedient aspects of peonage. Debt-bondage worked well as a method of recruiting labour and, when objections were raised, its apparent legality could be cited in defence. But while the Indian of the mountains was legally protected from the greater excesses of slavery, the forest Indian had no such protection.

The company which was eventually the subject of the enquiries of the Select Committee on Putumayo was very much the creation of one man, Julio Cesar Arana, who effectively controlled it until he lost the powers of liquidator in March 1913. Of Spanish descent he was born in 1864 in

Rioja, a town in the foothills of the Peruvian Andes. According to his own testimony[6] he began as a general exporter and merchant on the upper reaches of the Amazon in 1881. He entered into partnership with John B. Vega in 1890 and in 1892 there was an amalgamation with a French firm which lasted until 1896 when the business was liquidated. Arana, thrown back on his own resources again, first bought rubber from the Putumayo in 1899. In December 1901 he joined forces with the firm of Larranaga Ramires which had established itself on the river Igara-Paraná at La Chorrera, a place which eventually became the operational headquarters of the London registered firm, known as the Peruvian Amazon Company, which it fell to Casement to investigate.

Arana rose to a position of control in the Putumayo, if his own account is to be believed, because he arrived in the rubber-gathering environment just when 'Colonies' (a term adopted by Arana's solicitors) had begun to establish themselves along the banks of the rivers and were in need of supplies, credit facilities and transport: 'I entered into business relations with the said Colonies exchanging merchandise for rubber, buying produce and making advances.' Hitherto, he said, 'the Indians on the rivers Igara-Paraná and Cara-Paraná had resisted the establishment of civilisation in their districts', but 'from about the year 1900 onwards the Indians became more civilised, and a system of rubber collected by the Indians for European merchandise sprang up between the Indians and the said Colonies. From that time my business in the Putumayo district gradually increased, but by slow degrees.' In 1903 he took his brother Lizardo and two brothers-in-law, Pablo Zumaeta and Abel Alarco into partnership and traded very successfully under the name J.C. Arana and Hermanos until 1907, when the decision was taken to increase capital by forming a limited company in England. It was a time of impulsive speculation in rubber and without difficulty the Peruvian Amazon Rubber Company was incorporated in October 1907 with a capital of £1,000,000. Arana and Alarco remained on the board, Arana as managing director, and they were joined by three Englishmen and a Frenchman. In July 1908, the word 'rubber' was dropped from the company's title.

Arana's statement understandably makes no mention of the special relationship which he enjoyed with regard to the Peruvian Government. Many of the Colonies along the rivers were Colombian and, by force or straightforward purchase, he was able to take them over; the 12,000 square miles acquired by 1906 cost him £116,700. At the height of his powers he was alleged to have boasted that his monopoly of the steamers in the area had enabled him to gain squatters' rights over a territory larger than France.[7] Recurrent territorial disputes between Colombia and Peru ceased for a brief period after an agreement of May 1904. When trouble started again the two governments submitted their case for arbitration to

Pope Pius X and a temporary arrangement was made whereby both countries agreed to withdraw their military authority from an area of some 200,000 square miles. However, the degree of encouragement and support accorded to Arana's commercial undertakings made it plain to many, including Casement, that the Peruvian President, José Pardo, was inclined towards company rule – which for the most part meant Arana rule – as a means of establishing Peruvian sovereignty.

Evidence shown to the Select Committee of Arana's close collusion with the Peruvian Government included a book called *In the Putumayo and its Tributaries*[8] by a French explorer, Eugenio Robuchon. Arana admitted that the motive behind the publication of this book was to show 'that the Putumayo now belongs to Peru'.[9] Robuchon was commissioned by the Peruvian Government to survey the Putumayo, but died (mysteriously) before his book was completed. Rey de Castro, formerly Peruvian consul at Manaos and close friend of Arana, edited the book and 20,000 copies were published as a semi-official government document, with photographs of Arana, his brother and Abel Alarco among the illustrations. Swift MacNeill, MP for South Donegal and the most forceful member of the committee examined Arana about entries in the company's accounts; he thought it sinister that de Castro had been allowed to run up debt which at the time of liquidation was in the region of £5,000. Attempts to disentangle a web of political and commercial intrigue were to occupy much of the committee's time.

During the early stages of the rubber-gathering industry rumours of atrocities perpetrated in the Upper Amazon basin did reach the ears of those in the cities, but they generated little response: in some areas traditional attitudes to the Indians encouraged indifference, in any case exaggerated accusations made by territorial rivals were commonplace and little creditability was attached to sensational news items of 'Backlands' newspapers, some of which were short-lived enterprises.

The earliest publicly available reports of atrocities were published in Iquitos in July 1907 by Benjamin Saldana Rocca in his news-sheet, *La Sanción* ('Sensation'). The issues were crude productions which appeared at irregular intervals; Rocca was proprietor, journalist and printer and waged something of a campaign against Arana's firm until the police expelled him from Iquitos early in 1908 and he made his way to Lima to find employment in a junior capacity with *La Prensa*. *La Sanción* became little more than a series of testimonies of former employees on the Putumayo; much information was supplied anonymously, but the declaration of 29 August 1907 had been sworn before a notary public. In December 1907 the name of the paper was changed to *La Felpa* ('A Drubbing') and publication continued with a modified format until the issue of 5 January 1908. Content was probably without precedent in terms of horrifying descriptions of torture. The enslaving of Indians might not have shocked a large section of South American opinion, nor the excessively hard working of peons; what might have jolted the public conscience, had it been believed, was the perverted nature of mutilations of men, women and children. The initial motive for torture – to ensure increased rubber yield – had, according to the accounts, long since given way to an orgy of sadism. What was convincing in the testimonies was that men trapped in the middle of the rubber-gathering hierarchy were, in their efforts to destroy the system, willing to incriminate themselves.

Although it might be thought that an Iquitos newspaper would have a limited readership, in fact the allegations did spread beyond the Upper Amazon basin. There is no doubt that the Colombian authorities, for instance, made quite sure that a wide public heard of the sufferings of members of their 'Colonies', including the 'domesticated' Indians, and when the Manaos newspaper *O Jornal do Commercio* published an account of Peruvian atrocities in its issue of 2 June 1908, it cited the Colombian consulate as its source. Two days later much the same account appeared in the *Provincia do Pará*, where it was read by Casement. The difficulty, as has been seen, lay in everyone's awareness that information from the disputed frontier areas was suspect, and the British Government might well have heard nothing of the serious allegations levelled against a London registered company had it not been for the persistence of an American railway engineer, Walter Hardenburg.

Walter Hardenburg, with a friend, W.B. Perkins, had left the Cauca Valley Railroad in Colombia to seek more profitable employment on the Madeira-Mamoré railway and crossed the Putumayo by canoe during late 1907 and early 1908. On his way he accepted hospitality from Colombians, suffered an attack from a Peruvian Amazon Company military expedition and was taken prisoner. His friend, Perkins, from whom he was temporarily separated, witnessed a massacre at El Encanto and both men attributed their survival to their American citizenship. While prisoners of the Peruvian Amazon Company they had all their luggage stolen, a circumstance which encouraged Hardenburg to stay in Iquitos and demand compensation from Arana, and it was during this period that he made a point of enquiring about the company and obtained – from Rocca's son – the original texts of the declarations which had appeared in print and several other documents, as yet unpublished.

Hardenburg had seen much evidence of abuse of the Indians and his first call on arrival in Iquitos had been on the acting United States consul, Guy T. King, but he had received no satisfaction. King's predecessor, Consul Charles C. Eberhardt, had forwarded details of local conditions to Washington in December 1907 and the official response had been that there was no sovereign power to which the US Government might

81

complain. When, therefore, King declined to forward to the US Minister in Lima the eighteen sworn depositions which he had collected, Hardenburg decided that his complaints, which were already the major part of a manuscript entitled *The Devil's Paradise*,[10] should be lodged in London.

British Foreign Office responsibility in the Putumayo did not simply derive from the fact that the Peruvian Amazon Company was incorporated in London and had British directors; in 1904 Abel Alarco had visited Barbados and engaged a number of Barbadians as indentured labourers for work in the Putumayo. In all 196 were recruited and, after arrival, they soon found themselves in debt to the company. They were the third level in the local hierarchy. Above them were the chiefs of sections and the 'blancos'. Below the negroes were 'racionales', usually half-breeds, who could read and write. These in turn controlled groups of about six 'muchachos', selected Indians whose function it was to discipline the 'wild' Indians. The man whose 'protective' consular duty it was to safeguard the Barbadians was David Cazes, at Iquitos, and through him the Foreign Office should have been alerted.

Hardenburg, as an American citizen, had made no headway with his own Consular Service and turned next to publishers. Not surprisingly his potentially libellous folder of documents did not immediately find favour and he went therefore to the Anti-Slavery Society, where he was received and encouraged by the Rev. John Harris, Casement's friend and co-worker in the recent Congo revelations. The Rev. Harris thought that there was a need for maximum publicity and advised Hardenburg to approach the magazine *Truth*.[11] The advice proved sound and a series of sensational articles provoked the desired result: the first of a series of parliamentary questions which helped to persuade Sir Edward Grey to intervene.

Casement subsequently testified that he had read the *Truth* articles in Rio de Janeiro and therefore had 'the ordinary knowledge which the public had'[12] of events in the Putumayo, a statement which he found it necessary to modify. When he left Buenos Aires on 4 April 1910, he sailed to Liverpool, and then stayed for only five days in London before he crossed to Dublin on 18 May. On 22 May he recorded in his diary: 'At *Tara* with *Harris* and family.'[13] On 17 June: 'At Ballycastle – up to Magheranteampul (sic) by myself. Got letter from Anti-Slavery people about Putumayo River & the Amazon Rubber Coy. Answered by wire at once and wrote also.'[14] The idea of repeating his Congo achievement seems to have had an immediate appeal and within a week he wrote: 'To Anti-Slavery & H. of C. Dilke, Wedgwood & the other M.P.s – Splendid talk.'[15] The nearness of these diary entries, the family outing with the Harrises and the speeding up of Anti-Slavery developments, coincided with renewal, in an allied sphere, of Congo Reform Association fervour which was reaching its climax in 1909.

The Foreign Office had reacted without undue haste to the clamour which had begun to build up since the publication of the first *Truth* article on 22 September 1909. When the parliamentary question put by Hart-Davies on 29 September (the date of the second *Truth* article) appeared in the Foreign Office file, it prompted the unsigned minute: 'We know nothing about the Peruvian Amazon Co.; neither do the Commercial or Consular Dept.'[16] Following this confession of ignorance efforts were made to rectify matters. Sperling noted, perhaps nervously, that Honorary Consul Cazes was employed by a rubber firm 'whose agents regularly trade on the Putumayo',[17] and plainly the Foreign Office was anxious to find some reliable independent source of information and not depend, as the less cautious bodies were depending, on sensational magazine articles derived from an American with no credentials.

There was a period of delay whilst independent witnesses were sought. One was found, thanks to the efficiency of George Pogson, Casement's successor at the Pará consulate. A search of consular despatches, although it did not produce anything from Casement on Arana, did reveal that Pogson, eight days after his arrival in Pará, wrote a detailed report[18] on a Captain Thomas Whiffen, of the 14th, the King's Hussars, who, though previously believed to be dead, passed through Pará on 2 June 1909, after having made careful exploration of the Putumayo. Captain Whiffen, away from official army duties on half-pay, because of troublesome old wounds from the Boer War, made the exploration whilst subsidized by his father. It had been a nine months' journey and during it Whiffen had discovered that Robuchon had died; the French Government had expressed their thanks to him for this information via the War Office.[19]

Whiffen returned to England with a large quantity of material intended to form the basis of a travel book and as he had made maps and phonograph recordings, and taken photographs, he was on the face of it an ideal independent witness. One of his main assets from the Foreign Office point of view was his acquisition of one of the Barbadian indentured labourers as interpreter and personal servant. This man, John Brown, was to return with Whiffen to Montserrat, where Whiffen had the lease of an estate, and eventually became Casement's interpreter. Although John Brown himself confessed to participation in atrocities and was described by Casement as a 'useless brute',[20] plainly the experiences of the Whiffen expedition, which confirmed Hardenburg's overall case, were exactly what the Foreign Office needed.[21]

Despite a report[22] from Captain A.W. Craig, RN, who said that Senor Arana 'struck me as a strong, clever and capable man and a gentleman', the Foreign Office decided to ask the company what it proposed to do about *Truth*'s allegations. Sir Edward Grey's hesitation was well-founded as members of the board were attempting to defend themselves in the columns of *Truth* by accusing Rocca and Hardenburg of blackmail. In the case of Rocca the charges were vague; in the case of Hardenburg there was some embarrassing evidence, later used to considerable effect before the Select Committee. What the Foreign Office did not know, or they might not have acted at all, was that the most incriminating evidence of black-mail would eventually be brought against Captain Whiffen. As it was, they had every reason at this time to trust him, and may also have been influenced by an account, plainly libellous if untrue, of an incident reported in the *Morning Leader*,[23] to whose reporter, Horace Thorogood, the office secretary of the Peruvian Amazon Company had offered a bribe, on the instruction of a Spanish-speaking director.

In the face of public clamour and pressure from the Foreign Office and the Anti-Slavery Society, the board as a whole decided that they had no option but to send a commission of enquiry to the Putumayo. The company commission which actually made the investigation consisted of four men: L.H. Barnes, a tropical agriculturalist, who was leader,[24] W. Fox, a botanist with a special knowledge of rubber, E.S. Bell, commercial expert, and H.L. Gielgud, formerly a clerk with Deloittes, who had kept the books for the company but had changed employers and accepted the post of company secretary and manager.[25] The commission's brief was 'To report on the possibilities of commercial development of the properties of the Company, and also to enquire into the present relations between the native employees and the Agents of the Company.'[26] (A wording which in part could be thought to divert attention from the matters which had called the commission into existence.)

Comparisons with the Congo situation were so obvious to all inter-ested parties at the time (indeed, *Truth*'s first revelation had been sub-titled 'A British-Owned Congo') that, even without influential advice from the Anti-Slavery Society and supporters of the Congo Reform Association, Casement would have been the obvious choice to head a government commission of enquiry. Later he dismissively remarked: 'Some consular officer had to go and I was the one he [Sir Edward Grey] selected.'[27] But a government commission was not set up. Instead the diplomatically easier course was taken and Casement was asked to accompany the company's commission. This was less likely to impinge on the Monroe Doctrine, on the other hand it might easily have limited Casement's activities and made it difficult for him to differ from the company's findings. Accordingly his own terms of reference gave him unusually wide powers. As originally drafted, however, they did not entitle him to investigate treatment of the native Indians. The Barbadian employees assured him of consular access and there, strictly speaking, his responsibilities, outside the investigation of the British Company and its officials, ended. He had to report separately from the company's commission on the system of rubber collection in the Putumayo and it was not in his character to limit himself to the letter of instructions when humanitarian principles were at stake. Although cautioned to avoid offending the governments of the states visited, he was granted complete freedom when it came to moving about the country, and with regard to his methods of acquiring information.

Despite Casement's later disavowals of merit (when merit in a British setting had become an embarrassment to him), he now began, on the large scale, to practise in the South American context what, as a conscientious consul, he had always believed in and preached: the great need for a consul to travel. Milne Cheetham, in his report on the consulate-general of Rio de Janeiro,[28] had stressed this need and had commended Casement for having 'ascended the Amazon';[29] and Casement had anticipated Cheetham in the sentiments of his annual report from Pará. The Congo investigation was his personal precedent. There was a fundamental distinction between his Congo and Putumayo enquiries, however; in the latter case he was not accredited to the country or district in which he was making his investigation. In view of the disputed nature of the territory concerned it was all to the good that he approached from a consulate-general established in a (theoretically) non-involved state; at the same time it might have been thought irregular that enquiries within the Peruvian consular district (as it was classified by the British Foreign Office) should be made from a consulate-general elsewhere. That these possible transgressions of protocol did not amount to anything was attributable to Casement's unrivalled reputation as the champion of exploited native labour. Cazes might reasonably have felt at a disadvantage, but Casement was generally accepted as the man for the task; he was also setting interesting consular precedents, later to be noticed favourably by the Select Committee.

Foreign Office records[30] reveal one major disappointment with regard to the British enquiries. It had been hoped to act jointly with the United States in the Putumayo. Of two reasons given for American avoidance of the issue, one, that no American citizens were involved, was singularly unconvincing to those who had derived most of their information from the sufferings of Hardenburg and Perkins; the other, that the United States (with Argentina and Brazil) had been requested to mediate in a boundary dispute between Peru and Ecuador, was accepted as valid. There seems little doubt that, having forged strong links of friendship with Brazil in particular (during the period of Rio-Branco's foreign policy) the United States was unwilling to hazard her improved diplomatic position in South America on the basis of, as yet, slight evidence. Later, when the case seemed clear, she was more forthcoming in her condemnation of slavery.[31]

The commission left London for South America on 23 July 1910. Brief diary jottings from among Casement's entries for that day summarize his commitments: 'Expect to sail by *Edinburgh Castle* ???. . . . Typed copy of Anti-Slavery matter. To Southampton. Mrs G., E.D.M., Harris'.[32] Next day the commission embarked, Casement armed with a copy of Robuchon's book, lent to him by the Anti-Slavery Society and Enock's *The Andes and the Amazon*. On 27 July the *Edinburgh Castle* docked at Madeira; four days later the commissioners embarked in the *Hilary*, Casement having indulged himself several times with a local homosexual, Carlos Augusta Costa, whilst the opportunity presented itself. Pará was reached on 8 August and the party had to wait for another four days, during which time Casement dined with Consul Pogson and his old school friend Barry, of the vice-consulate at Victoria, saw Pickerell, the American consul, and seized further opportunities for nocturnal assignations. The party departed on 12 August and reached Manaos on 16 August. From this point onwards they were to be wholly dependent on Arana for transportation.

CHAPTER 8

COMMISSION OF
ENQUIRY

Casement made some effort to travel apart from the commission after Manaos, embarking on the *Huayna* while the four company commissioners travelled in the launch *Yurumaguas*. This did not, however, prove to be a practical or comfortable arrangement and before Iquitos he had changed vessels and was soon passing the time playing bridge with Barnes, Gielgud and Fox.

Iquitos, where the company had its headquarters, was the first really significant stopping point of the commission and the five men stayed there for a fortnight. Casement stayed at Le Cosmopolite hotel and was able to start the investigation proper. Honorary Consul David Cazes, who it turned out had complained to the Foreign Office of ill-treatment of Arana's employees as early as May 1905, immediately extended hospitality. This was only to be expected, but he and his wife went beyond the minimum official requirements of the Service and Casement's diary makes reference to several happy associations of a social nature in their company.[1] A ready understanding between the two consular officials had hardly been expected by the American Department of the Foreign Office, whose witness at the Select Committee enquiry, Gerald Spicer, testified that the Foreign Office received no information on the Putumayo prior to September 1909 – a serious error which, subsequently, he had to correct in detail before the committee. The diary, however, shows that Casement was superficially influenced by the honorary consul's personality, rather than his innocence; Cazes could have done more: 'After dinner, Cazes & I talked till 11.30 on this Putumayo Horror. He explaining his reasons for not having taken action.'[2] Was Cazes simply trying to win Casement to his defence? Three months later a more characteristic response to the attentions of an honorary consul appeared: 'I am as sick of the Cazes as a man can be!'[3]

Now came the first of the many testimonies which Casement was to hear before he left Iquitos for Manaos on 6 December. By way of introduction, as it were, the late acting French consular agent Vatan, who had spent fourteen years in the region, visited him and explained how the rule in the Putumayo was unadulterated slavery, the inevitable sequel of conquest of a race which stood outside the law: the Indian must be civilized and slavery was the means to this end. The first two Barbadians to testify gave entirely contradictory accounts: one described atrocities, the other 'gave a clean bill'.[4] From this time onwards, as Casement's presence became known, there was a steady stream of Barbadians anxious to reveal the horrors of the system and seemingly indifferent to the consequences of incriminating themselves.

Basically the task ahead of Casement and the company commission at this point was twofold: an on-the-spot inspection of actual conditions and the collecting of depositions from witnesses. The 12,000 square miles of territory defied exploration, let alone inspection, and therefore the commission concentrated mainly on the two main centres and their more easily accessible sections. This meant two distinct tours of inspection: the first, which Casement accompanied, was of three months' duration and embraced La Chorrera on the river Igara-Paraná; the second, which lasted two months, took in El Encanto at the junction of the rivers Cara-Paraná and Putumayo. Although 'supreme authority', in the words of the commission's own report, was vested in the manager of the Iquitos office, the managers of La Chorrera and El Encanto had a great deal of autonomy, if only because they were seven to ten days from Iquitos. Their vast territories were subdivided into a number of sections under the command of a white chief, with several white assistants, the 'blancos' mentioned above. According to the company's summary there were only two more levels, the native assistants and the Indian labourers. But Casement was to delve deeper into the real state of the hierarchy to find the function of the Barbadians and the literate half-breeds, known as 'racionales'. He seemed to get more quickly to the heart of things than his fellow investigators, because of his Congo experiences. It is arguable, however, that, just as Gielgud at least seemed to have a preconceived notion of a commercial system, Casement was predisposed to draw horrific conclusions on the basis of the methods of organization alone. As Arana's steamer, *Liberal*, brought Casement and the commission into the vicinity of La Chorrera, however, all were brought face to face with the physical proof of Hardenburg's accusations.

At Indostan, the last port of call before La Chorrera, the commission saw one Indian (a young boy) kept in heavy chains for attempting to escape downstream, the others, male and female, starving, except for one woman, the white overseer's concubine. Interviews on board intimated that worse was to come and, on their first day in La Chorrera, where they were welcomed by Juan Tizon, the company's chief overseer, the commissioners saw on the backs of the Indians the scars which were known locally as the 'marks of Arana'. One of the Barbadians in Iquitos had warned that all the worst evidence had been concealed from Captain Whiffen, and Casement was concerned that his dependence on the local company officials for so much should not inhibit full acquaintance with the actual state of affairs. A 'safe-conduct' pass had been provided by the prefect of the Department of Loreto in which the Peruvian authorities had been ordered to give the consul-general every assistance. Other than a few soldiers who eventually arrived at La Chorrera, however, the only Peruvian authorities were the agents of the Peruvian Amazon Company. This was a serious impediment, but, thanks to the information already contained in received depositions, the vast extent of concealment necessary, and general inefficiency, the commissioners were soon unanimous in their acceptance of *Truth*'s main charges.

Casement's work-load at this time was prodigious. Not content merely to hear statements, he assumed responsibility for a multiplicity of small physical tasks which, put together, took their toll: he measured the 'cepo' (stocks) personally, weighed and attempted to carry the Indians' rubber loads, took detailed measurements of the Indians themselves, photographed evidence whenever possible and undertook arduous journeys by horse or mule. Thirty Barbadians were principal witnesses when it came to the report, but far more statements were heard and Casement was all the time cross-checking references and confronting individuals in order to eradicate areas of contradiction. Throughout this period, when his health was frequently poor, he was checking the company's accounts, corresponding with the Foreign Office and writing three concurrent diaries. Another of his activities, letter-writing, was causing concern at the Foreign Office. Because of a leakage of information to the Anti-Slavery Society (with whom the Foreign Office had a sensitive relationship) on 24 October a telegram[5] was authorized by Sir Arthur Nicolson urging 'greatest discretion in communicating with correspondents in England'.

Merely hearing the catalogue of horrors – ingeniously designed variations of the 'cepo', carefully prolonged deaths from starvation, drowning or hanging, and mutilations of various kinds – would be too much for most civilized men to endure for long, without the extra tasks which Casement imposed upon himself. It transpired that the chiefs of sections were paid entirely in accordance with the amount of rubber collected and their respective 'estates' were run as autonomous units. The background of men attracted to this sort of work was often criminal and the commissioners drew the conclusion that corruption and cruelty were virtually built into the system from the start; each stratum of the hierarchy exploited the one beneath it in order to relieve pressures from above. A seemingly endless stream of accusers and accused passed before Casement, though ultimately, after the Peruvian Government investigated the company, by means of a commission headed by Dr Paredes, only 215 warrants were issued.

Among the most notorious of the chiefs of sections was Armando Normand, whose imaginative cruelties were probably not excelled. He deserves mention by name because for nearly seventy years he has been used to throw doubt on the authenticity of Casement's diaries. The forgery school of thought, whose most distinguished advocate was Alfred Noyes,[6] based a major part of its thesis on a conversation which Casement had with Bulmer Hobson whilst writing part of the Putumayo Report when in Dublin.[7] It was claimed that Casement had had in his possession a perverted diary of Normand's (Normand had had part of his education in England) which he sent to the Foreign Office as evidence; later, for propaganda purposes and to prevent Casement's reprieve, extracts from that diary, possibly in Casement's own hand, were used as evidence against him by agents of the British Government. Hobson's sister believed this until she died.[8] An explanation of the origin of this idea may be found by contrasting the Dollard's diary in London[9] with the parallel document in Dublin.[10] The Dublin version states that, on 28 October, at La Chorrera, the Barbadian, Bishop, brought Casement 'a sort of written Diary' of what he had observed there since 22 October; and the Dublin version, as a whole – with the possible exception of the entry for 31 October 1910 – contains no homosexual passages. In the London diary entry of 28 October, shortly after some erotic material, incongruously adjacent to mundane details of the journey, is the sentence: 'Bishop brought a written statement of all that has transpired since he left me.' Bulmer Hobson, who had access to the Dublin version (the London diaries were classified until 1959, and are still restricted) would have found it easy to regard the reference to Bishop's 'sort of written Diary' as confirmation of his half-century old memories of there being another diary which might have been attributed to Casement. But reasonably effective refutation of the Normand diary hypothesis, which did not in any case resolve the confusion between Bishop and Normand and depended on the hearsay evidence of two men,[11] lies in the nature of the atrocities committed by Normand: sadistic exercises of a heterosexual nature; his unambiguous masculinity was never in doubt.

During this burdensome period in his life Casement had to restrict indulgence in his personal proclivity to observation, for which there was plenty of scope, and diary-writing fantasy. Another area of inhibition involved attempting to hold his growing commitment to the Irish cause in suspension; it was never far below the surface. In this connection the discovery that one of the worst criminals of the Putumayo was a black man of part-Irish descent, called O'Donnell, shook his recently expressed con-viction[12] that the world consisted of men of two categories: compromisers and Irishmen. 'Thank God I am an Irishman.' The distinction had arisen in his mind because Fox and Gielgud were comparatively slow in accepting the full consequences of what they had seen and heard. Perhaps more reasonably than Casement they were prepared to regard the more out-rageous cases as exceptions caused by peculiar circumstances, until they heard more evidence. Casement's attitude was also confused by the fact that if the Indian slaves of the Peruvians were to be saved by anyone, it would be the British Government who would bring this about. He actually looked forward to the sight of the British flag on his return to Iquitos 'since there is no Irish flag',[13] an omission he would personally rectify four years later.

He was still 'British' in personal as well as public ways. On 15 February 1910 he had been godfather, necessarily by proxy, to Roger, son of Lieutenant Colonel F.R. Hicks, a member of the general's staff at the Fermoy Garrison and brother-in-law of Casement's closest English friend, Dick Morten.[14] Roger Hicks, now Captain R.B.N. Hicks, DSO, RN, received a handsome silver porringer and his photograph as a healthy toddler was subsequently stuck on to the fly-leaf of the 1911 Cash Ledger, where, with the inscription: 'My godson "Roger" Hicks',[15] it continues to be a strong piece of evidence for the genuineness of the volume. Two years later an invitation to forge such a close personal alliance with a member of the garrison occupying Ireland would have stood slim chance of accep-tance; in 1912 Casement, for a mixture of motives, declined to be god-father of an old 'Black Protestant' friend's son, who was none the less christened 'Roger'.

Comparisons between the plight of the Indians and that of the Irish would have seemed far-fetched to most observers. In this, though, Case-ment was perceptive and based his beliefs on what he actually saw and heard. He had already drawn attention to the rapid extinction of the Tupi-Guarani language in his annual report from Pará. Now, in the Upper Amazon basin, he recorded in his diary another sad consequence of conquest:[16]

> The young Quichua[17] pilot on Liberal is named Simon Pisango – a pure Indian name – but calls himself Simon ['de la' crossed out] Pizarro – because he wants to be 'civilised'!
> Just like the Irish O's and M's dropping first their names or prefixes to show their 'respectability' and then their ancient tongue itself, to be completely Anglicised.
> Simon Pisango still talks Quichua but another generation of 'Pizarros' will speak only Spanish! Men are conquered not by invasion but by themselves and their own turpitude.

Anglicization was a subtle form of mental and cultural enslavement which Casement found especially abhorrent; he was only too aware of how Anglo-Saxon his own attitudes had been at the time of the Boer War. The anti-slavery impetus, which was the most consistent feature of his life, pointed him more and more towards Ireland until the time came when he witnessed physical resemblances to the Putumayo in Connemara, where starvation and squalor caused an outbreak of typhus. Then the lot of the Indian and the Irish peasant seemed to him to be much the same. He christened the locality the 'Irish Putumayo' and wrote that 'The "white Indians" of Ireland are heavier on my heart than all the Indians of the rest of the earth.'[18]

The only official of the Peruvian Amazon Company in whom Casement felt that he could place any faith was Juan Tizon who, although nominally in charge of the company's vast territories, had, in fact, only been appointed a few months before the commission arrived. Previously he had been sub-prefect in Iquitos, in which post he later confessed, he had heard unpleasant rumours from the Putumayo. He professed himself to be totally convinced and appalled by the commission's findings (he had been present while many of the Barbadians were questioned) and assured Casement that he would 'polish off Zumaeta, Arana & all'.[19] It was therefore in a cautiously optimistic frame of mind that Casement left La Chorrera on 16 November in Arana's steamer, *Liberal*, accompanied by all the remaining Barbadians save four. The company commissioners stayed behind, ready to set off overland for their inspection of El Encanto.

The *Liberal* took Casement as far as Iquitos where there was a week's wait until he could continue in the *Atahualpa* as far as Manaos. Cazes accommodated him in his own house during this enforced delay and the consul-general found himself, not surprisingly, the centre of much attention. The prefect, Dr Paz Soldan, invited him to describe what he had found in the Putumayo and reacted suitably. He told Casement that a Peruvian government commission would now make a thorough investigation and bring the wrongdoers to justice; had the Peruvian authorities guessed for a moment that his findings would be positive, they would, of course, have made their own enquiries long ago. The pause in Iquitos was frustrating in some ways, useful in others. Casement had forcefully brought home to him by Vatan the extent to which his life had been in danger during his expedition; apparently only his status in the British Consular Service had saved him. Characteristically he took advantage of his more settled circumstances, temporary though they were, to put pen to paper for the benefit of the Peruvian commission which was to follow and he advised the company commissioners and the Foreign Office of the situation so far. The duplication of reports was a consular habit which was second nature to him now.

Relationships with the Cazes were strained, partly because David Cazes did not share Casement's faith in Tizon, but mainly because Casement had brought with him two Indian boys he had acquired and whom he naively imagined he might educate in the United Kingdom; unfortunately, Mrs Cazes found their presence embarrassing. 'Omarīno', later 'Hamurummy', was an orphan, and was sold to his new master for a shirt and a pair of trousers. 'Aredomi', 'Pedro' to some, 'Ricudo' to Casement, was scarcely a 'boy' except in the sense of British imperial terminology; he was nineteen and married. The Dublin Putumayo diary's details of part of the Omarīno transaction are believed by some to be the one and only example of deviant inclinations to be found in that document. However, without the revelations of the other diaries it is doubtful if such thoughts would spring to mind:[20]

> He clasped both my hands, backed up to me and cuddled between
> my legs and said 'Yes'. After much conversation and crowding
> round of Indians it is fully agreed on, he will go home with me.

Whatever the degree of affection felt for the two Indians, there is little evidence to suggest that they were ever the subject of advances, welcome or unwelcome. Their owner should rather be criticized for parading them about London as curiosities. They lived with him at 110, Philbeach Gardens and he took them to William Rothenstein to have their portraits painted. The artist's son, Sir John Rothenstein, still remembers them: 'they spoke no English, but I was sent for to try to divert them while they posed, wearing nothing but beads and feathers.'[21] The decision to make Irishmen of them had been taken in haste and their owner soon repented of it and took them back with him on his last visit to Iquitos.

After short breaks at Manaos and Pará, the return to England, with a detour to allow a long week-end in Paris, gave Casement much opportunity for reflection; he was unencumbered for most of the voyage as he had decided to leave Omarīno and Aredomi in the care of a Catholic priest in Barbados for some months, so that they might be prepared for European ways. He had time not only to think about the position of the Huitotos and other tribes of the Putumayo, whom he felt he might have saved, but to consider the plight of South American Indians generally and the aborigines of other continents. He knew that the Congo and the Putumayo were not the only blemishes of this nature and his diary reveals that his worries now extended beyond the rubber regions into the wider realms of colonial and ex-colonial possessions, particularly those of Spain and Portugal. His was a wholly humanitarian concern and the extent of the problem continued to worry him after the journey home, during the long period of delay between the writing of his report and the publication of it. Sir Edward Grey was also worried, doubtless for the same reasons, but while he was to postpone publication ostensibly for fear of doing more harm than good, his clerks were looking into worrying allegations about other British companies, whose activities elsewhere were reported to equal or excel those of the Peruvian Amazon Company.

Early in 1911 *La Prensa*[22] drew attention to the practices of the Inambari Pará Rubber Company[23] in the Carabaya Region. Travers Buxton, of the Anti-Slavery Society, took up the case with a letter to *The Times*[24] and Foreign Office enquiries led to Lucien J. Jerome, British Minister in Lima, being convinced that the accusations were well-founded. Worse was to come; a fortnight later another British company, the Tambopata Rubber Syndicate,[25] was drawn into the correspondence; missionaries were claiming that conditions were worse than those of the Putumayo, and mention was made of two American companies. The situation was becoming more sensitive than Casement, usually impetuous, would be patient enough to tolerate for long. And yet it was Casement's semi-private diplomacy which poured oil on these troubled waters. Never content to be a bystander he maintained direct communication with Jerome in Lima and soon discovered that the British Minister was having second thoughts about some of the stories he had heard. Casement therefore took it upon himself to quote, in a long letter to Spicer,[26] an illuminating passage from a 'Very Confidential' which he had received from Jerome.[27] In it the minister showed that he believed that one source of atrocity accusations, the Peruvian Society for the Protection of the Indians, had motives which were not exclusively humanitarian: 'Entrenous the Sociedad Pro-Indigena is a farce. It is more or less a political society whose *real* object is to *embêté le gouvernement*.'

In going along with the playing down of atrocity stories, Casement was to risk laying himself open to charges of operating a double standard as far as things Peruvian were concerned. The most outrageous allegations carried much weight with him, except when they came from a Peruvian source with a high-sounding name. Such an assessment, however, would not have done justice to the man. One of his virtues was his determination to translate theory into practice and, despite the occasional fanatical outburst, he was able to realize that, far from strengthening the hand of reformers, those who saw atrocities everywhere were only confusing the issue and delaying action. His letter to Spicer may have been a minor breach of confidence; it was, however, calculated to keep Foreign Office eyes firmly focused on the Putumayo.

After his brief visit to Paris Casement had reported to the Foreign Office on 5 January 1911 and had told Louis Mallet of the terrible nature of his findings. Previously he had decided on a short-list of seven[28] of the worst characters in the Putumayo; now he decided that the evidence was strongest against Aguero, Fonseca, Montt[29] and Normand and, when

Grey asked for a short preliminary report, he named these four and reiterated the charges against the agents of the company. This information was transmitted to the British Legation in Lima, with instructions that pressure be brought to bear on the Peruvian Government for effective action.

Casement then began his penultimate consular report, his last major document. It promised to be of even greater significance than his Congo disclosures, which had lost much of their strength because of the decision to substitute a letter code for the many names which Casement had named. In the case of the Putumayo where in a sense Britain was putting its own house in order, there were no such qualms. The shorthand typist was soon dismissed and Casement fell back on the longhand of the majority of his consular communications. This time the organization of material, the actual writing, the revision of the first proof and the submission of transcripts of oral testimony straddled three months. He began in the second week of January and received the proof of the revised version on 5 April.

The report which was finally approved still bore Casement's own distinctive vocabulary and style. Instead of letting the facts speak for themselves in the matter-of-fact way favoured by bureaucrats, perhaps with some justification, it abounds with emotive terms (e.g. 'revolting', 'unspeakable', 'atrocious', 'terrifying') and other, more fully expressed, moral judgments are to be found. Interestingly, in Gaelic manner it speaks of so many hundred 'souls' and, when an individual is found culpable he is a 'villain' – in another context he may sarcastically be referred to as a 'gentleman'. As Casement's feeling for the cause intrudes, one may feel that the power of his argument is lessened. And yet there are passages of lucid exposition which convey with great clarity matters of some complexity, for example, his analysis of the development of the Upper Amazon tribes and their interaction with the 'conquistadores'. Objections on grounds of exaggeration, other than those made by accused parties, tended to come later, and were largely generalizations coloured by hindsight.[30] Casement's use of hyperbole was apt to attract such charges. In this connection it is worth noting that, even with its dramatic epithets, the report which finally appeared had, thanks to Spicer's tactful criticism of the first draft, come a little way towards meeting the English preference for understatement.

The long gap between the appearance of the confidential print and the publication of the Blue Book on the Putumayo was caused by a variety of diplomatic considerations. Although the report underlined Great Britain's involvement, without which no effective pressures could have been exerted, Casement had assumed Peruvian responsibility throughout, and had mentioned the participation of Peruvian soldiers in one of the atrocities. At first the Peruvian Government seemed far more easily convinced than King Leopold had been; it was arguable that if the allegations were true it was all the more important that their sovereign rights over the area be recognized so that the administrative system which they claimed already existed there might be strengthened until it was capable of maintaining the rule of law. The converse was that Lima, separated from the Upper Amazon basin by the Andes, was not in a position to exercise effective control, in which case a territory might reasonably be ceded to Colombia (which, in fact, eventually happened as far as the Arana holdings were concerned).[31]

Aware of the ambiguities involved, the Peruvians moved cautiously. Following the first official British notifications of the state of affairs existing in the Putumayo, they set up the Paredes Commission to find out things for themselves. Dr Paredes returned to Iquitos on 15 July 1911, having visited all the twenty-six sections. A report of 1,300 pages followed (condensed from some 3,000 pages of depositions and other records) confirming Casement's findings; the information was placed in the hands of Judge Valcarcel and the British Government was informed.

Sir Edward Grey's policy during this difficult period was to try to force the Peruvian Government to put the Putumayo to rights by threatening them with international pressure which would follow the publication of Casement's Report; the implication was that, if thorough reforms were carried out and criminals brought to justice, minimum fuss would be made. It was a reasonable policy if effective action could be seen to be taking place. Casement, however, felt sure that the only thing actually happening was the escape of men responsible for the atrocities, possibly heading for alternative areas in which to practise the same trade by the same means. These fears began with a letter[32] which he had received from Tizon before he had even started writing his report. 'I am very busy dismissing all these people,' Tizon had said. Later came information from Jerome in Lima to the effect that of the many for whom warrants were issued, only four were named as being actually arrested.[33] Accordingly on 16 August, to satisfy himself and the Foreign Office, the consul-general set sail once again for Iquitos, taking with him Aredomi and Omarīno.

Casement's brief stay in Europe had been a very busy one. He had spent much of it actively attempting to raise money for the Morel testimonial, an endowment scheme intended to free the famous anti-slaver from worldly problems so that he might concentrate wholly upon his work. Other anti-slavery activities led Casement to devise a list of awkward parliamentary questions to keep the issue of the Putumayo alive in the House. Then, when the Peruvian Amazon Company's commissioners returned from the second part of their tour of investigation, he accepted their invitation to attend meetings of the board. His most important work, though, was aimed at the creation of a Christian mission which he hoped would be set up in the heart of the Putumayo to watch over the welfare of the Indians. He felt that this would inevitably have to be a Catholic undertaking in Peru, but that did not stop him from trying to rally support from the Archbishop of Canterbury. Not surprisingly the archbishop prevaricated, but so, also, did the Catholic Archbishop of Westminster. Casement was thoroughly disillusioned by the reactions to what seemed to be the only practical way of maintaining continuous benevolent observation of what really went on in the Putumayo.

At this point in his career Casement was given, and politely accepted, a knighthood. Later, at his trial, great play was made of his letter of acceptance[34] by the attorney-general, Sir Frederick Smith, who described it as 'fulsome', a term which has been uncritically accepted.[35] Among his friends, however, there was little doubt that the distinction would place him in a stronger position when it came to furthering the cause. His misgivings were more about what the Irish response would be than whether he should accept or not. He pretended to hate it and yet was obviously flattered. The opening sentence of the letter which was used with such great effect against him: 'I find it very hard to choose the words in which to make acknowledgement of the honour done to me by the King', can be seen to provide something of an escape clause with a slight touch of Gaelic humour. Most biographers have found the letter a stumbling block and yet it proves no more than that Casement was, like any other consular official, fully acquainted with the pompous phrases which convention demanded. In so far as the donor was Sir Edward Grey, he was genuinely grateful and the timing of the honour could only give his efforts on behalf of the Indians the stamp of approval and respectability.

CHAPTER 9

THE PUTUMAYO REPORT

Casement's return to Iquitos confirmed his worst suspicions. He left England on 16 August 1911 and on 28 August his ship docked in Barbados, where he found the black Irishman, O'Donnell, living in great luxury and popularity, in no way hampered by the authorities for his crimes in the Putumayo. Leaving Barbados on 5 September he found that a fellow passenger, Herbert Spencer Dickey, MD, who subsequently signed himself 'late medical officer of the Peruvian Amazon Company, Limited, Encanto, Putumayo' in at least one letter[1] to Mr Gubbins, one of the British directors, was returning to his practice in the Upper Amazon. Conversation with Dickey, an American citizen, although apparently based largely on hearsay, served only to increase Casement's impatience with the ineffective measures so far taken.

From his earliest experience of consular practice in South America, Casement had developed contempt for the 'honorary consul' and, despite the unexpectedly happy relationship which he had at first enjoyed with Cazes, it was predictable that he should seek the appointment of a consul proper in Iquitos. This was now achieved and the choice, George B. Michell, was wholly Casement's. The two had been friends years before in Africa and had renewed their relationship during Casement's recent visit to Paris, where Michell was vice-consul. It was a happy choice and Michell was soon to make his own tour of inspection in the Putumayo and submit a perceptive report.[2] He was quick to notice that some witnesses became uncommunicative when certain spectators were present.

After arrival in Iquitos on 16 October there was a seemingly long drawn-out period of disillusionment. Of the named accused only Aurelio Rodriguez was awaiting trial. Then, on 1 November, came the news that Judge Valcarcel, who had ordered Zumaeta's arrest, had been dismissed by the Iquitos court. Much time was spent with Paredes, the only Peruvian of genuine influence whom Casement felt he could trust. Paredes's vast dossier on the Putumayo went into far greater detail than Casement's report, uncovering cannibalistic aspects of torture which had not been discovered by Casement, but Paredes too was convinced that nothing would be done. The only real achievement of this visit to Iquitos was the practical help which Casement was able to provide when the Michell family arrived on 30 November. Even that was marred by guilty feelings about bringing them to such a terrible part of the world and he was relieved when his final departure occurred on 7 December.

At Pará he found instructions to go, via Barbados, to the United States, where he was to bring home to the Americans the unwillingness of the Peruvian Government to take any positive action. Always impatient with 'that abominable Monroe Doctrine'[3] he made the most of his present opportunity and, whilst in Washington, was somewhat surprised to find sympathetic ears. The way was well-paved for him by the British ambassador, James Bryce, whose Irish background was very similar to his own, and whose writings[4] reveal that he, too, was well-acquainted with Santos and Rio de Janeiro. There was an immediate feeling of trust and common cause between the two men and it was Bryce, naturally, who made sure that Casement's message was delivered personally to President Taft, so that the British view of the Putumayo could be presented by its most ardent advocate. Casement had discovered that the Americans generally had too easily been fobbed off by Peruvian assurances and was able to bring them up-to-date details to correct their false impressions. One detail which probably carried more weight with his listeners than the now too familiar atrocity stories was the inescapable fact that Zumaeta was not in prison, despite reports to the contrary. Within a week of these discussions in Washington, the United States was urging the government in Lima that, unless it acted immediately and effectively, Casement's report would be published. No more delays would be allowed.

In January 1912 Casement returned to London, where he stayed until he left for Ireland in July. He spent part of his time advising the Foreign Office that they should devote their energies now to encouraging the setting up of a real system of local government in the Putumayo, rather than pursuing the criminals, most of whom would never be seen or heard of again anyway. He saw the Putumayo as a test case, from which guidelines would emerge for the protection of primitive peoples elsewhere in the world. Then, apart from dealing with family matters – Casement's brothers, Charles and Tom, repeatedly sought financial aid from him – he devoted most of the rest of his time to the establishment of the Christian mission. Here his determination to translate high flown ideas into action was wholly successful. Eventually, when armed with his Blue Book, he was able to rally support from Catholics and Protestants alike, often from influential personal friends, such as William Cadbury;[5] a Franciscan mission was established by the end of the year.

The Peruvian response to complaints from both Great Britain and the United States was merely the proposal that yet another commission be set up, this time to formulate a general scheme of reform prior to new legislation. Sir Edward Grey had now reached the point of unequivocal acceptance of Casement's assessment of the Peruvian attitude to the Indian; two statistics served to convince him that publication should be delayed no further: one of the largest consignments of rubber to be shipped from Iquitos in recent years had left that port in April, and the total tonnage exported during the first four months of 1912 equalled three-quarters of the output for the previous year. It was felt that only a resumption of the old methods could have produced such results and Sir Edward Grey himself believed that a Christian mission was the answer and needed the encouragement that a Blue Book would provide. The date of publication was 13 July 1912.

The general public had known of the alleged state of affairs in the Putumayo since September 1909; even so, the gap of nearly three years did not dissipate interest and the Blue Book created a considerable stir. Casement's findings, with the imprimatur of His Majesty's Stationery Office, went much further than anything *Truth* had revealed and were accepted even by accused parties as generally true. The newspapers sang Casement's praises and an outspoken sermon in Westminster Abbey commended him personally.[6] The investigations which followed were largely about the allocation of responsibility for the atrocities. In so far as the report was challenged at all, it was in small matters of detail which might affect the degree of responsibility of a particular individual. Peru, Colombia, the English directors of the Peruvian Amazon Company and even, with some reservations, Julio Arana, accepted Casement's overall findings.

The House of Commons Select Committee was appointed 'to inquire whether any responsibility rests upon the British Directors of the Peruvian Amazon Company in respect of the atrocities in the Putumayo district, and whether any changes in the law are desirable to prevent the machinery of the Companies Acts being used in connection with similar practices in foreign countries,' and began its enquiry on 6 November 1912, under the chairmanship of Charles Roberts. The first witness to be examined was Gerald Spicer, who appeared as senior clerk at the Foreign Office and head of the American Department. Questioned by the chairman as to when the Foreign Office began to interest itself in the atrocity stories emanating from the Upper Amazon basin, he stated that its attention 'was first drawn to this question by the articles in *Truth* which appeared towards the end of September, 1909'.[7] But on 16 November Spicer had to submit a correction to his testimony and admit that the Foreign Office had in fact been notified by David Cazes in May 1905 of ill-treatment of Barbadian workers by the firm of Arana; the notification had been referred to the Colonial Office which had, in turn, passed the information to the governor of Barbados. The outcome had been representations to the government in Lima, a complaint by Cazes to the prefect of Loreto and a meeting between Cazes and Arana. The allegedly cruel agent of Arana, Ramon Sanchez, was dismissed but not otherwise punished, and Cazes followed up the incident by complaining to the Foreign Office that it was difficult to obtain reliable information from the Putumayo as all trading was in the hands of Arana's employees, and the firm also owned all means of transport.

Spicer's initial error and the implications which might have followed from its uncritical acceptance put the committee on its guard from the very first; as witness followed witness it became clearer that the dating of awareness of cause for concern and the degree of responsibility which followed from such awareness were crucial issues to be considered. Plainly culpability of the British directors of the Peruvian Amazon Company could only date from October 1907 when the firm of J.C. Arana and Hermanos became incorporated in London and changed its name. The committee had to try to decide to what extent after that date a British director ought to know something about the conditions of those who laboured for the company, or to what extent he might plead justifiable ignorance of all matters which were not purely financial. However, exemption from responsibility prior to October 1907 could not necessarily be accorded to the Foreign Office, nor, in purely moral terms, as was demonstrated when Travers Buxton was examined, to the Anti-Slavery Society.

The minutes of evidence reveal a degree of evasiveness on Casement's part when it came to pinpointing the date of his own awareness of atrocity allegations, all the more puzzling in the light of his letter to Milne Cheetham quoted above (page 69). Questioned by Willoughby Dickinson[8] he described how, by coincidence, when travelling by steamer to take up his post at Pará, he sat at dinner beside Julio Arana. Later, during 1908, the captain of the vessel called at the consulate officially and said that 'shocking stories' were coming from Arana's part of the Upper Amazon basin:

> indirectly, you see, I had heard in 1908, but it was not my business; it was not in my consular jurisdiction at the time, and I had no authority to investigate and report at all.

Why in his answer did he not refer to the newspaper cutting and letter which he had sent to Milne Cheetham? The invariably punctilious adherent to regulations may have realized that he had not fully complied with Consular Instructions (1893), Chapter XXI, 'Slave Trade', paragraph 3. This obliged consuls to keep the secretary of state 'fully informed . . . on all matters of interest in connection with slavery and the slave trade'

– not only the diplomatic representative. Consular despatches in the Public Record Office, Spicer's testimony and Casement's testimony show that an early publication of Arana's activities went no further than Petropolis – a circumstance which recalls the clash between Chapman and Haggard about communication priorities. Casement had indicated on the cutting and in his covering letter what proved to be the most significant paragraph:[9]

> David Serrano trabalhava, ha 8 annos, na sua propriedade La
> Reserva, tendo domesticado os indis Jabayenas, hoje reduzidos a
> condição de escravos pelo terrivel syndicato peruano

and had underlined the sentence which stated Arana's involvement. Although it remains arguable that the Foreign Office would have attached no more significance to the newspaper account than did the Legation, Casement did do less than he should have done. The excuse that the cause of the captain's complaints was 'not in my consular jurisdiction' is hardly in line with Consular Instructions and, if it were, why did he notify the Legation when the same stories reached him via a source which he himself described as highly unreliable?

Dickinson followed up his line of enquiry and Casement was pressed to admit that he had had in his possession copies of *La Felpa* and *La Sanción* and, as the latter ceased to appear under this name in 1907 – a fact apparently not appreciated by his questioner – Casement had clearly known about the Putumayo longer than he cared to say. This awkward inconsistency is unlikely to be resolved as the best source, a diary for 1907 or 1908, will have been destroyed, along with other sexually incriminating material,[10] after being concealed during the period leading up to the trial for treason. Shortcomings in the public official may have been caused by disappointments in private life, but there is no proof that this was so.

As the witnesses passed before the committee until the last examination on 30 April 1913, it gradually became clear that the defensive stance of the board had been based on disbelief of unpleasant information because it was derived from blackmailers. On the one hand it was accepted as axiomatic that Casement's report was generally true; on the other it was claimed that all who had attempted to bring home the horrifying facts to the directors had demanded a high price for silence: therefore the directors, who now accepted that the Putumayo was a 'Devil's Paradise', as Hardenburg had christened it, had been justified in not believing what they had been told. Remarkably convincing documentary evidence was produced, but it was stretching the committee's credulity too far to expect them to believe that three individuals, from different walks of life, who had never previously met each other, should all choose Arana as victim.[11] The British directors had, though, believed the statements of their Peruvian colleagues about the company's enemies and, to their credit, did not try to let what guilt there was rest upon them alone.

Apart from establishing the degree of culpability of the directors, the committee sought to discover whether the protective functions of the Consular Service might be modified to prevent similar abuses of native labour occurring elsewhere. The British Empire being so extensive at the time, it seemed that a gentle policing of the world might occur if Great Britain looked to its own colonies first and, through the Consular Service, watched carefully the movements of its native populations when they strayed into foreign territory. This was all right for Barbadian migrants but, unless international law with regard to slavery and the slave trade were generously interpreted, a more militant consular presence which took direct interest in indigenous peoples would inevitably alienate the host country. Harris, questioned by the chairman,[12] wanted travelling consuls, paid for by the Colonial Office; initially he saw the problem as one which was applicable to coloured migrant workers, but he went on to say that treaties should be concluded, giving consuls generally an obligation to care for native peoples. Like Casement he felt that the honorary consul too frequently had divided loyalties; by way of example he cited the case of one who was in charge of a telegraph station, an appointment which required him to observe complete secrecy. How could he fulfil his obligation to report anything amiss to the Foreign Office? In the Putumayo, in the words of Swift MacNeill,[13] 'a Consul with a foreign name, 1,200 miles from the scene of operations, was the only person with whom these people could communicate if they could escape from the hands of these company exploiters.' And, to make matters worse, Cazes was in many ways beholden to Arana.

Casement did not share Harris's view of the specifically appointed travelling consuls; he had always shown, by word and example, that he believed travelling to be a duty incumbent upon all consuls anyway. What he wanted was for British control to be exercised abroad on the basis of a document deposited at Somerset House whenever a company employing labour overseas was registered in London. This was to be 'a schedule of all the labour conditions; first, the number of labourers they employ, and then the conditions on which that labour is engaged, whether it is contract by indenture or merely verbal arrangements; the rate of pay, the provisions made for feeding and housing'.[14] In making this suggestion he was mindful of the second part of the committee's brief, to consider possible improvements in Company Law, and his practical recommendations recall his respect for precise regulations during his early career in South America.

Assuming that, with the help of the Consular Service, Company Law (strengthened by new legislation) could be effectively administered wherever British firms were to be found, still no direct account had been taken of what would today be termed the 'human rights' of the primitive native – whether or not he were officially an employee; the problem of national integrity remained insuperable. As Joynson-Hicks reminded Casement: 'the only way in which England has been able to interfere was in consequence of the Barbadian natives, and that was our only *locus*.'[15] The Indians who were employees of the company were subject to Peruvian law; improved terms of employment might only protect them from exploitation by British subjects, and then only if consuls were vigilant.

In a personal letter to Charles Roberts, written some months after he had testified before the Select Committee, Casement revealed that he had forced a retrospective widening of his terms of reference on to the Foreign Office: '*I far exceeded my instructions*. I had no instructions to investigate the treatment of the Indians at all.'[16] He went on to say that the sentence empowering him to enquire into treatment of Indian labourers 'was inter-polated just before the Blue Book was issued'. The original wording only authorized him to investigate the condition and treatment of British subjects:

> All the rest was off my own bat – & the responsibility for it rested on
> my shoulders. Had I failed or got into trouble with the Peruvian
> authorities I could have been disowned – in any case the Br. Govt.
> could have rightly said I had exceeded my instructions. . . . When I
> came home and told Grey & the Under-Sec. of State they were with
> me heart & soul & from that on they practically acted on my advice
> right through.

Thus, by setting a powerful precedent, Casement helped to widen the scope of future legitimate consular activity.

Naturally much of the evidence volunteered by witnesses was repetitive, partly because they had not always had the benefit of hearing what had gone before. Members of the committee, however, only repeated themselves to the extent of checking the consistency of testimony about past iniquities. When it came to discussion of preventive measures there was a gradual development of ideas. To a certain extent, instead of bringing forth definite proposals, questioning tended to reveal the differences between how a consul actually performed his duties (and traditional grievances were aired) and his personal attitude to what might in theory be expected of him. In this area Casement's instinctive practice anticipated the more sophisticated suggestions of the committee. Very much a man of action, and, as far as most of his South American career was concerned, a conscientious public official, he had by habit worked with consular representatives of the different nations almost as though they were all part of some international organization. Perhaps it was simply part of his nature that he got on well with the other side; or it may have been his unconsciously British feeling for a Diplomatic (Casement would want a large 'D') 'Old Boy network' such as he showed when appointing Barry to a consular post. As has been seen (page 55) the General Consular Service lacked *esprit de corps* and, as if by way of compensation, some consuls were inclined to establish strong links, socially, and, as it were, professionally, with their opposite numbers from other powers. Even in Iquitos Casement found himself ministered unto by consular officers, past and present, of the United States, Brazil and France; in Pará he was happier to work with America's Pickerell than Great Britain's Pogson.[17] Despite differences of practice and the obvious built-in rivalries, there was an accepted code which crossed national boundaries and might have been utilized in practical ways against a common neutral foe, such as famine. It might be felt by some, however, that slavery was not yet in the neutral zone.

The committee, however, went further than Casement's personal feeling that something beyond an 'aggregation of posts' was desirable and pushed the theoretical potentialities of the Consular Service in the field beyond what the actual practitioners were prepared to contemplate. Matters came to a head at one of the last sessions when, on 22 April 1913, Dickinson was pressing Sir Harry Johnston about the possibility of some sort of 'international protectorate over all these particular regions that we are concerned with':[18] 'would it be practicable to have an international Consular Service for that purpose by agreement with other nations?'[19] Sir Harry Johnston rejected the idea. He did go so far as to admit that British consuls did make it their business to look after the welfare of those who were not British subjects when 'gross abuses' occurred, but consequent action seemed to be limited to a letter to *The Times*: then 'the parties involved sit up.' The level of enquiry had not reached so advanced a stage when Casement had been examined and the questions put to him were mostly assumed to be restricted to exploitation by British firms. When the chairman attempted to pin him down to practical recommendations, he at first claimed that the Consular Service as it stood was in no condition to be a watchdog against slavery: 'it would have to be strengthened, and more money spent on it.'[20] Granted these improvements, however, he came out unequivocally in favour of accepting the responsibility: 'Undoubtedly. I can only see that action could be taken through the Consular Service.'[21] By action he meant making investigations, and he characteristically added that they would be outside the scope of honorary consuls. It was in his view a question of a more positive interpretation and implementation of Consular Instructions as already written: 'There are general instructions which all Consuls have requiring them to investigate and take care of British labour ... when in the Congo ... I took long journeys, frequently of several hundred miles, to see conditions under which British labour was working.'[22] And it was not lost on the committee that the Congo reforms had been wholly for the benefit of the native population, nor that the political context was Belgian, not British.

The committee realized from time to time that it was straying a little from its terms of reference in giving so much attention to the Consular Service as a possible vehicle of native protection, but it did not shrink from giving this part of its deliberations due emphasis in the report which appeared on 5 June 1913. Quoting Sir Harry Johnston and E.D. Morel it emphasized that it was consular reports 'backed by public opinion' which had been the 'true levers of reform in the Congo'. The trouble in the Putumayo could, it implied, have been averted if there had been more diplomatic and consular activity there before 1909. It referred to specific Consular Instructions about the slave trade and stressed that both the secretary of state and the diplomatic representative had to be kept fully informed about these matters. The main recommendation echoed Casement: enlightened implementation of instructions would require strengthening the Service and, in areas like the Putumayo, career consuls should be employed.

As far as the second part of its terms of reference went, the committee made no recommendations for alterations in Company Law. It concluded that the company was already liable to be held responsible in law for atrocities committed against Colombians or Barbadians and 'in the abstract' to Indians. But, evidently worried by the notion of abstract responsibility, it added that it was 'doubtless the fact that wild forest Indians could not possibly use their legal rights' (though none had been discovered) and even the Barbadians were in fact wholly restricted to 'such redress as Sir Roger Casement secured for them'. Under the heading 'The Precedent of the Putumayo Case', the committee summarized its main conclusion: the Commercial Department of the Foreign Office was, it said, the natural channel of information. As it had no policing authority, it should pass on the information (gleaned by consuls) to the Board of Trade and the public prosecutor. Existing law need be modified only to the extent to which it should be made easier to compel directors to institute enquiries.

In a narrow sense Casement's Blue Book and the Select Committee Report which followed it were less successful in their effects than Casement's achievements in the Congo. The directors[23] were found guilty of 'culpable negligence' but of no overt act punishable under the Slave Trade Acts; public disgrace was their punishment. Arana, although dismissed as liquidator, continued to enjoy the style of living to which he was accustomed and, in 1916, on hearing of Casement's impending trial for High Treason, sent a long telegram asking him to recant. The Anti-Slavery Society continued to receive reports of guilty parties conveying Huitotos to other parts of South America, where the old system, somewhat diminished in scale, was perpetuated; as late as 1974[24] attempts were being made by Survival International to buy out of debt-bondage 120 Andoke rubber-gatherers, the last remnants of their tribe. (Their 'patron' was a man named Zumaeta.) The Upper Amazon boom ended in the year of the Select Committee's Report, or shortly afterwards, but it was the Malayan plantations, not a cessation of peonage, which brought about its decline and fall. It is not, however, necessary to go all the way with Sir Edward Grey in the conclusions which he drew from the increase in rubber output after the commission's tour of inspection; kindly administered methods of collection, if indeed Tizon did insist upon them, would be expected to produce a higher yield, given the nature of the Huitotos and the amount of wastage inherent in a cruel system.

Despite the outbreak of war, the event usually accepted as having brought the Putumayo campaign to an unsatisfactory conclusion, the Foreign Office, through the new British Minister in Lima, Ernest Rennie, kept applying pressure to the Peruvian Government. The Peruvians, for their part, successfully avoided taking any genuine action against the accused parties. Those who were arrested invariably escaped, and newspaper articles[25] championing the most notorious of the rubber-gatherers had not been lacking in the months which followed the publication of the committee's report. But even in the midst of all the problems created by a world war, the Foreign Office persevered in its efforts on behalf of the Amerindian, right until the news of Casement's arrest cut the ground from under its feet. When the author of the Putumayo Report was found guilty of High Treason, it was generally felt in Peru that Arana was vindicated; the Foreign Office, without altering its stance on the need for reform, was then realistic enough to cease agitating for the punishment of the guilty.

Even when the many unsatisfactory and inconclusive aspects of the campaign for reform in the Putumayo have been taken into account, there remain substantial benefits in the sphere of consular efficiency and in the broader, less easily defined, area of world attitudes to coloured native peoples. As far as the former went, Casement found that the members of the Royal Commission on the Civil Service were predisposed to heed his advice when they examined him in May 1914. As many witnesses were called and many recommendations were made in their report,[26] it is obviously not possible to see exactly where Casement's testimony formed the basis of what finally appeared. It is difficult, however, not to see him behind recommendation 30: 'In the appointment of unpaid Consular officers preference should be given to persons of British nationality, and all unpaid officers should be under the supervision of a salaried Consular officer of superior rank' (a reversal of the attitude adopted by the Walrond Committee in their report of 1903)[27] and recommendation 33 (page 41): 'The practice of employing at certain posts Consular Officers with

Diplomatic rank should be extended', recalls the Casement whom Hambloch knew. The commissioners, like Casement, felt that the Consular Service had, in one sense, to stand aloof from matters of trade, a sentiment which ran contrary to much received opinion:[28]

> The Consular Service like the Diplomatic Service exists for the
> benefit of the community as a whole, and the influence and
> efficiency of either service are impaired when it becomes identified
> with the interests of individual traders or concessionaires.

There was more general acceptance of the diplomatic role of the consul, and the Putumayo Case can only have helped this. Nevertheless, the commissioners, like the Ridley Commissioners before them,[29] drew back from the idea of amalgamation of the Consular and Diplomatic Services and this did not occur until another quarter of a century had elapsed.

What did in fact occur was the extension of the protective role of the consul (see Appendix A); the precedent of the Putumayo had helped to give it a new dimension. The umbrella which protected British interests could, with appropriate diplomatic action, be extended to protect what amounted to stateless persons. There was, as a result of the stir created by the events in the Putumayo, a revival of awareness of the continuing validity of the Slave Trade Acts as applicable to the British Empire,[30] that these were not archaic instruments of another age was brought home to educated British opinion with some force. Nor was the message wholly lost in the world at large, which had been shocked by the Congo revelations, but might have been tempted to think of them as an isolated aberration. Now it was seen that in other places, where modern civilization had impinged upon the territory traditionally occupied by primitive peoples, cruel exploitation could occur. And it was appreciated that native coloured races generally, not merely the very primitive, were vulnerable. For the second time Casement had demonstrated to the world a need for a new kind of international law with regard to the individual. He had done his best to awaken his contemporaries to a problem which has yet to be solved:[31]

> These people have absolutely no human rights, much less civil rights.

CHAPTER 10

IRELAND AND GERMANY

The beginning of the last stage in Casement's journey towards a total commitment to the cause of Irish separatism is best illustrated by recourse to the letters which he wrote to John Morgan in 1912–13, and which were not seen again until 1979. From lodgings at 45, Ebury Street, SW, on 18 December 1912 came a 'Private & Confidential' (this instruction added as an after-thought in a different shade of ink) with intimations of what was to come:[1]

> I am in bad need of some friendly counsel – from one like
> yourself – . . .
> My future depends on the decision I come to in the next few days
> – and I do not want to leap impetuously or follow my impulse
> alone. . . .
> I am in great doubt how to act – and in much trouble of mind.

Superficially the problem was whether or not to retire from the Foreign Office at this particular time, but later correspondence shows the nature of the retirement he had in mind. The letter goes on to discuss his poor health (which was an important consideration when the pension rights were taken into account) and to ask whether Morgan would like to come to lunch the next day, when Morel was already coming: 'supposing Morel is *persona grata* to you'. The discussion at that luncheon is knowingly referred to again six months later when Morgan is expected to meet some Irish friends in Dublin: 'if . . . you are the same man who lunched with me in London you must repeat the process here in Dublin.'[2]

Casement had been undergoing medical checks and was inclined to exaggerate the findings of those he consulted. The first result of all the advice he received during early December was a decision to take an extensive holiday until he was his old self again. Accordingly he wrote to Morgan on Christmas Eve, saying that he would be sailing for Las Palmas on 27 December. He was en route to his brother Tom's inn in South Africa, still unable to see his way to a consistent course of action in the future. The holiday, taking in Teneriffe and St Helena, restored him to a more optimistic frame of mind and Morgan next heard from Ebury Street in May 1913.[3] 'Here I am back again – ever so much fitter and strong – Mrs G tells me you will be with her on Friday [crossed out] afternoon. . . . I saw Dick Morten on Sunday & Parry[4] & heard of you.' He expected to be off to Dublin on the Saturday, but, finding that he still had not managed to get away a week later, wrote again. The letter[5] (four quarto sheets) continued to reveal that his 'mind was still in fluctuation', largely about severing the link with the Foreign Office, which was now regarded solely as a source of income, not so much for Casement himself, for whom the pension would suffice, but 'for all the obligations I have contracted'. The traditional respectable alternative of directors' fees is rejected in blunt terms:

One must *earn* what one takes – and it is occupation as much as money or more than money my mind seeks.
If I could see clear what to *do* with myself once I am free from Consuling I'd go tomorrow.

The same letter gives some indication of what the future may hold. 'Now that I am back I am obsessed by Ireland! I've been on the wing for Ireland all through the week . . . I hope tonight shall see me crossing the Irish Sea.' And that thought led naturally to the next: 'Mrs Green gave me word of you and so did my friend Sydney (sic) Parry. . . .' But he was now toying with an idea which might postpone any real decision making for some time: a tour of his old haunts in Africa 'to record en passant how I found Leopold', an understandable enterprise for one who had occasional yearnings to be a writer. The idea had a strong sentimental appeal to him and easily displaced any prospect of a resort to the conventional post-consular activity, a business career. However, after a page of what proved to be only a dream he returned to the obsession with which he began: 'I am busy in Ireland for next three weeks probably when I daresay I shall be back in England & probably staying with Dick Morten in Denham.' And the letter concluded after the almost inevitable allusion to Mrs Green.

Within the week Casement was replying from 55, Lower Baggot Street, Dublin to Morgan's letter of 20 May. Morgan was expected in Dublin, wrongly as it turned out, on 4 June and his friend had persuaded the Foreign Office to grant leave of absence until 30 June. Enjoying a period of self-confessed good health and freedom of action, Casement was busying himself with 'a little enterprise of despair that may result in a mission of hope',[6] a reference to his efforts to improve the lot of the 'white Indians' of Connemara. This was the letter in which he invited Morgan to meet his 'Irish friends' and alluded to the lunchtime 'counsel' session, before his recent travels, at which Morel had been present. He wrote during the week in which one Irish friend, or rather acquaintance, who lunched with him was Major MacBride, and he was able to hear the first-hand account of MacBride's Irish Brigade, raised to fight the British on behalf of the Boers. He was delighted to learn that MacBride's antecedents were much the same as his own; not only was he an Ulsterman, but he came from the same Glen, and Casement discovered that he already knew the family. Certainly this was a week which saw a hardening of his views on Irish affairs. Although still undecided about leaving the Foreign Office there is a feeling in the letter that things are coming to a head. He felt that while he might easily retire '& spend the next ten years . . . in doing just those things I like best to try to do . . . I don't know that I am justified in pleasing myself, or following an inclination . . . I've got a month still to think of it – & I don't worry about it. Things always come right in the end – the fatal optimism of an Irishman I feel!' Then the mere thought of Ireland stimulated an outspoken statement about the Irish Question and his attitude to it:

> The truth is nearly every Irishman one meets is now a Home Ruler of some sort – the Ulsterians worst of all. They go in for the Whole Hog of Sinn Fein – ourselves alone & war to the last bolt – and rivet – against compromise. What an extraordinary people we are.
>
> The 'Unionists' one meets often say 'if this were *real* Home Rule – a Colonial Parliament, we could accept it – but this bill is neither one thing nor another' – so that their objection to Home Rule is that they are not offered enough of it.
>
> Personally I am a Separatist – I want Ireland on her own – on her own pocket too. We want the grave responsibilities of life to be thrust on us – and I never fear that once we had to face the problem of doing for ourselves we should manage.
>
> The thing to fear is that under the present measure causes of friction between the two Parliaments will increase not diminish. . . .
>
> . . . If I am in Dublin I shall be delighted to hear your speech[7] on the subject.

Having heard again from Morgan, and thinking that he was due at 10, Herbert Street, Dublin the next day, Casement wrote to that address in mysterious and dramatic vein on 3 June: 'I want to try & entice you into an adventure with me. . . . It will be a serious & great adventure too & one you won't forget.'[8] He intimated that it was for Ireland. But he had mistaken Morgan's date of arrival and, calling at Herbert Street, was told by the maid that the professor had arrived the previous day, was now out, would not be back until late and was off to Belfast the next day. In desperation he went back to Lower Baggot Street and wrote a letter attempting to sort out the problem: 'I had hoped to lure you away with me tomorrow on a great adventure. . . . I am going west – and I wanted to get you with me. Can't you come? Give up the Black North & its Ulsterians & come with me to Connacht!'[9] The 'adventure' was by his own standards scarcely worthy of the name, and Morgan had already slipped through his fingers. It was no more than the 'mission of hope' previously mentioned, but had, largely because of his sister's agitation, rapidly assumed greater proportions in his mind. It was a very worthy cause, some fifty peasants had already died of typhus because of the poor conditions in which they lived. Sadly a crusade on behalf of these unfortunates had political potential, but the dominant motivation of the veteran anti-slaver was undoubtedly humanitarian. £2,440 was raised by opening a relief fund, much of it coming with the assistance of a newspaper subscription appeal. The 'adventure' unavoidably brought the King of England uncomfortably close to Leopold in Casement's mind; and in so doing it had made it easier for him to sever his links with the Foreign Office. On the last day of his leave he had posted his letter of resignation.

In August Casement was back at Denham and anticipating a journey 'to "Ulster"'[10] for a few days to inspect the rebel troops'.[11] In the meantime he beseeched Morgan to join him at The Savoy; he was writing to reinforce his host's letter of invitation.

The remaining correspondence is a pencilled letter headed 'On the way to Ireland' and an ink postscript of greater length; the first is dated 29 August 1913, the other, though undated, is believed to have been written shortly after arrival. The pencilled letter reveals a little more of Morgan's own position: 'I will drop you some lines from "Ulster", and if anything of real interest is likely to transpire on "Ulster Day" (28 Sept) I'll ask you over in good time to take a hand in the fray. Between us we might rout a phalanx'.[12] After more in that vein he concluded that as it was the season of mellow fruitfulness, 'our pens should all be dropping matured reflection. Mine, when it comes to Ulster will be found to have a wasp in it.' In his postscript he put aside the pencil and took up his pen.

The final item in the Morgan Letters shows the extent to which Casement had gone in thinking through the implications of Protestant reaction to Home Rule. Carson is not mentioned, but plainly he, or the position which he occupied on the political stage, gave rise to the more radical thoughts which now found expression. Casement had crossed over from the Moses Room at Denham to an equivalent retreat at Ardrigh, Francis Bigger's house in Belfast. The physical journey was matched by the sentiments which he expressed to Morgan:[13]

There *can* be no compromise on the principle at issue, 'Ulster' will never assent to an Irish Parliament until it is a fact. Once it is then she'll go into it & make it hers – but to get her beforehand to say that is impossible.

If England doesn't settle the 'Irish Question' soon it is possible Germany may. I mean if a war comes & Ireland [is] still as she now is, & that war goes against Great Britain – not an impossible contingency – then Ireland goes for ever.

If the present effort at Home Rule is wrecked through the timidity or indifference of Gt. Britain I think it will be the last occasion the chance will come – & that the ultimate complete separation of the two countries will become the way out of the difficulty. One of the biggest linen merchants in 'Ulster' a Protestant & a 'Unionist' said to me last Sunday that what *he* wanted was to see Ireland entirely independent & Ulster ruling that Ireland – & what's more, he said it *must* come. Home Rule removes all hope of that for it will make Nationalist Ireland 'loyal' – & there are still plenty of men in Ireland [who] are not Home Rulers because they feel like the linen man.

The Casement who felt in the Amazon basin that compromise was an undesirable English characteristic was now fully restored to that opinion, after finding early 'Ulster' refusals to compromise tiresome. He was also becoming firmer in his previously expressed opinions that Germany might provide the key to the Irish problem. In June, 1912 he had invited Hambloch to visit him at the Mortens' and had given his fellow guest his impressions of Germany as he had found it in May of that year. After mentioning the official car at his disposal (page 75), he went on to praise the Germans at the expense of 'You English'.[14] According to Hambloch's account of the conversation, he said, 'I may be going over there again soon,' and suddenly refused to talk any more.

By the end of the correspondence with Morgan the time had come for more positive efforts for Ireland; the cumulative effect of years of discussion with like-minded individuals had helped to narrow down the courses of action open to him. Belfast, where he now found himself, was the scene of the clash between British troops and strikers which had so distressed him when he had been on leave in Antrim in 1907. Once again feelings were running high and guns were brought to the root of the trouble, but this time the weapons were Unionist, or 'Carsonite', and were slowly trickling in for the benefit of the Ulster Volunteer Force, the Peace Preservation Act of 1881 having lapsed in 1907. Moreover, the approach of the anniversary of the signing of the Covenant by nearly half a million Ulstermen was generating excitement. He had already given his services as a writer to Ireland (with the help of various pseudonyms), the next step, partly influenced by Morgan's example, was to speak publicly on her behalf, and he first did this at Ballymoney in October 1913. The purpose of the meeting was to rally Protestant Nationalists of the province in a show of strength against Carsonism and in favour of a united Ireland. Mrs Green was another speaker and the evening was generally regarded as a success. Unexpectedly, it was the moderation of the speeches which impressed. Of Casement's contribution, William Cadbury later observed that every sentence was 'in a most conciliatory spirit, with no suggestion whatever of hatred of England'.[15] Cadbury, who had met Casement in connection with the Congo Reform Association and given him much hospitality at his home in Kings Norton, spent some time with him in Ireland towards the end of 1913, when he was instrumental in convincing him, though only temporarily, that 'it was a mistake to dwell too much on the wrongs of the past.' The issue arose as a result of the two men attending the Abbey Theatre together.

The Ballymoney meeting and the publication, the following month, of 'Ulster and Ireland',[16] properly signed by the author, were the last overt acts necessary to draw him into the mainstream of the various agencies which had a hand in the creation, organization and, finally, arming, of the Irish Volunteers. By virtue of international standing, proven loyalties and influential friendships he was almost at once in the upper hierarchy of the movement which was Nationalism's answer to the Ulster Volunteers. That he was regarded as something of a prestige symbol was indicated on St Patrick's Day, 1914, when 'I reviewed the Limerick Volunteers – 1000 strong – and marched at their head!'[17] On 24 April the Ulster adversaries, emboldened by the Curragh incident, successfully imported and distributed a massive quantity of arms, and on 1 May Casement was writing in unaccustomed seriousness to Richard Morten:[18]

> It is quite clear to every Irishman that the only rule John Bull respects is that of the rifle. . . .
> If they think – as they do – that any political sham called 'Federalism' is going to settle the 'Irish Question' – the question they both [Liberal and Conservative] made – they are grimly mistaken. Before I die, please God, I'll raise the English Question – & make *its* solution the chief case of Europe.

Similar gun-running plans were already afoot in the Nationalist camp, as a result of a meeting at Mrs Green's house. She was treasurer of the operation and the main agents were Casement, Darrell Figgis and Erskine Childers. The arms were landed at Howth in July and Kilcoole in August, by which time Casement was on a mission to America.

In February, Casement's article, 'The Elsewhere Empire',[19] had been published in Dublin. Citing both J.R. Green and his widow as inspirations of a 'message of hope' to Irishmen, he arrived by a circuitous route at the conclusion that: 'The true alliance to aim at for all who love peace is the

114

friendly Union of Germany, America and Ireland. These are the true United States of the world. Ireland, the link between Europe and America, must be freed by both.' Home Rule Assemblies and Indian Legislative Councils were denounced as a futile means of prolonging 'the darkness' and he argued that: 'The jailer of Ireland seeks Irish–American support to keep Ireland in prison; the intriguer against Germany would win German–American goodwill against its parent stock.' Accepting his premises, it made sense that he should go to the United States and attempt to seek more help from Clan-na-Gael in particular and Americans in general, but there were other important contacts to be made; Bulmer Hobson had already been over there in January and had taken with him a memorandum of Casement's on Irish–German relations in the event of war. Devoy had given this to von Bernstorff, the German ambassador in Washington. At first Casement was delayed by the understandable attempt by Redmond to gain control of the Irish Volunteers, but July saw him welcomed warily by John Devoy in New York, and then, enthusiastically, by Joe McGarrity in Philadelphia.

The rejoicing which followed the safe landing of arms for the Irish Volunteers was swiftly succeeded by a protest meeting in Philadelphia, organized because of the shootings in Bachelor's Walk. This occurred nine days before war was declared and Casement was chief speaker. The fact that he was, apparently, a Protestant went down well with his audience at this and other meetings which followed, and he proved to be a reliable fund-raiser. He was shocked, however, to discover what he regarded to be the fickleness of the American press, when the outbreak of war drove Ireland off the pages of the newspapers and donations began to dwindle. To try to put this right, he wrote an open letter[20] in which he urged support for Germany rather than Great Britain, and was dismayed to learn that the Irish leaders to whom he showed it advised against publication in America, where they feared its intemperate language might provoke the opposite reaction to the one intended. His effort was not wasted as he had already sent a copy to Ireland. Nevertheless, the episode served to hasten his disenchantment with America and encouraged him, in a negative way, to concentrate on the part which Germany occupied in his beliefs and hopes. A meeting with von Bernstorff took place, at which the possibility of raising an 'Irish Brigade' from among prisoners-of-war was discussed and on 27 September a telegraphic despatch was sent to the Foreign Office in Berlin. It was intercepted, as a matter of routine, by Room 40 in the Admiralty Old Building in London and found to express the view that 'The formation of an Irish Legion from Irish prisoners of war would be a grand idea if only it could be carried out.'[21]

Restored to optimism, now that his beliefs were to be translated into action, Casement moved rapidly towards what was to be his final goal.

Partly because he had acquired, for a mixture of motives, a Norwegian manservant, Adler Christensen, and partly because it was more discreet to enter Germany through a neutral country by means of a neutral shipping line, it was decided to set sail on the *Oskar II* for Norway. Clan-na-Gael, not without misgivings, gave the emissary their official blessing and financial support, and also took care of formalities, such as a false passport. The date of departure was 15 October; a fortnight later, having survived the close attentions of HMS *Hibernia* on the way, the two men disembarked in Norway. There then followed 'The Findlay Affair', and this long, involved and futile series of exchanges between Casement and the British Minister at Christiania (now Oslo), instigated and sustained by the doubly treacherous Christensen, displaced for far too many months the main object of the visit to Germany. The initial stage of the Norwegian episode was summed up in a handwritten letter from the minister, Mansfeldt de C. Findlay, in which he referred to a memorandum by F.O. Lindley[22] on the subject of a conversation he had had on 29 October 'with a young Norwegian–American who gave certain information implicating a well known Englishman in an Irish–American–German conspiracy. . . . He implied that their relations were of an unnatural nature and that consequently he had great power over this man who trusted him absolutely.'[23] Apart from anything else, this was the first intimation which British Intelligence received that their opponent had an alleged weakness in his armour. It came to them twenty-one months before his execution.

Although later correspondence, over Sir Arthur Nicolson's signature, stressed that the informer must be warned that Casement must come to no physical harm and that on no account must Christensen receive any written communication, Findlay only heeded half his instruction. In London, Kitchener was consulted and his holograph letter records, 'I think we better (sic) promise to pay the £5000 in case of successful capture of Casement and his accomplices.'[24] Findlay not only made this promise to Christensen, he wrote it out fully in his own hand on Legation headed paper and signed it 'M. de C. Findlay, H.B.M. Minister'. Christensen had cleverly played the two men off against each other while the price had crept up. Meanwhile, Casement, not knowing that his manservant had betrayed the secret that was ultimately to convince the British Cabinet that he did not deserve a reprieve, plagued the German Foreign Office to make full use of what he believed to be a powerful propaganda weapon, the attempt of a British Minister to have him killed (that was how Christensen put it to him) in a neutral country. Although the Germans under-valued the power of propaganda in World War I, they could hardly be blamed for making little of a matter which revolved around such a character as Christensen, who was seen by nearly all, except his master, to be transparently unsavoury.

At first the German enterprise seemed to have all the makings of a success. There was an enthusiastic welcome from von Zimmermann and then the practical details of the recruitment of the brigade were discussed with von Wedel, head of the Foreign Office English Department. A statement was soon published announcing the arrival of 'The well known Irish Nationalist' and repudiating Redmond's remarks about what would happen to Ireland if Germany were to win the war. Casement then drew up and successfully negotiated a 'treaty' of ten articles, one of which stated that the Irish Brigade would in no circumstances fight for Germany; presumably, as its sole purpose was to promote the cause of Irish freedom, the charge of 'treason' was, on a technicality, avoided. Everything appeared to be going even better than anticipated, but from this point onwards his own nature, and a series of disillusioning experiences, led to periods of despair and, ultimately, after the failure of his mission, to two suicide attempts.

Once again, Casement's unconscious awareness of social marginality became apparent. In Berlin his only happy experiences were those which elevated him from a retired consul to the diplomatic representative of a hypothetical state. He was soon worrying about the one act of recognition which had not been bestowed upon him; he had not been received by von Bethmann-Hollweg, the imperial chancellor. When, eventually, the meeting did take place, his enthusiasm was dampened by the extent of the delay which had occurred. Living in prestigious hotels he compensated from time to time by issuing challenges to Sir Edward Grey and making the theatrical gesture of returning the insignia of his decorations. The ramifications of the Findlay Affair (Christensen was carrying doctored papers back and forth) seemed to haunt him and he devised a scheme to lure British warships into a maze of non-existent minefields (charts provided) to capture him, whilst German ships lay in wait. Doubts about the morality of such a venture surfaced in his mind and nothing came of it in the end. Whenever possible, he sought to participate in the social round; initial access was a simple matter as an old friend from Africa and the Putumayo Mission Appeal Committee, Count (later Prince) Blücher, was in Berlin with his English wife, Evelyn, née Stapleton-Bretherton. He was duly invited to functions, but it was not long before his popularity was marred by the boldness with which he persisted in his relationship with Christensen. Whatever the compensations of life in Berlin did for him, they were divorced from the real world and, when he went to Limburg, where the Irish prisoners had been separated from their fellow British subjects, he found ample justification for disillusionment.

The decline which followed may be illustrated by Casement's correspondence with Father Nicholson, an Irish–American priest recruited by the German Embassy in Washington. Two Irish priests, of Nationalist persuasion, Father Crotty and Father O'Gorman, sent by the German Embassy at the Vatican, were, for the most part, restricting themselves to spiritual ministration. The Rev. John T. Nicholson, described by von Bernstorff as 'in full sympathy with the work we want done'[25] had fewer qualms; in 1918 an eye-witness was to recall that 'he perverted every influence that belonged to him on account of his status as a priest to persuade the prisoners to perjure themselves.'[26]

On the first visit to Limburg, at which Father Nicholson was not present, the suggestion of fighting for Irish independence naturally provoked references to Home Rule. In a sense, everyone present might reasonably have been assumed to be Unionist or Redmondite or they would not have volunteered. Many were veterans of famous Irish regiments and they understood that, for better or worse, Home Rule was already on the statute book. It was therefore hardly wise for Casement to remark that Redmond was a traitor, and not surprising that the men 'retaliated in a manner characteristic of their class'.[27] It was later reported that Sergeant Murphy, of the Second Munster Fusiliers, went so far as to pick up some mud and throw it into his face.[28] When, in January 1915, Father Nicholson received a welcoming brief from the man he had come to serve, it was not encouraging; 'Consult Fr Crotty in all difficulties. He does not think that anything will come of the attempt . . . that the men are not the stamp of Irishmen to appeal to. I think so too. But there is a chance. . . .' He had had a great shock and he could not bring himself to try again until the men were 'willing minded'. Already he was paving the way towards the delegation of virtually all responsibility for recruitment to the new priest. He advised him to take the line that the views so far expressed were shared by the majority of Irish–Americans; they supported the German Declaration in favour of Irish Independence, which had been made at Casement's request, and shared the opinion that Redmond's act should be termed 'An Act for the better recruitment of Irishmen in the ranks of the British Army'.

From the more congenial atmosphere of Berlin there next came a long letter which began by politely asking about Father Nicholson's impressions of 'our fellow countrymen in Limburg? Not very hopeful I expect'[29] and then went on to describe at length how the 'affair at Christiania' was progressing. A letter to Sir Edward Grey had related the whole story and charged him with full responsibility; a photograph of Findlay's attempt to bribe Christensen had been enclosed. Copies had been made of the correspondence and had been sent to twelve embassies and legations, to three Irish priests at the Vatican, to press agencies, to Washington direct and 'to Ireland'. Such were Casement's priorities at the time. He was obviously relishing the thought of a major court case and could not resist saying: 'there has been no diplomatic scandal like this for a very long time.'

In America the old Fenian, John Devoy, soon had his worst fears confirmed about the type of amateur whom the Clan had allowed to represent them. Although, thanks to his Foreign Office experience, he achieved more success at the diplomatic level than the enterprise deserved, when it came to the practical side of the mission, the man of action found that he did not understand the Irishmen he had come to serve. And it was, sadly, as Nicholson saw, a matter of class. His education for the Irish cause had taken place in the Glens of Antrim and in dialogue with people like Morgan and Mrs Green; although *Feisianna* might offer something for everyone, the vocabulary of a man imbued with the values of the cultural renaissance carried no weight with the mass of ordinary Irish soldiery who now confronted him, and was certainly no preparation for the secretive methods of wartime emissaries. The unrealistic world in which he lived is shown in one of the last optimistic messages which he was to write. It is hardly credible that it was a cover note for an important secret document intended for Eoin MacNeill and goes some way to indicate the extent of his naivety:[30]

> With much love and affection from the Man of Three Cows. He is well and has convincing assurance of help, recognition, friends and comfort for the poor old woman. All that he asks for will be given her and the stranger put out of her house for ever. He has seen the big men, and they are one with his views, and if successful they will aid to uttermost to redeem the four green fields.

Use *ad nauseum* of the pessimistic term 'poor old woman' for Ireland alienated Devoy from the start. Casement's own pseudonym, derived from a recent version of an Old Irish ballad about a 'woman of three cows' was no better (it tells us that the addressee was Mrs Green; he could never bring himself to call her 'Alice'; instead he used variations on the 'woman' theme, for example, 'Woman of the Stern and Unbending Purpose'). Moreover, it is doubtful whether anyone in Room 40 was unaware that the 'four fields' were the four provinces of Ireland or did not know who the 'stranger' was. The imagery of the Celtic Revival had no place in his new environment, which both sides of his Anglo-Irish nature found increasingly hard to bear.

In his letter to Father Nicholson of 8 February 1915, he had prefaced his progress report on the Findlay Affair with the remark, 'I have finished it, as far as I can,' but his next letter to the priest showed that this was by no means the case. Fortunately for the relationship between the two correspondents Father Nicholson was one of the few who believed in Christensen's integrity (which suggests that he did not meet him) and his anti-English sentiments were such that he shared Casement's attitude to Findlay and, unlike practically everyone else, did not believe the Findlay

119

Affair to be an annoying irrelevance. Many years later, in a letter to Julius Klein, who had been a young newspaper reporter in Berlin at the time of Casement's arrival, the priest observed that it had been a 'tussle of wits between the skilled diplomat and the plain man. The plain man won, although not by himself alone.'[31] And the evidence of Christensen's alleged victory was enclosed with this next letter on the subject: a photocopy of Findlay's £5,000 offer. Then, as if to demonstrate the breadth of the gulf between him and the men he sought to recruit, Casement said, 'I don't know what better proof the Irishmen at Limburg could want.'[32] He went on to boast that, rather than face him in the Norwegian courts, the British Government had withdrawn their minister from Norway.

CHAPTER 11

IMPRISONMENT AND TRIAL

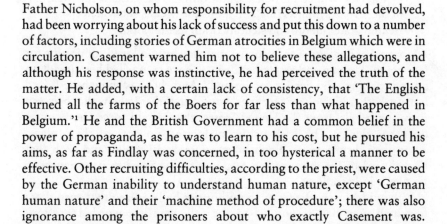

Father Nicholson, on whom responsibility for recruitment had devolved, had been worrying about his lack of success and put this down to a number of factors, including stories of German atrocities in Belgium which were in circulation. Casement warned him not to believe these allegations, and although his response was instinctive, he had perceived the truth of the matter. He added, with a certain lack of consistency, that 'The English burned all the farms of the Boers for far less than what happened in Belgium.'[1] He and the British Government had a common belief in the power of propaganda, as he was to learn to his cost, but he pursued his aims, as far as Findlay was concerned, in too hysterical a manner to be effective. Other recruiting difficulties, according to the priest, were caused by the German inability to understand human nature, except 'German human nature' and their 'machine method of procedure'; there was also ignorance among the prisoners about who exactly Casement was. Although this was, again, partly a question of class, he was not as well known in Ireland as elsewhere, and was sometimes frustrated by being taken for a famous Englishman.

Although Casement's behaviour sometimes lacked consistency, and declining health had something to do with this, there runs through his actions and beliefs even during this muddled period the thread of a sense of honour, which, for example, precluded him from doing anything which he deemed unnecessarily hazardous to others. Seldom aware of his own contradictions (the overall pattern of his life was, it would be difficult to deny, governed by a wish to emancipate) he found inconsistency in his opponents' policy quite intolerable; expediency was no excuse. News had reached him that, in order to protect British shipping from U-boat attacks, 'the Irish flag' was being hoisted on vessels. 'They hoist a flag that has no existence in *Law*, and for flying which in Ireland they have often sent Irishmen to prison.' This was done to save lives and yet he was branded a traitor because he had come to Germany 'to ask this country to respect

Ireland and as far as possible to keep my own poor country neutral'. This last sentence, had it been made available as evidence would have given substantial aid to those who had eventually to work for his reprieve; a major part of their campaign exploited the idea that he went to Ireland to stop the Rising, to prevent useless bloodshed.

The letter went on to say that there was no point in 'discussing the future of Ireland with the men in Limburg'. They are, 'when they are honest, hypnotised by the word 'Home Rule'. They did not realize that unless Germany were to win the war 'No Home Rule will come to her – Ulster will see to that and the English Aristocracy'. There would simply be a substantial increase in taxation and fewer people to tax:

> The *only* hope for Ireland to save her from complete bleeding white
> by England will be the defeat of the latter as the latter is the Mistress
> of the seas. As long as England holds the oceans she will keep
> Ireland at her mercy and steadily drain its lifeblood.

But hatred of England was no longer matched by unalloyed admiration for Germany: 'I, alone and single-handed . . . have compelled her already to do many things she detests for Ireland.' And then, as though he feared hurting Father Nicholson's feelings, he added, rather lamely, that between them, with help from the United States, they would force Germany to do other things. The Irish prisoners formed no part of these plans. They were dismissed as 'Englishmen, pure and simple', and with that he returned to the encouraging response of the Swedish newspapers to Findlay's indiscretions.

By mid-March, the German authorities had realized that even those few Irish who had responded to the call were not worth the effort. Casement felt low morale was unreasonable; the prisoners were blaming the Germans for food shortages which were common to the nation as a whole. Suffering from an attack of influenza which, his doctor later advised him, was bordering on pneumonia, he was finding Father Nicholson's reports increasingly depressing and again said that it would be futile for him to visit the camp. Instead he would send 'a friend from New York'[2] who, he hoped would arrive in time for St Patrick's Day and give some help with a concert. The German administration had refused to permit a St Patrick's Day Parade to the Dom, but had agreed to allow a holiday. The friend, who was not named in the letters of Casement which refer to him, nor in Father Nicholson's denunciation of him to Klein, was Joseph Plunkett, who had been sent by the inner circle of the IRB, quite independently of Casement, to negotiate for arms and to survey the situation. Plunkett, who suffered from tuberculosis, had no difficulty in moving around Europe as though in search of a cure, and the priest took an instant dislike to him, though he did not say so to Casement. Father

Nicholson saw him as some sort of spy upon his activities, which in one sense he was, although 'inspector' would be a better word, and he may have sensed that his immediate loyalties were fractionally different from Casement's. Plunkett saw the recruiting efforts first hand, was shocked by the political blandishments of a spiritual mediator and not at all surprised by the paltry results. The brigade numbered about thirty at this time, many of whom were barefacedly in search of easier conditions or, as in the case of Bailey (who was to accompany Casement to Ireland), looking for a means to escape. Plunkett, who was much better informed as to real rebel intentions, nevertheless struck up a happy working relationship with Casement and, when the time came for him to move on to Dublin, they were good friends.

Moving rapidly from one worry to another, there was now a new British iniquity to provoke Casement's rage. He had ordered 500 copies of the *Irish World* to be sent to the camp every week. Their safe arrival was, however, threatened by 'the latest development of British "freedom of the seas" – no vessel of any flag may carry any German Mails'. The 'Mistress of the seas' was now the 'Harlot': 'this war was let loose on the world by her shameless greed for gold.' On the question of money, in his next letter he gave his reply to prospective brigade members who had begun to enquire about 'back pay'.[3] This was guaranteed to them; it would come from an American fund. A more important question for him to consider was their political status. What he called 'political freedom' in his view automatically devolved upon anyone pledged to fight for Ireland. He tried to explain this by saying that while no act by a volunteer or by the German Government could free any of them from their British nationality 'till the end', it was possible to become 'an Irishman' and 'be recognised officially as such by the German Govt'. And to prove it, he enclosed a photograph of his imperial passport, which was, he claimed, the first ever example of 'an Irishman' being officially recognized by a great power. Clearly he was worried by the prospect of leading men into high treason. The word 'traitor' he often applied to himself over the years, and he was not afraid of it; in his mind it was not far removed from 'martyr': it was quite another thing to make martyrs of innocent young men. Ill in bed, he consoled himself with the thought that the brigade's function might well be 'as far as this war is concerned only a political and moral one':

> Germany may never be able to land us on the shores of Ireland – but the fact that men came out and joined me in an Irish Brigade on the Continent would have an enormous effect on the war.

Were it not that his modified conception of the brigade's aims arose from his failure to raise sufficient numbers of committed nationalists to make it viable, his reasoning might have carried some weight. As it was, he was doing little more than rationalizing his failure, and he overlooked entirely the almost universal contempt felt for turncoats, whatever their origins. This aspect alone reduced to a minimum the propaganda value of his mission.

In the same letter there follows a tirade about the 'Tyrant of the earth' and the 'World Enslaver'. He was greatly incensed by the admission in *The Times*, 'the organ of the Foreign Office', that England was fighting for English interests and not just for Belgium. When he had said as much in his open letter to the Irish people, it was a hanging matter, when *The Times* admits it, it is called 'statesmanship'. By this time virtually all his old friends had heard of his activities and some of them were wondering if ill-health had unhinged his mind. They were wrong, at any rate from the legal point of view, but there was an acceleration in his hysterical use of vocabulary, which indicated emotional deterioration: 'Ireland is being bullied, coaxed, befooled, coerced and starved into fighting this selfish, damnable fight . . .', and so on. He was desperate to strike a blow to England's prestige that will 'go around the world'. Two hundred men would be enough. (There were never more than fifty-four.) But he felt betrayed by 'recreant Irishmen'; they were 'cads and cowards'. The statistics did not bear thinking about and so he closed his mind to them and set about designing a uniform for the brigade. He reminded Father Nicholson to 'have the flag hoisted tomorrow – the big green flag I left with Fr C'.

Before Father Nicholson had finished his ministrations in Germany, friction between brigade recruits and their former comrades-in-arms made it necessary to move to separate quarters at Zossen. Another motive was to free the brigade members from some of the restrictions which, as they had ceased to be foes of Germany, were no longer appropriate. Casement had complained of 'red tape' and at Zossen it was hoped to cut through it wherever possible. A change of scene was desirable for the men and for Casement's peace of mind. Some of those who resented his approaches had told him what they intended to do when 'their demi-god Kitchener goes to Limburg', and he could not forgive the 'curs'.[4] However, at Zossen the men responded to new freedoms as might have been feared. Even Monteith, an experienced volunteer organizer sent to assist Casement, admitted that they indulged in drunken brawls.[5] By June 1915 Father Nicholson had had enough of his part of the mission and, before he returned to America, he received a last letter thanking him for his efforts. In it Casement asked him to remind McGarrity and Devoy of 'the great importance of backing up the handful of men in arms'.[6]

When the German general staff learned of the date chosen for the Rising, it was as if as an afterthought that Casement's senior officer, Monteith, was told of it. Germany had been asked to supply, by Easter Monday 24 April, a shipload of arms, a U-boat escort and German officers and men. Casement was ill in Munich when Monteith arrived with the news; but immediately hurried to Berlin where his worst fears were confirmed; as he saw it the German side of the operation was only a token to encourage the Irish to commit themselves. There were to be no officers, no men; 20,000 rifles instead of the 200,000 he had requested. The whole enterprise was obviously only seen as a diversion to keep British forces from France. It was inconceivable that the brigade should go, but he asked that he might precede the arms ship by U-boat. At first the Germans resisted this move, saying that no U-boat was available.

The wish to return to Ireland in person has in it much that implies suicidal intent; while his companions could hope to dissolve into the background after an unobserved landing, Casement knew that his activities in Germany were known to all and made no secret of the fact that he expected to be hanged; in an hysterical interview with Princess Blücher at this time he said as much. By this date (4 April) he knew that he could go after all and he was told that the U-boat accommodation would, at a stretch, permit the presence of two others; these places were taken by Monteith and Bailey.[7] Aboard the U-20 seven men occupied a cabin designed for four. They had not travelled far before the submarine broke down and had to put into Heligoland for repairs. There they were transferred to the U-19, a less spacious vessel.

The arms ship, the *Aud*, succeeded in avoiding the British blockade and arrived at the correct place off the Kerry coast at the time which had originally been arranged; but as the IRB military council had made no contingency arrangements for an arrival three days earlier than their revised date (the *Aud* carried no wireless) contact was not made. After a wait of twenty-four hours, the *Aud*, having been intercepted by HMS *Bluebell*, was scuttled. Meanwhile the U-19, which had also failed to rendezvous with the *Aud*, despatched its passengers towards the shore by means of a collapsible boat, which soon capsized. British Intelligence was better informed than the IRB and within a few hours Casement was in custody, having made virtually no attempt to evade capture. Bailey was soon picked up, but Monteith eventually made his way to New York. Casement spent the night of Good Friday in Tralee police station, where he was visited by a doctor and a Dominican priest. Dr Michael Shanahan assumed that Casement would wish the Irish Volunteers to rescue him, but the local leader, Austin Stack, was not inclined to depart from his orders and risk a premature start to the Rising. A close look at all the subjective testimony relating to the prisoner's first night in captivity shows him to have been more intent on self-sacrifice than on escape – though a message about the futility of the Rising was conveyed to Dublin in his name. The nominal Protestant was wondering whether he should continue to progress towards an almost inevitable hanging, or kill himself straightaway;

he had brought the means of suicide with him, but could not bring himself to take such a step without prior spiritual discussion with a Catholic priest. Inevitably such discussion acquired the confidentiality of the confessional and what is known of it is derived from Casement's Notes to Counsel.[8] Father F.M. Ryan became entangled in controversy about Casement's political motives; naturally he revealed nothing that he and the prisoner had talked about on the subject of spiritual values.

Next morning saw more behaviour characteristic of a man who did not expect to live for much longer. That he should offer no less than five of the policemen involved in his capture and custody cash or gifts is in keeping with one side of his nature with which friends and acquaintances alike would have been only too familiar. It was a life-long feature which contrasted dramatically with the extreme meanness suggested by his diaries, in which there is an almost fanatical attention to the spending of individual halfpennies – yet another dichotomy. But to give away one's watch, waistcoat and walking stick to the RIC, on one's way to trial for treason, has more in keeping with the traditional word of forgiveness given to the public executioner by the condemned man.

The prisoner then set off on his journey to Dublin by rail. It so happened that on the way he had to change trains at Mallow and this led to a brief reminiscence with his police escort which revealed his first-hand acquaintance with the locality. On the basis of the conversation which ensued one can deduce that he did go to stay at Mallow Castle with Louisa Jephson-Norreys in July 1895[9] in order that he might pursue his quest for his maternal origins. Four RIC men with carbines guarded Casement on Mallow station and they were observed by an armed member of the Irish Volunteers, who felt powerless to act. The volunteer boarded the train for Cork and watched while the prisoner and his escort crossed the footbridge to board the Dublin train. Later the observer, who was a resident of Mallow, sent a description of the scene to Brigadier Jephson, signing his letter 'SENEX'; he sent an almost identically worded letter to Alfred Noyes, over the signature 'D.J. Hegarty'.[10] Understandably, in the difficult months ahead, when Magherintemple severed all connections with the traitor son, thoughts of his mother came increasingly to him, and his Jephson cousins were his main support.

After some humiliating experiences in Dublin (he was very roughly searched at Arbour Hill Military Barracks), Casement was transferred to London and, during a period of temporary accommodation at Brixton Prison, he was taken daily to Scotland Yard to be interrogated by Basil Thomson, assistant commissioner of Metropolitan Police, and Captain Hall, director of the Naval Intelligence Division. When these investigations were completed, he began a period of imprisonment in the Tower which was to last until the completion of the preliminary magisterial enquiry. Some accounts of this stage of his confinement have made much of allegedly appalling conditions in which he was kept; from them it could be inferred that it was these circumstances which brought about a suicidal frame of mind, and not a predisposition on his part to take his own life. If it were true that he was 'in solitary confinement' in a 'verminous subterranean dungeon' wearing garments 'infested with lice and vermin',[11] there would be some evidence to support the idea that he made a sudden decision to end everything. However, inspection of the accommodation itself, and recent testimony given by one of the soldiers detailed to occupy the room with the prisoner, shows that such statements do not fit the facts.[12]

The room in which the prisoner was held was in the Casemates, that is to say it was encased within the outer wall of the Tower. Prior to, and after, occupation by prisoners, the rooms in the Casemates were used to accommodate warders; the Provost Marshal has occupied one and another has been used to house the military police. The one occupied by Casement, Number 2A, was adjacent to the Byward Tower which forms the main entrance through the outer circuit of walls, and it was therefore possible to bring him in and out with the minimum of formalities. From within the Tower the general aspect of the Casemates is modern brick, rather than ancient stone; only from the moat is the impression distinctly medieval. His own room was used for a period after 1937 for resident staff; nevertheless, despite the addition of wallpaper and the removal of bars, it remains basically the same; the old bar slots, now filled with cement, can still be seen. The windows look out on to a street-like space between the outer and inner circuits of walls; an admittedly drab view. The original floor remains and it is difficult to accept that the cell was ever verminous or even damp. The subject of rats in the Tower is, however, a bone of contention among resident staff even today.

Although the circumstances of imprisonment were less harsh than has been represented, Gertrude Bannister can readily be forgiven, and not only on emotional grounds, for her interpretation of the prisoner's conditions. When she first saw him he was still wearing the suit in which he had fallen into the sea, a state of affairs which could, and should, have been rectified. But appearances were made worse by the normal precautions taken in the case of prisoners deemed suicidal in inclination; tie, bootlaces and braces had been removed; furthermore, her cousin's physical condition had deteriorated because of the necessity of keeping the light burning continuously throughout the night. As it transpired, there was ample justification for these precautions, which cannot be regarded as the cause of the two suicide attempts which occurred.

First-hand testimony has been forthcoming from Corporal King,[13] for whom Casement developed affection and respect. The corporal's duty was

127

to occupy the cell with another soldier, a Welshman who spoke little English, and observe the prisoner from close quarters. During the first of King's watches Casement became agitated and confessed that he had swallowed bent nails which he had removed from the kindling wood used to light the fire in his cell (the fireplace is still there). This clumsy and futile attempt had, King was told, been made because of the failure of the method which had been planned while he was still in the care of Germany. He had brought with him a phial of poison which, he said, he had concealed in his hair. He went on to explain that the poison had had to be introduced into the bloodstream to take effect; while lying on his bed with his knees up, he had secretly sawn away at his finger with a broken lens from his spectacles and tried to rub the poison into the wound. Like everything else to do with the German mission, this had failed and, in desperation, he had swallowed the nails, with a similar lack of success.

There was another means by which Casement could have smuggled the poison for the major part of the journey. In June 1915 he had offered Joseph Plunkett a walking stick with an iron point containing a hollow tube which might have been useful for carrying secret papers. Plunkett returned the stick, as the cavity was too small, and Casement brought it with him to Ireland, finally presenting it, as has been mentioned, to the RIC Sergeant who arrested him in Kerry. Whatever his means of concealment, the successful smuggling of the poison shows that suicide was seriously anticipated, and the crude second attempt, by means of nails, underlines the fact that his intentions, unlike those of many who fail in such efforts, were more than a mere cry for help.

The advent of the preliminary enquiry at Bow Street Magistrates Court on 15 May 1916 brought with it a transfer of the prisoner from the Tower to Brixton prison hospital and a general improvement in his spirits. A solicitor had been difficult to find and Gavan Duffy's agreement to act for Casement brought about the dissolution of his partnership. There was no difficulty in finding one counsel to instruct; a rallying of old friends brought John Morgan this unwelcome brief. He was led, at Bow Street, by another Welshman, Artemus Jones. The proceedings lasted three days, after which both Casement and Bailey were committed for trial. On the first day the attorney-general read a statement by Bailey which obliquely indicated that he had done some effective bargaining for his life and, though he was to appear at the trial, the Crown brought no evidence against him. To strengthen the case against the accused, testimony was heard from Irish soldiers recently exchanged for German prisoners in England, and this lasted for much of the second day. Artemus Jones acquitted himself well, particularly on the last day, when enquiring into possible enticements offered to Bailey, and Casement was later to regret that he had not left everything to the two Welshmen.

A King's Counsel now had to be found to lead for the defence and at first this proved no easier than finding a solicitor. However, Duffy was able to persuade his own brother-in-law, Alexander Sullivan, to accept the brief, despite problems arising from his position as Second Serjeant of the Irish Bar, an office extinct in England. Under the Treason Act of 1351 only two counsel were allowed to appear, and so, while Artemus Jones could be the junior, Morgan had to be relegated to *amicus curiae*. In addition, at Mrs Green's suggestion, and Gertrude Bannister's written request, Michael Francis Doyle of the American Bar came over to act in an advisory capacity and to bring much-needed funds which he obtained from Devoy.

Casement, who was undergoing a resurgence of confidence, had had to be dissuaded from conducting his own defence. Short-lived despair had been replaced by delusions about his degree of responsibility for the Easter Rising. He saw his political preaching behind the actions of those who had already achieved martyrdom and saw himself as an embodiment of the Irish Nation awaiting ritual sacrifice. It therefore went against the grain that Sullivan should wish to defend him strictly in accordance with the wording of the act. The nub of Sullivan's defence would be that, as defined in 1351, treason could only be committed 'in the realm', not 'elsewhere', in the final reckoning it would be a matter of punctuation. But all this was anathema to the prisoner, who had all along recognized that his actions were treasonable; he sent a mass of paper to his counsel, citing historical references and precedents, which can only have hindered the preparation of the case.

At this stage the Bernard Shaws were approached by Gertrude Bannister and Mrs Green, mainly for funds. Instead of subscribing money, however, Shaw presented the outline of a defence, which the prisoner was delighted to receive, although he did not entirely agree with it. His reactions to it, at first incompatible with some of his own pronouncements, are better understood if one takes into account the conflict both of ideas and emotions which beset him at this time. Where there has been concrete evidence of suicidal intent, the intention must take its place as a relevant factor in assessing the rationality of motivation along the road to the scaffold. An outwardly expressed reversal of fundamental beliefs, even when the change has been wrought over a lifetime, must do some violence to the personality, and rival internal forces seemed to strive for dominance in the months before death became certain. It is said[14] that, as Casement left the U-19, the commander, Captain Raimund Weisbach, asked whether there was anything else he needed. The reply was 'Only my shroud' and, whether or not the story is apocryphal, it reminds one that the decision to return to the United Kingdom had to reckon with the idea of execution. And yet one is reluctant to think in terms of an unworthy death-wish, even if it can be partially excused on grounds of ill-health. Was it the wish for a martyr's crown? Put in such blunt terms, that would not be much better. Or was it a noble willingness to sacrifice oneself for a great cause? As with nearly everything to do with Casement, good reasons can be found for each motive, and it would probably be fair to say that all were present to some degree. Under the emotional stress inevitable during the imprisonment and the preparation of the defence, his underlying ambivalence was once more to be seen as he weighed up the different lines of defence which were open to him, and judged them on the one hand in terms of his own physical survival and, on the other, in terms of their value to Ireland.

Shaw was, as he put it,[15] 'in no sense a Casementite', because he neither believed that Germany could win the war, nor wanted her to win it; 'but I have no patience with judicial murders in which the infuriated accuser is also the judge, the jury, and the executioner.' In the draft[16] which he sent to his fellow-countryman he narrowed the possible lines of defence down to three: Counsel could plead that the prisoner was insane, Counsel could undertake the traditional defence and argue the case on its merits, or the prisoner himself could admit all the facts and claim that, as an Irish Nationalist, he should be treated as a prisoner-of-war. The first possibility would require medical evidence and was not open to discussion; the second was doomed; the third would not seriously be entertained by Counsel, and therefore the accused would almost certainly have to conduct his own defence. By doing so he would be granted much more freedom than Counsel would ever receive and would even be given some help by the Bench. The plea would be Not Guilty, but it would be necessary to make it plain that the essential facts as put forward by the Crown were not denied. All who fought for their country were guilty 'under the higher law of God', but that guilt was shared by all present in the court.

When Shaw advised him to express regret that the prosecution had called witnesses whose testimony the defence, far from disputing, would be happy to amplify, Casement noted on the draft that this was exactly what he had said when interrogated at Scotland Yard. He was also pleased when he read Shaw's suggestion that a comparison be drawn with Garibaldi. It had been hoped, Shaw went on, that the same would be achieved for Ireland that Garibaldi had been honoured in England for doing for Italy, though Casement felt that the Garibaldi analogy, which he used in his advice to Sullivan, was apt only in so far as it revealed England's inconsistency; both patriots seduced others from an allegiance; one was excessively praised, regardless of some of his acts. Shaw continued his argument to the effect that, while it might be thought vain for a Casement to attempt what a Garibaldi had achieved, it was necessary to imitate the liberation of Italy to the extent that a foreign alliance was essential. The present conflict revealed that even the Great Powers could not stand single-handed. An alliance between Ireland and the German Empire had been the obvious fulfilment of a strategic need, partially achieved; in furthering this end the prisoner had merely been carrying out his patriotic duty. The accused should stress the handicaps which had bedevilled his dealings with Germany; he had had little to offer in exchange for help and did not want German troops in Ireland; Germany was to provide money, arms and repatriated Irish prisoners-of-war (Casement vigorously crossed out the word 'money' and appended a strongly worded note, emphasizing his most definite wish to import German troops). The Irish prisoners had been collected together and asked for their assistance – no English soldier was approached, as an Englishman's nationality, too, is to be respected.

Shaw insisted that any suggestion that the prisoner had compromised himself by the acceptance of money and a knighthood (the latter acknowledged in a normal gentlemanly manner) from the British Empire, was illogical. The attorney-general himself must have accepted fees from clients who were potentially liable to be prosecuted by him. He would not confess that he had betrayed his former client should the situation actually arise. Similarly, Englishmen who have accepted moneys from Germany are not now traitors to Germany because of their English loyalty in the war.[17] The prisoner's position was, in fact, stronger than that of these examples, because he had been denied any other outlet for his public services than that afforded jointly by England and Ireland. His record revealed that his only quarrel with England was political. But here, again, Casement dissented, though he seems to have misunderstood Shaw's intention. Other quarrels were with England's right to India, Egypt and similar nations; as well as an Irish Republican he had become an anti-imperialist. Doubtless Shaw would have regarded the latter as a generalization of the former. By way of conclusion the prisoner was advised to argue that if Ireland were merely a province of England then he would be an Englishman and deserve hanging. But Ireland is a nation and the prisoner was captured while making an attempt to achieve its independence. On this general principle he claimed to be found not guilty on the indictment and requested that he be transferred to a prisoner-of-war camp.

The tenor of the Shaw defence has a teasing quality; and there are several gibes at the attorney-general which may, or may not, have appealed to the average juror. In the concluding remarks the Dublin Rising is equated with the Gallipoli Campaign. The climate of opinion being what it was, perhaps this, too, was unnecessarily provocative. To Casement, at any rate, the basic argument was misguided, and his remaining notes, whilst conceding that many individual points were excellent, reject the prisoner-of-war thesis because – though it might have saved his life – it did not face the Crown sufficiently squarely. Though he could not say so to the prisoner, Shaw felt that, for his proposed line of defence to stand any real chance of success, it would have to be put to the test in a neutral court in a neutral country. The outcome of the state trial was, to him, a foregone conclusion. Both men wanted a demonstration of their belief that an English court had no right to try an Irishman. The realities of life, however, demanded that such sentiments be reserved, in accordance with heroic tradition, for the Speech from the Dock, delivered after a verdict of Guilty has been pronounced. As Shaw observed, Casement must have felt (and, indeed, he said as much to his friends) that there was really 'nothing left for him but to go through that old ordeal called "dying for Ireland" '.[18]

There now occurred a reversal of Casement's long held conviction about his ultimate fate; he was sufficiently familiar with the ways of British diplomacy to become convinced that the British Government, though bent on his destruction, would not hang him. The executions of the other rebel leaders in Dublin had had the unforeseen effect of generating a wave of sympathy for the cause, not only in Ireland but in America, and he was sure that, however much he was hated as a traitor, the British leaders would not compound their error. He would be found guilty and sentenced to death, and then the sentence would be commuted to life imprisonment. Whatever happened (he knew his diaries were at Scotland Yard), he would be disgraced in the eyes of friend and foe alike. It was to be a sham trial, designed purely for propaganda purposes, and with this realization he resigned himself to Sullivan's defence. His only consolation would be the Speech from the Dock.

Three judges presided when the trial began in the King's Bench Division at the Law Courts in the Strand on Monday 26 June 1916: The Lord Chief Justice (Viscount Reading), Mr Justice Avory and Mr Justice Horridge. Counsel for the Crown were the attorney-general (the Right Hon. Sir Frederick Smith, KC, MP), the solicitor-general (the Right Hon. Sir George Cave, KC, MP), Mr A.H. Bodkin, Mr Travers Humphreys and Mr G.A.H. Branson. The attorney-general, in his opening and closing speeches for the Prosecution, was able to outline what were in the main undisputed facts about the prisoner's recent conduct. Although he claimed that rhetoric would be improper and unnecessary, his quiet use of sarcasm was particularly effective. Generally his method was to appear to let the facts speak for themselves, a pretence he fairly consistently maintained except when handling Casement's knighthood acceptance, and he was, of course, wrong about the supposed suddenness of the prisoner's conversion to Republicanism. For the most part prosecution witnesses, including several of those who had been thoughtlessly provided by Casement's recent allies in the prisoner-exchange, corroborated the facts, though the prisoner did make a short speech correcting certain 'misstatements'.

Sullivan moved unsuccessfully to quash the indictment, the wording of which permitted more than one interpretation. Then, when it came to his Speech for the Prisoner, he began with a somewhat unrealistic analysis of the Prosecution witnesses' testimony, in order to show that the Irish Brigade was only to be landed in Ireland if and when Germany won the war. He next moved on to what he thought was stronger ground; he clearly felt it fortunate for the defence that the attorney-general had himself been involved in the shipping of arms to the Ulster Volunteers and made great play of the fact that the gun-runners of Ulster had been seeking to oppose the rule of United Kingdom law whilst the Irish Volunteers were upholding an act of parliament. His argument stressed the paradox of Ulster's disloyalty and the Nationalists' loyalty within the context of the Home Rule Statute, an approach made all the more telling by the presence of F.E. Smith in the courtroom. But despite his admitted eloquence – though on one occasion his use of uncorroborated statements led the Lord Chief Justice to intervene – it remained irrefutable that the Larne landings, whatever their legal perspective, took place before the declaration of war.

Towards the end of the third day Sullivan broke down, completely exhausted, and the conclusion of his Speech for the Prisoner was made on the fourth, and last, day by Artemus Jones. He reinforced Sullivan's line of argument by stating that it was the inability of the executive government to protect Irishmen from coercion within Ireland which had brought about the necessity to import arms. There had been a serious breach of the law, but high treason had not been committed. Next came the Closing Speech for the Crown and the attorney-general was quick to point out the changed circumstance which rendered false the analogy between the actions of the two rival volunteer organizations. At the beginning of the trial he had asked: 'Why did the prisoner ever go to Germany at all?' and at the end he claimed that this question remained unanswered. Sullivan had warned the unsophisticated English jurors that 'We do not in a moment throw off the atmosphere in which we have always lived' and in wartime that is particularly hard to do. They may have had reasonable doubts about the attorney-general's main contention, but, if so, Lord Reading, in his summing up, put paid to them:

> It is necessary that you should pay particular attention to this
> direction, which is a direction of law to you . . . if he knew or
> believed that the Irish Brigade was to be sent to Ireland during the
> war with a view to securing the national freedom of Ireland, that is,
> to engage in a civil war which would necessarily weaken and
> embarrass this country, then he was contriving and intending to
> assist the enemy.

Sullivan had largely succeeded in showing that Casement's motive was solely to aid Ireland, but the incidental aid to the king's enemies was a stumbling block which he could not remove from the minds of the jurors.

It took the jury less than an hour to arrive at a verdict of guilty, after which the prisoner made his memorable Speech from the Dock, heard sentence of death and was removed to Pentonville to await execution. The next day he was degraded from his knighthood, an event with only three analogous precedents. In court he left behind a parcel of papers including his 'treaty', in which he agreed to employ the Irish Brigade in the Egyptian fight for freedom from British rule, should his original plan be frustrated; it was as though he were ensuring that there should be no second thoughts about his guilt. Nevertheless, Morgan managed to persuade him to appeal and the Court of Criminal Appeal met on 17 July to hear Sullivan reiterate his arguments about the troublesome words: 'adherent to the King's enemies in his realm giving them aid and comfort in the realm and elsewhere'. As they were translated from Norman-French, which lacked punctuation, it was difficult to tell whether the words 'giving them aid and comfort in the realm' should be understood as though enclosed between commas. Before the hearing, Mr Justice Darling, who presided, and one of the four judges who assisted him, Mr Justice Atkin, examined the rolls in the Public Record Office. They found a gap which might be regarded as equivalent in force to a comma, after the second 'realm'. But two commas were needed; the appeal was dismissed on the grounds that the appellant 'is the King's liege wherever he may be'.

Gavan Duffy at once applied for permission to appeal to the House of Lords. By an anomaly of the Criminal Appeal Act 1907, the application for a convicted appellant to be given leave to appeal to the highest court in the land required permission to be obtained from Casement's prosecutor, the attorney-general. Sir Frederick Smith considered the application for two days before his refusal to grant a certificate was conveyed to Gavan Duffy on 24 July. Now, with one appeal dismissed and the other lacking authorization, all depended on petitions for reprieve. At this time, although he was accommodated in the condemned cell, and obliged to wear the traditional convict's uniform, marked with broad arrows, Casement's spirits began to revive; he could sleep more easily. But for his friends, desperately striving to attract influential signatures, the outlook became steadily darker. As they made their way to every conceivable source of help, they met more and more rebuffs. The diaries had gone before them.

CHAPTER 12

DIARIES AND DEATH

Setting aside the fact that the use made of the diaries prejudiced the chances of a reprieve, one might be forgiven for asking what possible value it is to know whether Casement was, or was not, addicted to the homosexual behaviour set down in such detail. However, a series of disclosures in the 1960s and 1970s has shown, not only that a man's political career can still be cut short by allegations of this nature, but that there is a high correlation between being a traitor and suffering from Casement's 'disease'. The Cambridge Apostles constitute the largest identifiable latter-day group in which these dual characteristics are to be found, but they are not alone. Casement, if his diaries are genuine, set the grand precedent for the twentieth century, and this is one reason for needing to know that the written evidence is neither wholly nor partially forged.

Although in recent years it has become easier to see that the disjunction 'Saintly Patriot or Treacherous Pervert' is a bogus one, there is still a large section of the British population of all classes who find it difficult to tolerate this minority group; and many who try to accept the democratic position (the 'consenting adults' viewpoint) find the whole idea distinctly obnoxious. During the reigns of Victoria, Edward VII and George V, Casement had to suffer under a climate of opinion which was far more oppressive and, if his private confessions are to be believed, during the latter two reigns was prone to such practices for not less than nine years. This means that during the decade which saw his transition from the model imperialist to the committed subversive nationalist he was frequently driven to transgress the law, he had to lead a meticulously maintained double life, and habits, comparable to those of a secret agent, had to be cultivated. Who can say for sure that the appeal of a 'secret mission' was not influenced by private acts which involved consistently sustained furtive, illegal behaviour? Shaw stressed that Casement's mission to Germany made diplomatic sense, but one can take the view that Ireland's interest might have been better served by a more open, less treasonable, act. If the man who devised the mission and carried it through was a habitual lawbreaker and, more significantly, was behaving in a manner contrary to the instincts and beliefs of virtually all his friends, of all classes (other than the shadowy figures who were his partners) the effect on his personality must be taken into account. And this remains true whatever one's view of his private acts may be; individual reaction to an intolerant climate of opinion is likely to be decisive in the formation of character.

For a reliable assessment of the man, then, the authenticity of the diaries must be verified; they are important primary sources and all conclusions about their author are suspect until this is done. There were many suspicious circumstances which caused their genuineness to be in doubt. Why did successive British home secretaries – all of whom knew that the diaries, or copies of them, had been made available to many people, including heads of church and state – pretend for over forty years that they did not exist? And why did Basil Thomson, the assistant commissioner of police who had interrogated Casement, publish several contradictory accounts of how he came by them? To answer these questions many elaborate theories were developed and it soon became embarrassingly obvious that there were two main schools of thought, each with a racial or religious bias; in general terms: the Irish, who believed the diaries to be forged, and the British, who were of the opposite opinion. Only in comparatively recent years have the barricades been crossed by brave men in search of the truth, however unsavoury it might be.

The initial publication[1] of the forgery thesis had one unexpected outcome: it inspired Yeats to write a poem entitled *Roger Casement*, with the stanza:

> Come Alfred Noyes, come all the troop
> That cried it far and wide,
> Come from the forger and his desk,
> Desert the perjurer's side.

Noyes, who had been shown a copy of part of one of the diaries in 1916, so that he might use it for suitable propaganda purposes in America, wrote an open letter to Yeats, and soon a revised version of the poem appeared, beginning: 'Come Tom and Dick, come all the troop'. But Noyes felt that he had not done enough and, twenty years later, he constructed and published a perceptive analysis[2] of all the evidence available to him, including a comparative study of Thomson's published indiscretions; his development of the Normand diary theory was so well argued that, in a modified version, it survived the production of the originals. To those who continued to adhere to the forgery thesis, Normand was the author of a source-diary, which may have been in the form of a rolled manuscript, as shown to Ben Allen of the Associated Press by Captain Hall, but the forgery lay in the interpolation of erotica in whatever spaces were avail-able in a genuine bound volume. All that remained was to identify the individual or department responsible.

One of the strongest arguments for the forgery school of thought was based on the widely held – to this day – conviction that there was an official Forgery for Propaganda department at work during World War I. The belief was revived in 1959, when, on 27 July Emrys Hughes, MP stated categorically in the House of Commons that there had been 'a special intelligence department at Scotland Yard which carefully forged diaries and letters and placed them on the corpses of German soldiers'. To test the veracity of such a statement it seemed wise to approach Richard Crossman who, as British Director of Political Warfare against the Enemy and Satellites or as Assistant Chief of the Psychological Warfare Division of SHAEF, might reasonably have been expected to inherit whatever machinery was used in the previous war. He elicited help from Donald McLachlan, who had held a number of propaganda posts which came loosely under the heading 'Naval Intelligence', and while no Forgery Department *per se* came to light, it was his guidance which led to the discovery that Hall had heard of Casement's alleged proclivities twenty-one months before the execution, and not long afterwards Hall discovered the whereabouts of the traitor's personal luggage. The Director of Naval Intelligence and the head of the CID were close friends and those who might seek to exonerate them from the charge of forgery are not helped by a typical indiscretion in Thomson's published diary.[3] The entry for 2 March 1917 tells a grim tale about what happened when a spy named Müller had been caught and shot. After the execution an intelligence officer who had 'a gift for imitating handwriting' was able to obtain money from Müller's employer for three months. The forger remained undetected until the Germans learned of Müller's death from another source. The story gives some support to McLachlan's opinion that such enterprises were not separately organized; they were part and parcel of counter espionage methods which embraced a wider field.

Perhaps not surprisingly, production of the originals in 1959, although it destroyed a major part of Noyes's case, made matters even more controversial. There was renewed clamour: this time for *proof* – the real proof that could only be demonstrated by use of an ultra-violet ray machine. The home secretary still refuses to sanction such an examination. The cause of the clamour is not hard to see: on first inspection one's immediate impression gives support to the theory that a forger inserted the erotic passages in whatever gaps he could find between innocent entries – not a very different exercise from the Müller forgery. Three distinct handwriting styles are discernible and all are unlike the handwriting of Casement's contemporary Foreign Office despatches. One style even resembles that of Basil Thomson, who was an inveterate diary writer and was, incidentally, convicted for committing an act in violation of public decency in 1925. Every so often one comes upon the tell-tale smudge which eventually appears after an eradicator has been used. Some of the best examples of conflicting handwriting styles are to be found in the 1911 diary, which has not yet been published. There one can conveniently compare and contrast the three styles which, reasonably enough, correspond with the use of three media: a fine-nibbed scratchy pen, a broad-nibbed pen and a pencil. The scratchy style has survived the years better than the broad nib and is much darker and clearer.

After the diaries were made available to historians the modified Amazon transcript diary theory became popular; selected passages from this document must have been inserted where the subject matter tallied in some way and space permitted. Faced with three styles of handwriting, an investigator wishing to expose a fraud might have hoped that erotic entries were limited to one style and confined to the interpolated passages. That is not the case. However, it is true that the more dramatic entries are interpolations and, when the writer is apparently excited, they constitute almost a fourth 'ecstatic' style. The scratchy pale, the broad dark and the pencil largely report the day's event, and, when eroticism forms a part of this, it is either expressed in a matter-of-fact manner or ruthlessly abbreviated, as if with a sense of shame. Detailed examination suggests that the writer was given to going over and reliving experiences (or hoped-for experiences), underlining entries which especially appealed to him, adding comments, scribbling adjectives or exclamation marks (sometimes the letter X) in the margin. The notorious 1911 ledger entry of 13 May, has four underlinings, using at least two different pens. On 11 August 1910 there is a reminiscence where a pencilled addition has had the last words gone over with a scratchy pen. The overall impression conjured up by this internal evidence – of which only a few examples are mentioned here – is of a very lonely figure.

Although the forgery school has always depended on it, the strongest evidence for authenticity is undoubtedly internal. Many people, in their personal writings, have differing casual styles, and a 'best' style which might be used, say, for official reports. Just as it is likely that there will be a marked distinction between considered and spontaneous expression, it should not cause much surprise if entries written in tropical heat on an Amazon steamer differ from recollections inserted later in more temperate surroundings. Moreover, a forger would hardly be so stylistically provocative; nor would he be expected to leave in the manuscript two passages expressing sentiments running counter to his supposed aims; in one Casement denounces in Puritan terms the very activities in which he so frequently indulged, and in the other (the Hector Macdonald incident, page

37), he sympathizes, as though from a heterosexual standpoint, with a sufferer from this 'disease', as he calls it. Such inconsistencies, while they hardly surprise the serious student of the ambivalent Casement, would surely have been deleted by a forger. A great depender on the internal evidence was Herbert Mackey,[4] who claimed, amidst much elaborate argument, that the name Bulmer had been carefully altered to Miller (spelled '-er') in some outrageous passages; the important point was that the 'l', the 'e' and the 'r' were in common. He failed to notice that the character mentioned was Millar (spelled '-ar').

When he moved to the external evidence Mackey was no luckier. Another of his major arguments was based on the claim that there never was a Grand Central Hotel in Warrenpoint, the alleged scene of certain activities. It was David Rudkin, the playwright, who indicated[5] that the actions took place before the individuals left Belfast for Warrenpoint. There was, and is, a Grand Central Hotel in Belfast. But the external evidence has a habit of falling apart. Mrs Green's letter of 17 September 1910 cannot be found among the Green Papers, so it cannot help to authenticate the 1910 blotter draft; the Black Box kept by Bigger in Belfast has had its contents destroyed. The photograph of Roger Hicks stuck in the 1911 ledger gives the stamp of authenticity to the document, but no more. All these examples only form part of arguments which are inconclusive.

One wants certainty and to find it one has to go to the man who forced the British Government to admit that the diaries existed. After they had served their purpose everything might have drifted into the realms of myths and legends, had it been possible to gather all the incriminating material in again. An astonishing amount was destroyed: Sir Basil Thomson burned his copy 'in case my executors should find it'.[6] But, in 1922, an unknown official presented copies of two of the three diaries and – which is even more remarkable – a transcript of the interrogation at Scotland Yard to Peter Singleton-Gates, then a Fleet Street reporter. The material was then carefully arranged and a preliminary notice of its impending publication appeared in 1925. Immediately the author was summoned to a personal interview with the home secretary, Sir William Joynson-Hicks, in the presence of his legal adviser, Sir Ernley Blackwell, and the Official Secrets Act was invoked. He refused to reveal his source, and has never done so ('I gave my bond of secrecy. I shall keep it till I die'),[7] but publication was prevented and shortly afterwards his flat was searched (he had hidden the typescripts elsewhere). In 1959, he risked prosecution by publishing them in Paris and presenting forty copies to various members of parliament. This gave interested parties, such as Montgomery Hyde, MP, the weapon they needed and the home secretary, Mr Butler, not only admitted the existence of the diaries but placed them in the Public

Record Office, where they still bear yellow labels stating that they may not be seen until the appropriate years in the twenty-first century. However, armed with a special permit from the under-secretary of state at the Home Office one may examine them, in the presence of an invigilator.

Singleton-Gates has been the traditional provider of vital material for almost all researchers into Casement's life and it is only right that the final proof of the authenticity of the diaries should come from him. In an interview which has had no publicity[8] he solemnly testified that, not very long ago, in his presence and in the presence of a well-known witness, the ultra-violet ray machine was used. This was a secret and highly unofficial exercise, but it established that, without any doubt at all, the diaries are entirely in Casement's own hand. Armed with such knowledge one can see at once that the Irish Government have known the truth for a long time; it explains why they tried to silence Casement's loyal supporter, Herbert Mackey. The British Government, who suppressed the diaries for as long as possible, because of a private and humane agreement between Gertrude Parry and Prime Minister Baldwin, are not likely to modify their policy until the Northern Ireland problem is resolved.

The diaries, or copies of them, were first brought to the notice of carefully chosen individuals, like Noyes, while Casement was in the Tower; those who might be influential in the organization of petitions or as potential signatories were given early priority. Among these was Clement Shorter who, as editor of *The Sphere*, was present when Hall first showed photographs of selected pages to a number of English and American journalists whom he invited to the Admiralty. At a later date, Shorter was shown the originals at Scotland Yard by Basil Thomson and was prompted to declare that the handwriting bore not the faintest resemblance to Casement's. The original rolled manuscript shown to the Associated Press representative and which Noyes came to believe was the Normand diary, was later found to have been twenty-two pages torn out of the 1903 diary. For the most part the early viewers were journalists or notable public figures. Recently Noel Harris, son of Sir John Harris of the Anti-Slavery Society, found in his desk a letter[9] from the Archbishop of Canterbury, dated 14 July 1916, in which Dr Davidson said that, instead of signing the petition, he had written to the home secretary, not directly requesting a reprieve, but 'calling attention to' three aspects of the case. The first of these was the value of Casement's services in the Congo and the Putumayo, the second was Harris's own testimony regarding the condemned man's character, the third – which was also very much in Sir Arthur Conan Doyle's mind – the possibility of 'mental disease, taking . . . a vicious form'. As it turned out, a lot depended on what was meant by 'vicious'.

Within a week, John Harris had read the diaries himself, at Dr

Davidson's request and on his behalf. Harris was astonished and deeply hurt by the discovery that the Congo sections (which covered a period when his career and Casement's had overlapped, and during which their friendship had been cemented) were completely convincing. Noel Harris recollects that it was the naming of a particular 'boy' in the 1903 diary which most distressed his father; and thus the second argument of the archbishop's letter to the home secretary lost its point. Harris's reaction was typical of his day and, despite the understandably heated response to treason during England's time of difficulty, it is borne in upon one that unnatural vice was the greater sin and crime. Captain Hall, however, was more pragmatic; he was sensitive about American reaction to Casement's predicament (it was Hall's manipulation of the 'Zimmerman telegram', it will be remembered, which did so much to bring the United States into the war); his friend Thomson lost no time in getting typed copies of specimen pages before the American ambassador in London, and one of Hall's staff, Captain Walcott, personally delivered a set of photographs to the British ambassador in Washington. Couriers were sent out in many directions. Later the trail was to be both revealed and confused by Thomson's contradictory statements about how this material came into his hands. The reason is almost too simple to be grasped; he was a prolific author, and his writings abound with errors of detail.

Despite the smear campaign there were many petitions for clemency and distinguished names appeared upon them; a copy of one, found among the effects of a former PPS of Lloyd George, is reproduced as Appendix D. However, although knowledge that the prisoner had frequently indulged in illegal and unpopular sexual activities was widespread throughout the period of the trial, it is not necessary to conclude that the object of the exercise was to get Casement hanged. That it achieved this end was, paradoxically, partially the responsibility of the defence. F.E. Smith, in a somewhat irregular gesture, had offered the diaries to Sullivan, in case he might wish to offer a plea of insanity; the defending counsel refused to entertain the possibility, preferring the prisoner's death to his dishonour. After the trial the attorney-general expressed his disapproval of any scheme to use the diaries to influence opinion. Against a confusing background the petitions stood little chance of success, although they raised strong points to justify exercising the royal prerogative of mercy, especially in connection with Casement's declared wish to stop the rebellion. In the event the diaries had the last word; their usefulness to the nation was succinctly expressed in a memorandum put before the cabinet by Sir Ernley Blackwell. Its substance was that Casement was a proven degenerate, justice should take its course and the diaries should be used to prevent martyrdom. One of the official typed copies is dated August 1916; Casement's date of execution was fixed for 3 August.

Hatred of the prisoner reached a peak of intensity which has seldom been equalled in England. One unique outcome of it serves to illustrate the nature of the reaction against him: his is the only entry in *Who's Who* which has not been carried forward to *Who was Who* after death; he became therefore, in a sense, the first and, as far as is known, the only, non-person of the western world. At a more personal level, the Herbert Ward family, friends since the Congo days, went so far as to petition parliament to change the name of Ward's third son, who had been christened Roger Casement Ward.[10] His christian names became Rodney Sanford, so they could still call him 'Roddie'. Many, to whom Casement's treason was either wholly acceptable or could at least be explained away as misguided, found his private actions impossible to forgive. To Magherin-temple both crimes were sufficient to put its celebrated son beyond the pale. The Great War had seen a flowering of the Casement tradition of loyalty, within the British definition, and the many naval Casements were naturally appalled by R.D.'s treachery. After the initial shock had subsided a little, they began a well-sustained policy of silence. In their subsequent record of distinguished, courageous service they have shown how a family tradition can surmount even a disaster of this magnitude.

On his first day in Pentonville Casement wrote a long letter to his Bannister cousins which alluded to many of the influences which had brought him to that place. Understandably it is an emotional document, and yet it is helpful in showing the thoughts which immediately surfaced in his mind when directly confronted by the prospect of death. After thanking 'Eily' (Elizabeth) and Gertrude for their unfailing devotion to him, his first thought was of their common maternity in the Jephson sisters, Anne and Grace: 'only God – and *your own dear Mother* who stood with us, too, at the last – and mine know how entirely one we are – when I looked at you – [in Court] – it was not often, I thought of her and I saw her wee face in yours – looking at me too.'[11] The next thought was of 'Mrs G.', and she came to mind again in three other paragraphs on the more mundane topic of books about Curran and Parnell which she had lent him. Other sources of books mentioned are Sidney Parry (who was soon to marry Gertrude) and Robert Lynd, his friend from the earliest days of his separatist involvement. Another Ulster friend in this category was Stephen Clark, and he too received an expression of gratitude for moral support.

The letter was written in the knowledge that 'this is *not* like Brixton' and he felt that he would be unable to write much more. Accordingly, a large part of it is a series of disconnected messages to those who mattered most to him. Love was sent to Alice Milligan, with whom he had started on the cultural side of the nationalist path at the first *Feis*. A more revealing message was sent to Richard Morten, with whom he had had an agonizing reunion in Brixton in the presence of Morgan:

all this has come by sure & certain stages – an irresistible destiny, appointed since I was a little boy. I felt it then & have often felt sure of it in later days.

And his acceptance of what he saw now as the inevitability of his death was emphasized to Gertrude and Elizabeth:

I knew this was certain & sure. I came back to meet it, the happiest hearted man in the world in some ways.

Although the initial salutation is to both cousins, the special relationship with Gertrude is shown by the repeated use of the singular in contexts only applicable to her: 'You must go back to Caversham & be good & kind to all there', a reference to Gertrude's post as senior mistress at Queen Anne's School. It was not to be as, although she had risen steadily up the ladder of seniority there, she was about to be dismissed, without explanation; and to this day the school authorities find it impossible to talk about her. Gertrude predominated in his affections, but the situation of his sister was a great worry to him: 'do everything in your power now & hereafter for the dear old N. I feel so deeply about her away out there by herself.' In the United States, she was working hard to raise American support for him and was to continue to labour for his good name long after his death. Although 'undying love' is sent to Ide (Ada NcNeill) and Margaret (Dobbs), first thoughts and penultimate ones were for family rather than friends; and the romantic image of 'Kathleen' for Ireland appearing to him during the nights of his trial, was credited with saving his sanity. But the last remark was a gibe at England: 'As for Shawn Bwee [John Yellow, a Nationalist version of John Bull] – well I wish him joy of his victory. He won it finely!' There was no mention of Magherintemple.

Incidental references to 'Crucifix' and 'Scapulars' (sic) and 'A statuette of the Blessed Virgin sent me by Fr Murnane,[12] I think', draw attention to the arrangements being made for admission to the Roman Catholic Church. He was anxious to convince himself that his was not a death-bed conversion; he had been moving away from Protestantism and becoming increasingly sympathetic towards Catholicism all his life, and yet he had to know that the final step was taken with full conviction. At first matters went well in so far as his recollection of the Welsh baptism meant that the question of conversion did not arise. What had to happen was reconciliation, and was on the face of it a simple process, once any doubts had been resolved. However, when Casement had satisfied his conscience and asked to be reconciled with the church of his mother, he met with a cruel obstacle: Cardinal Bourne required, as a prerequisite, an expression of sorrow for acts, public or private, which might have caused scandal, and this Casement felt unwilling to give. It must have seemed to him that, armed with the diaries, his enemies were able to reach even beyond the grave. But, once his appeal had been dismissed and the date of execution fixed, a new avenue of acceptance into the Catholic Church opened up. With or without Cardinal Bourne's approval, he could be received *in articulo mortis*.

Casement went to his death bravely on 3 August, after receiving his first Catholic Holy Communion. The German mission which led him to the condemned cell was, in its own terms, a failure. The execution, however, had positive effects of which he would have approved and which he had anticipated. Added to the executions which had already taken place in Dublin, it went some way to influence the hitherto largely indifferent body of nominal Home Rulers towards radical Republicanism. True, the diaries, which had been shown to Redmond, and were later shown to Collins and Duggan, took away some of the force of the last sacrifice; but equally powerful, though false, rumours of forgery, made England's crime seem even greater. So, while Casement's statements of policy did not, as he wrongly believed they did, pave the way to the creation of the Irish Republic, his death, aided by the irregularities which surrounded it, helped to hasten its arrival.

Looking back over his life, one can attempt to draw some conclusions about the inevitability or otherwise of the course which it followed. His life certainly had more shape and purpose to it than the lives of his siblings. Nina, as mentioned, was never emotionally stable. Tom, like his sister, had a broken marriage; later he remarried. Charlie went to Australia and Roger did not see him again after their last childhood contact. Both brothers solicited help from Roger, and both were subsidized by him from time to time. It was typical of Roger that, when Tom and his first wife, Blanche, were on the verge of divorce, he found himself agreeing with both parties. All four orphans spent their lives searching, in much the same way as, in Victorian novels, orphans do search. Charlie's life was essentially Australian; Tom's, during Roger's lifetime, was often South (or Southern) African; Nina pursued her quest in the United States. Tom came back to Ireland, where his death had about it more evidence of a death-wish than Roger's. The children had a common ancestry and early upbringing; why did the youngest child become a flawed hero?

The key to the answer to this question lies in the conditions of the Consular Service, which brought out both the best and the worst in Roger Casement. Looked at from the point of view of his origins, the General Consular Service, with its history of strained social relationships with its Diplomatic superiors, was the last occupation in which he might have been expected to feel at ease. And yet he made a success of all his consular postings, other than Rio, and achieved successes on an international scale in two great anti-slavery campaigns. The problem of the Service for him did not only lie in the region of social ambivalence; while his sister and brothers severed their ties with Magherintemple almost completely, by permanent or temporary emigration, Roger was true to the career stereotype of his paternal antecedents and the Service repeatedly brought him back, both to Magherintemple and to the cultural and political melting pot of the Glens of Antrim. The uncongenial side of the 'Cold North', as he described it, turned him against the religion and the politics of his father's family, while neighbouring influences drew him towards his third and final great cause. But for long consular leaves and the loneliness engendered by his 'disease', he might have fulfilled the playwright's fanciful retrospective prophecy[13] and become the first Lord Ballycastle.

The 'disease' is more helpful to analysis of the man and his achievements than one might like to admit; it explains a large part of the generally accepted contradictions of his life. He has long been known in terms of these contradictions: the imperial official who embraced the rebel cause, the Protestant of Catholic persuasion, the Northerner of Southern temperament, and, of course, the prude who practised perversions – the list can be prolonged indefinitely. There is little doubt that initially the effect of family tensions on the youngest orphan helped to produce the deviation from the sexual norm which accustomed him to commit frequent and illegal acts over many years; at the emotional and physical level he became a classic example of the effect of frustrated mother-love. Exactly when such behaviour began is not known; it was, however, a deeply rooted habit with him throughout the major part of his career as a public official and set him apart, in his own mind, from those who were otherwise his natural associates; it aggravated the problem of his social uncertainties and led to the gossip in South America which went some way towards alienating him from his colleagues. Another aspect of his sexual activities was that, with only one recorded identifiable exception, all his partners, regardless of nationality, were of the lowest social class. One can only estimate the effect of such intimate and frequent associations with those from a very different world on a man who was himself socially ambivalent; it threw him completely off balance when it came to his concurrent relationship with German aristocrats on the one hand and Christensen on the other. Against the late Victorian and Edwardian background, duplicity of thought and speech materialized into the double life illustrated in the diaries. And a strange sort of duplicity of emotion drew him back to the family seat, whose values he rejected. Vague feelings of resentment were nurtured from the time of the earliest manifestations of his inclinations and will have played their part in the creation of a rebel, especially when other resentments, of national relevance and scale, gave such notions respectability within the circles in which, when free of the Foreign Office, he chose to move.

DIARIES AND DEATH

It is as though the anti-slavery achievements of the Congo and the Putumayo, pursued within the context of the British Consular Service, were the substantial compensations for the inner sufferings of an individual flawed to a certain degree by a combination of social, political, religious and, above all, familial stresses in his formative years. From these difficulties sprang his sympathy for the oppressed which dominated so much of his thought and behaviour. When it came to the Irish campaign, however, on the one hand the sustaining organization was in many ways alien to him, and on the other the divisions within his nature were subject to greater stresses than those which he had to bear when emancipating Negroes or Indians. Throughout the latter part of his consular career there had been a struggle between the British and Irish elements within him and, in basic instinctive terms, the maternal Jephson-Bannister side of the family displaced the Ulster family seat as the focal point of familial loyalty as soon as he became a free agent. From that moment the already strained relationship between orthodox Casements and the offspring of the union between their most unconventional son and the Catholic daughter of the more elevated Ascendancy house deteriorated rapidly; when Roger David allied himself with the champions of the lower echelons who followed the separatist course, no point of contact remained.

Having had more than his share of ill-timed uncertainty, there developed a man who achieved remarkably well at several levels. As a day-to-day consul he was conscientious and humane; he protected British subjects and furthered British interests, making for the most part exceptionally enlightened use of his instructions. In one way, as a mere 'aggregation of posts', the Consular Service did provide him with an ideal setting, in that the amount of autonomy could, partly by default, allow a man to set his own goals. For some, like Consul Rhind, this led to a decline; but to a man greatly concerned with the plight of the under-privileged, it could bring unusual opportunities. With the exception of the embarrassments of the brief period of resident consul-generalship, when the powerful influence of friends such as Mrs Green, coupled with the social ambiguities of consular activity in Petropolis nearly brought about a crisis, Casement seized these opportunities, whether dealing with an individual British subject with a problem, or with whole races threatened with extermination. He used the British Foreign Office as a vehicle for reform, and modified that vehicle when it seemed inadequate.

Apart from the alleviation of human suffering in two extensive areas of the globe, and the sacrifice of his life in the interests of Irish independence, a major contribution of Casement's career was to the Consular Service itself. Within the context of the department of an imperial power which, towards the end, he came to despise, he marshalled world opinion behind helpless primitive peoples and argued for recognition of their

146

human rights. That he initiated this with the Nelson touch, by exceeding his instructions, was hidden by retrospectively tampering with the wording of his brief. Whatever the diplomatic propriety of doing such a thing, it was the deliberate action of the consul in the field which helped to raise the Consular Service to a new high point before the decline which accompanied imperial withdrawal. His greatest achievements, as he realized with some sadness, were carried out in the name of a benevolent imperialism.

The contribution which the Putumayo investigations made to the concept of the role of the consul, and, through discussion, to the wider implications of inter-state responsibility for the prevention of the exploitation of natives, can best be seen in the minutes of the proceedings of Charles Roberts's Select Committee. Much time was taken up in the search for safeguards and Casement's answers indicated that the worldwide problem of the vulnerability of backward peoples could only be investigated by a strengthened Consular Service; moreover, he felt that enlightened interpretation of existing instructions should be sufficient for the task. He had, in his own practice, shown that co-operation between the consulates of different nations could achieve good results; hence, by example, as well as advice, he helped to bring the committee to a consideration of something which was implicit in his own performance: the possibility of an international consular service. The prospect of such a collaboration between the Great Powers had an unreal ring about it some two years before the outbreak of the European War; nevertheless, what the committee came close to advocating, and might have done, but for the opposition of Sir Harry Johnston, was similar in principle to the United Nations agencies which endeavour to fulfil various humanitarian needs today.

The United Nations Economic and Social Council has in effect delegated part of its responsibilities for the protection of those least able to defend themselves from predatory public and private enterprises to the organization with which Casement collaborated: the Anti-Slavery Society for the Protection of Human Rights. And, as a non-governmental organization, enjoying consultative status at the UN, the society still tries to find something akin to consular access to enable it to penetrate the sovereign territory of governments which are often themselves the offenders; its task has been made no easier by the passing of the Colonial era. In all three of the territories with which Casement concerned himself, governments stood to profit from the exploitation of ethnic groups who had the misfortune to be within their boundaries of conquest, and what he, and members of the Select Committee sought (though few of the latter would have had Ireland in mind) was some kind of international watchdog which would safeguard the development of civil as well as human rights for the weak and inarticulate. With a rare combination of humane thought and positive personal action, he had stimulated general awareness of this need.

Consideration of Casement's career in the light of origins and family background shows him to have been a person of ambivalence right through life, one for whom it was not strange to have a foot in different camps simultaneously. There were therefore few moments of real choice between diametrically opposed policies; that is, until Irish Nationalism brought him to the brink, and beyond. The divergence of strains within him meant that, for long periods, he could embrace loyalties which, to others, were irreconcilable. This capacity eventually led to his personal downfall, but it enabled him, almost intuitively, to ignore contradictions of class and nationality when it suited him, and devote himself to the weak and the vulnerable.

APPENDIX A
CONSULAR FUNCTIONS
IN CASEMENT'S DAY

The Consular Service having grown up independently of planning or centralized direction, the royal commissions and other bodies which were appointed to investigate it were as much concerned to find out how it worked as to make recommendations for its improvement. In their efforts to understand it they naturally delved into the earliest origins of the Service to find their starting point. Thus the Select Committee of 1858 reported that at first 'Consuls were the elected arbiters of commercial differences and regulators of the mercantile marine in the ports of Spain and Italy'[1] and in their Fifth Report[2] the Royal Commission on the Civil Service concluded that their predecessors had correctly identified the beginnings of the General Consular Service. The consul in the field, particularly when his relationship with his Diplomatic colleagues became strained, might prefer to think of the term 'consul' as being in the direct line of the Roman of the same title, but Gibbon had observed that the name 'finally settled on the humble station of the agent of commerce in a foreign land'.[3] It will, however, be seen that while Gibbon may have been right at a given point in time (and with reference to specific areas), the functions of a consul from 1895 to the outbreak of World War I could not be so narrowly interpreted.

The banding together of overseas merchants in territories where, on the negative side, local law provided inadequate protection, and, positively, there was something to be gained from having a mutually recognized spokesman, led to the development of a consular system within the Levant Company, which became the Levant Branch of the Consular Service when the company was abolished in 1825. After inspection and investigation during 1876, carried out by Sir Philip Currie, senior clerk at the Foreign Office in charge of the Eastern Department, the Levant Consular Service became formally independent of the remainder of the Consular Service in 1877 (and remained so until 1934).

A development, in some ways similar, occurred with regard to the East India Company which had enjoyed a monopoly of trade with China.

The Far Eastern Service, because of the difficulty of oriental languages and for other reasons – part geographical, part traditional – was a 'close' service from the outset. It covered China, Japan and Siam and responsibility shifted from the company to the British Government during 1833–4. Like the Levant Service it survived as a formally independent entity until 1934, when the Japan Service and Siam Service (hitherto integral parts of the Far Eastern Service) lost their independence; but the China Service lingered on as far as existing consuls were concerned until amalgamation of all the Foreign Office Services took place in 1943. Even then, as full amalgamation applied only to new entrants to the unified Foreign Service, its traditional set-up persisted as long as the old guard remained in their posts.

Prior to 1934, consuls appointed to parts of the world which were outside the districts of the Levant and Far Eastern Services were members of the General Service. In Casement's time, then, there were three consular services – or three branches of the consular service, depending on the emphasis which one wished to make. Of these three, the Levant had the reputation of demanding diplomatic functions from its consuls; in the Far Eastern the diplomatic was blended with the commercial; in the General Service consuls were reputed to be well and truly subject to trade and mercantile considerations – but the truth of the matter was not so simple.

Consuls did not merely fall into three categories according to the branch or service in which they served, and from time to time there have been attempts to circumscribe their duties. When, in June 1914, Mr Richard Dunning Holt, MP, member of the Royal Commission on the Civil Service, questioned Sir William Tyrrell (Sir Edward Grey's principal private secretary and the civil servant for whom Casement had the most respect) in an effort to define a consul, Holt put it to him that the diplomatist should be described as being 'essentially a political officer, and the consul as being a commercial and shipping officer'. Sir William Tyrrell agreed.[4] Holt had, however, put the words into his mouth. In the previous month, Lord MacDonnell, the commission's chairman, had simply asked Casement: 'Would you briefly describe what his [a consul's] functions are?' Casement's reply, which, under pressure, he effectively withdrew, reflected the general attitude of practising consuls: 'they never have been defined and could not be defined. He is expected to do everything. They are not defined in any regulations.'[5]

Casement's answer would have been very popular with some of his colleagues in Africa and South America, but it was manifestly untrue. In fact, detailed regulations, covering practically every conceivable eventuality, were set out in *General Instructions for H.M.'s Consular Officers*, printed for the Foreign Office. Casement's consular career was guided in its early years by the 1893 edition and in later years by the 1907 edition. A much slimmer, but equally helpful, companion volume was printed for the Board of Trade. Its full title was *Instructions to Consuls relating to matters affecting the British Mercantile Marine, under the Merchant Shipping Act, 1894* and the 1905 edition of this book had between its covers the key to the solution of the Merchant Shipping problems which presented themselves to Casement during his South American career. Consuls were repeatedly upbraided by the Foreign Office for asking permission to do precisely what the regulations told them to do and the minutes on Foreign Office papers often reveal exasperation. 'Oh these Consuls! these Consuls!'[6] introduced the response to an enquiry of this nature from Consul Hewitt, whose failure to consult the *Instructions* simply brought to the surface the general dissatisfaction of the Foreign Office with the Consular Service as a whole.

Partly because of the background from which they were drawn, consuls tended not to be the sort of men who would look up the answer to a human problem in a work of reference and, as their despatches reveal, those in 'places pronounced unhealthy for purposes of superannuation' (which included all Casement's postings) felt free to write frank, near abusive letters to their superiors at the Foreign Office. One cannot help but suspect that these letters – the answers to which could have been found in the *Instructions* – reflect dissatisfaction with conditions of service (as was subsequently to be brought out by the enquiries of the Departmental Committee of 1912) instead of exemplifying the problems with which, superficially, they deal. At any rate they show that it occurred to few consuls to seek a definition of their functions within the printed Foreign Office and Board of Trade guidelines. Ernest Hambloch, who acted for Casement as consul-general at Rio de Janeiro during the Putumayo investigations, said that he found them 'an excellent guide to what a Consul might not do'.[7] But this does not square with the books themselves; by far the greater part of them is devoted to positive instructions. In an effort to be reasonable Hambloch conceded that most cases which came before the consul had some novel feature in them and therefore had to be assessed according to their merits; for this reason 'it would be impossible to lay down cut-and-dried rules for what is in many respects a Service to meet unforeseen emergencies'. But the *Instructions* do come near to reconciling the fundamental difficulties. They provide definite rulings whenever possible, but are written from a human standpoint: advocating discretion where necessary, without abdicating responsibility in the name of consular discretion. The Board of Trade Instructions of 1905, for example, under the heading 'Detention of Ships' (meaning 'by any foreign authority') gives the vague but necessary advice: 'the Consul . . . will do whatever is in his power to ensure safety and order on board' and then supplements it with precise regulations with regard to proper procedure.

Although Casement may have been right to say that the functions of a consul cannot be defined – that is, in the succinct way that is normally required of a definition – they can at least be described; and then the description reduced to the most essential features, in order to approach definition. In this connection use may be made of Hambloch's memoir; despite being basically a gossipy collection of anecdotes, coloured by hindsight, it does contain some useful insights and generalizations, as, for example, the predicament of a consul as seen by the man who sat in Casement's seat:[8]

> Though not enjoying the status of a diplomatist he is expected to be
> diplomatic, while more often than not he is called upon to make
> quick decisions on his own responsibility, with little to guide him
> except the golden rule of the Service – to protect British subjects and
> further British interests.

Lord MacDonnell, by 8 May 1914, when he was questioning Casement, had had his fill of generalizations and pressed the witness, as he put it, to 'endeavour to form a conception'. He enquired whether in some places the consul exercised political functions, and received the reply: 'Never by the letter of his instructions, but only by the fact of local conditions.'[9] On the previous day, in the context of the Levant Service and China and Japan, the commission had heard Sir Maurice de Bunsen, answering questions put by Sir Donald MacAlister, say: 'He is a political agent as well. If a British subject gets into trouble and is captured by brigands the local consul has a good deal to do with getting him out.'[10] This point was taken further when supplementary questions led to the conclusion that a consul's political judgment could be exercised without reference to the embassy.

In the dialogue between Lord MacDonnell and Casement the chairman sought to establish what he called the 'immediate functions'[11] of a consul. Casement would not agree that these were simply connected with the Merchant Shipping Act, and reminded his hearers that a consul was a marriage officer and registrar of births and deaths (those functions at least would form part of a precise definition), and then he had the immensely varied responsibility of caring for 'distress amongst British subjects'. This last item, as Casement's own experience might have confirmed, could include not only dealing with drunken and otherwise distressed sailors, but with problems such as tracing missing persons, investigating the misappropriation of inheritances and impeding the abduction of a minor.

The MacDonnell Commission gave some prominence in their examination of witnesses to the 'sorts of intelligence that consuls furnish'. There was a strategic aspect to this; they were expected to observe carefully the activities, especially naval, of other Powers, but this did not normally loom large in despatches. The Consular Act of 1825 had done much to create a unified service from the isolated consulates which had developed in their own ways, and George Canning had realized, and urged, the development of the commercial potential of the new organization. Translated into the realities of a consul's day-to-day existence, this involved the preparation of trade reports. These were transmitted by the Foreign Office to the Board of Trade, two of whose officials were examined. Two departments of the Board of Trade were concerned; the Commercial Department (represented by Mr H. Fountain) received the general annual report, reports on large subjects of commercial interest as they arose and replies to special enquiries; the Marine Department (represented by Mr G.E. Baker) looked into all activities of a consul which were connected with shipping and with seamen. Officially the consul was dealing with the Foreign Office and it was to his employer that he sent his reports, but he did send (without covering letter) copies of replies to business houses direct to the Board of Trade. Unknown to the consuls there was some informal, semi-official correspondence between the Board of Trade and the Foreign Office on the efficiency of the commercial work of consuls and this could influence promotion. In Casement's experience conflict never arose between the two sources of instructions because in trade matters the Foreign Office invariably referred him to the Board of Trade Instructions. But he strongly repudiated the suggestion that it was the 'sole function of a consul to push the individual interests of the traders of his nationality'. 'No, I should not admit that for a moment. There are many other British subjects abroad besides traders.'[12] His questioner (Mr Graham Wallas) then asked whether a consul was ever in effect a magistrate. Casement replied that that depended on the locality, but denied emphatically that in a port, in civil questions connected with the Board of Trade, a consul ever had to act in a judicial capacity; he could enquire into a maritime offence, but could not try the case. In this answer he was simply paraphrasing Board of Trade instruction 174: 'Though the Consul has no magisterial power he has the . . . authority to summon a Naval Court.'[13] And it is worth noting that should a problem of this nature arise, the consul was supported by another work of reference, namely the *Instructions relating to Naval Courts*.

A consideration of the various volumes of instructions with which consuls were supplied does undermine the prevailing prejudice of members of the Service that they received insufficient guidance. Casement went so far as to exclaim that there was no consular service: 'It is an aggregation of posts,'[14] and in his view there was 'no limit' to the functions of consuls in their highly individual situations. The limits were, however, quite clearly set out in *General Instructions*. After introductory chapters on matters of protocol, of which it might reasonably have been complained that too much information was given, detailed directions are set out concerning

APPENDIX A

the terms and conditions of service. General Instruction 2 was headed 'Subordination of Consular to Diplomatic Service' and made the relationship quite clear; there then followed specific guidance with regard to fees, accounts, correspondence and archives. Trade and commerce were dealt with only in general terms as there was a separate volume to take care of this part of consular activity, and much the same could be said of the chapter entitled 'Mercantile Marine'. Another section dealt with the consul's relationship with the Royal Navy; another with vice-consuls and their appointment. His responsibilities with regard to quarantine and cattle disease were explained and, as in most sections, the minutest details of clerical procedures were given. In countries where slavery existed, consular officers were advised that they should consult *Instructions for Guidance of Naval Officers employed in the Suppression of the Slave Trade* (1892).

Much of the remainder of the volume went thoroughly into the nature of assistance and advice available to British subjects, to protect them and their property. Naturalization, repatriation and extradition were important sections, and the issuing of passports was meticulously gone into. The rest was largely devoted to the functions of a consul as Commissioner for Oaths and Registrar of Births, Marriages and Deaths.

Returning to Hambloch's generalized view, given above, one may agree that an Edwardian British Consul of the General Service might reasonably be described as one chosen to protect British subjects and further British interests within a district of a foreign territory: to make this a more serviceable description – if not definition – a brief summary of the tasks performed might be added, viz:

(a) *Protective duties*: Care of distressed British subjects (granting material assistance only when the distress was not self-inflicted: otherwise advisory); such responsibilities as bringing the best advice to British subjects in legal difficulties or in prison; seeing that adequate hospital facilities exist; ensuring that religious rights are guaranteed, including the provision of burial grounds. Here too would come consular functions in the field of extradition and naturalization. As Board of Trade Instruction No. 5. put it: 'With a few exceptions the Consul is the representative of British law at his post'; in real terms this amounted to 'Power of Enquiry' which carried with it the responsibility of supervising practically all contractual relationships between Ships' Masters and seamen (both parties frequently being liable to £10 or £20 fines, should they not co-operate with consular rulings). And then there was the consul's function as registrar.

(b) *Duty to further British interests*: For the most part, as has been mentioned, this lay in the consul's obligation to collect the best available information for his annual report and to reply to specific enquiries from the Board of Trade, private businesses, or the Admiralty. The information

154

was gleaned from whatever sources were available – for example, local customs statistics or, in South America, the *Brazilian Review* – after which the task of compilation was, for many consuls, largely clerical; though some consuls waxed lyrical in their reports. Political matters were generally, but not always, left to the Legation. Consuls were, however, sometimes expected to be diplomatic with a small 'd' and promote British interests by subtle, social means.

APPENDIX B
A CHARITABLE APPEAL
ISSUED BY CONSUL
CASEMENT AT SANTOS

HIS BRITANNIC MAJESTY'S CONSULATE, SANTOS

December 12, 1906.

It is within the knowledge of the British community that a considerable number of our fellow countrymen who in one capacity or another have found their way to this part of Brazil constitute a charge upon the charity of many of us and a burden not alone upon the charity but upon the time of some few others of our number.

While in a great many cases these men are little deserving of charity, being themselves largely responsible for their unfortunate circumstances, there are among them cases which demand the attention and possible relief of this Consulate, and it is difficult to withhold some form of assistance from many of those who so constantly appeal for food, lodging or, more often, the means of leaving this neighbourhood.

Apart from the claims of ordinary kindliness which, I am sure, are no where more readily or more generously admitted than in this community, I think that as British subjects we cannot view with complete unconcern the degradation and demoralisation to which many of our fellow countrymen publicly expose themselves in the streets of a Brazilian city.

It is nearly always possible for this Consulate to deal with seamen who may be in distress, but for distressed British subjects who are not seamen there is no readily provided official means of relief.

Many of those who come to the notice of His Majesty's Consulate as destitute belong to the latter category and in dealing with them it becomes the Consul's duty to show 'that every effort has been made, by recourse to local charitable agencies or other available sources' before he is permitted to incur any expenditure which may fall upon public funds.

In these circumstances I would venture to appeal to the British community in the State of São Paulo, and more particularly to those resident in the cities of São Paulo and Santos, to assist His Majesty's Consulate to deal with such cases by joining the Consul in the creation of a fund which shall be at his disposal for the purpose of affording relief in urgent cases and which shall be primarily destined to getting all such needy applicants carried away from this part of Brazil.

I would propose that the principal of this fund should remain intact and that, after investment, the interest only be available for charitable distribution.

By this means it may be possible to deal with the discreditable state of affairs we are all cognisant of and, if a sufficient sum can be raised, to provide a means against its continuance and remove, in future, the reproach I fear we all incur today of being nationally identified with some of the worst elements of vagabondage and idleness in our midst.

Should, on the other hand, the suggestion now made prove unworkable either by reason of lack of funds or from inadequacy of such an attempt to cope with the evil, we shall be no worse off than we already are while we shall, at least, have made a combined effort to deal with an admitted evil by means within our own resources.

I propose, if this appeal meets with your approval and adequate support is forthcoming, to place the control of the fund so raised in the hands of a local committee whose co-operation could not fail to greatly assist this Consulate.

I am, Yours faithfully ROGER CASEMENT

APPENDIX C
G.B. SHAW TO
JULIUS KLEIN

The position taken by Sir Roger Casement in the war of 1914 was perfectly clear and logical.

His object as an Irish patriot was the freeing of Ireland from her enforced subjection to England, and the establishment of her national independence. As a diplomat by profession he understood perfectly that it was necessary to have a considered diplomatic policy and not a mere gush of patriotic sentiment. He had stated his policy at full length in American journals with all possible precision as follows.

England is Ireland's conqueror and enemy, and so much more powerful that it is impossible for Ireland to free herself by her own unaided efforts. Ireland must therefore seek an alliance with some anti-English Power or combination of Powers, and offer them her support, such as it is, in return for a promise to guarantee the independence of Ireland in the event of their coming victorious out of a war with England, Casement's calculation being that such a victorious Power or Powers would have a strong interest in weakening their defeated foe by establishing a hostile independent nation in the fairway of her foreign trade.

Accordingly, when England took the field against Germany, and for some time Germany seemed quite a likely winner, Casement took the German side and actually went to Germany and tried to raise an Irish brigade there. When the Easter rebellion broke out in 1916 he came to Ireland in a German submarine to take part in it and urge his foreign policy upon it. In Ireland he was captured by the British forces, sent to England, tried there as a traitorous British subject, convicted, and hanged. At least six separate petitions for his reprieve were sent to the Prime Minister, Mr Asquith; for so many different grounds were alleged for sparing him that it would have been impossible to procure signatures if they had all been combined in one petition. I drafted at least one of these petitions, and possibly revised one or more of the others. But I had no illusions as to the chances of success. I knew that his defence at the trial had been mis-

158

managed, and that the execution was certain. England is not magnanimous in such matters.

I did not know Casement personally; but I understood his policy, and, as an Irishman, held that he had just as clear a right to take the German side in the war as any Serb had to take the English side, even a Serb who had formerly been in the Turkish public service. And I was moved by the distress of his cousin Mrs Parry, who was a friend of mine. I therefore addressed myself to the question of his defence. I knew that the conventional legal defence which his lawyers were certain to advise would infallibly hang him after eliciting compliments from the Bench for its ability and eloquence. The facts were undeniable; but learned counsel would refuse to admit them and would cross examine the Crown witnesses at the utmost possible length so as to give plenty of value for their fees. The Lord Chief Justice would compliment; the jury would admire; and everybody except the prisoner would be perfectly happy in the obvious certainty that the facts were the facts, the witnesses unshakeable, and a verdict of guilty certain.

I advised Casement to conduct his own defence; to plead not guilty but admit all the facts; to assert his complete right to act as he had done; to claim that as he was a prisoner of war and not a traitor his execution would be a murder; to be eloquent about his right to take up arms for the independence of his country; and to finish with a defiant 'Now murder me if you like and be damned'. I believed, and still believe, that such a defence would have had at least a chance of disagreement in the jury. I knew also that the conventional defence was absolutely certain to produce a conviction.

Unfortunately, I could not induce Casement to give the requisite weight to my advice. As far as I can guess he was amused by it and did not quite grasp his own diplomatic position. The lawyers would of course have considered themselves professionally disgraced if they had advised such a course. They persuaded him that he must have the regular professional defence and that he could say what he liked *after the verdict*, when he was asked, in due form, whether he had anything to say against sentence being pronounced. He adopted this course, and had the satisfaction of making a fine speech from the dock before the Lord Chief Justice put on the black cap. His counsel was highly complimented from the bench, as I had foreseen, and actually had a breakdown in court from the intensity of his useless pleading. There was an equally vain ceremony before the Court of Appeal, of which Casement wrote a humorous account with extraordinary detachment. And then he was hanged. The rebellion had failed; his expedition had failed; his policy had never been understood; and I suppose he felt that there was nothing left for him but to go through that old ordeal called 'dying for Ireland'.

Some years afterwards the late Clement Shorter, who was a collector of literary rarities, and liked printing little private editions of anything that seemed sufficiently interesting, printed 25 copies of an account of the matter,[1] including, as well as I remember, a letter of mine to Casement. This is the explanation of the quite unfounded notion that I wrote 'a booklet' about him.

I did not agree with Casement's policy, because I never believed, after the hold-up of the German advance before Liège, that Germany could win; nor did I want her to win. The suggestion that an independent Ireland could be of any real use to a victorious Germany was not plausible enough for the German general staff, whose feeling evidently was 'You have a horse to sell, Sir Roger', though they were always too credulous as to the value to them of the Orange and Nationalist rebellions. I was therefore in no sense a Casementite; but I have no patience with judicial murders in which the infuriated accuser is also the judge, the jury, and the executioner. The crucial issue was whether Casement was or was not a prisoner of war in a struggle for the independence of his country. That issue, in the absence of an international tribunal, should have been tried by a neutral court in a neutral country. I was strongly of this opinion with regard not only to Casement but to all cognate trials.

As to the sort of British patriotism which expressed itself in dismissing Casement's cousin from the educational post she had held honorably for many years because she visited him in prison, I had no feeling for it but one of contemptuous disgust. The British Government discredited Casement shockingly by exhibiting photographs of a document found in his possession as pages from his diary. But this alleged diary has never been produced; and until and unless it is forthcoming the contention of Casement's friends that the document is a relic of his Putumayo days, when he had to copy and report many unmentionable confessions, remains unrefuted.

G. Bernard Shaw
19th December, 1934.

APPENDIX D

COPY OF A PETITION FOR CLEMENCY FOR ROGER CASEMENT, FOUND AMONG THE EFFECTS OF JOHN HOWARD WHITEHOUSE, A FORMER PARLIAMENTARY PRIVATE SECRETARY TO LLOYD GEORGE

On April 6th Casement was in a Nursing Home in Germany when he heard through a spy's report that there was going to be a rising in Ireland. He went straight to Berlin where with great difficulty he got a submarine to take him to Ireland. The submarine broke down, off Heligoland, and he had to wait for some days to get another. His object in going was to stop the rising which he considered a fatal mistake. The Captain of the second submarine did not know Ireland and landed him on a part of the coast where he knew nobody. Nobody of course expected him. He hid himself while Bailey and Monteith went to Tralee to get a motor-car. They found a shop with Sinn Fein colours, went in and arranged for a car. One went in the car, the other cycled, but they were followed by Police and never found Casement who was meanwhile arrested. Meanwhile another car nothing to do with Casement, met with an accident and two men were drowned. When Casement, in the train, heard someone mention this he thought it must be Bailey and Monteith and broke down.

Casement begged to be allowed to communicate with the Leaders to try and stop the rising, but he was not allowed. On Easter Sunday, at Scotland Yard, he implored again to be allowed to communicate or send a message. But they refused, saying, 'It's a festering sore, it's much better it should come to a head'. It is quite clear from this that if Casement had not been so frightfully anxious to stop the rising he would not have been caught and be in danger of being hanged. This was not told at the Trial because Casement would not allow it. He said the Irish people would think he was going back on them and trying to save his neck by telling the world he did not approve of the rising. Anybody knowing his character would understand this, and the almost fantastic sense of pride and honour that he has.

These are the absolute facts. Whatever people think of the Sinn Feiners, they must know that they are courageous to a fault and incapable of trying to save their lives by shuffling.

May I ask your support for an appeal that is being made to the Government on behalf of Roger Casement on political and human grounds. From the political point of view, it is felt by many that in the present state of excitement and restlessness in Ireland, the execution of the sentence would cause a real national danger. It must be remembered that Casement is in no sense an ordinary criminal under the ordinary criminal law. In Ireland, at all events by the mass of the people, the question of the reprieve is looked upon entirely as a political question. Willingness has been shewn by the Authorities to make some kind of political settlement conciliatory to the various parties in Ireland. But anyone who knows the country must realise that any settlement made with the present political leaders which ignores the wishes, sentiments and indignation of the mass of the people will be as far as a tranquilising effect is concerned, so much waste paper. It would be hard to over-estimate the bitter feeling and misery caused in Ireland even among moderate Nationalists by recent executions, and when the country is in such a state surely an act of clemency would be an act of the highest political wisdom.

Indignation and bitterness in America have, of course, no direct bearing on the case like the Irish feeling, but surely from a statesman's point of view it might be well to pause before insisting on an act of rigor which must inevitably bring down the prestige of this country in the eyes of a neutral hitherto friendly but whose sympathy has already, on trustworthy evidence, been partially alienated by what they consider the excessive severity of the recent executions.

Surely many calm minded people in this country itself, who feel sadly that the Government has erred on the side of severity especially in the execution of innocent people like Mr Sheehy Skeffington, must think that it would be an act of grace to reprieve Roger Casement, even if they considered this to be erring a little on the side of clemency, giving as it were a life in exchange for the other they now allow was wrongfully taken.

As far as Roger Casement's own claim to consideration is concerned surely anyone who followed the trial must be convinced of the absence of any sordid or criminal motive on his part. It seems a terrible severity for anyone who has any respect for patriotism or loyalty amongst Englishmen to hang a man for his reckless love of Ireland, even if that patriotism has made him in the end act in a manner hostile to this country. The fine character of his previous career, his great work for the world in the Congo and at Putumayo, should surely also weigh with the Government. The horrors he was brought in contact with combined with his twenty years' uninterrupted work in the unhealthy climates so told on his constitution that he had a complete break down in health, and by 1914 he was an utterly broken man.

In this condition he faced the horrors, hardships and dangers of Putumayo with the same disinterested eagerness he had always shewn. He came back in a state of absolute nervous collapse so serious that he often wakened shrieking in the night, and there were certain photographs and notes he brought back that he could not look at without terribly intense mental agitation and physical emotion. In this state he was faced with the news of the Ulster arming which had brought Irish affairs into a very critical state, and the prevailing agitation was bound to react on him in his weakened condition.

Surely his long record of splendid work for humanity, and the way in which in the past he sacrificed health, comfort and all thought of the ordinary happiness of home life, should tell in his favour, also the fact recognised by authority that his self devoted work was of great use to this country. If anyone thinks there are enough grounds here to ask for a reprieve they are urgently requested to write to the Prime Minister and the Home Secretary, and to use all their influence on the side of clemency.

NOTES AND REFERENCES

ABBREVIATIONS

NLI National Library of Ireland
PRO FO Public Record Office, London, Foreign Office
PRO HO Public Record Office, London, Home Office
PRO WO Public Record Office, London, War Office

CHAPTER 1 ANTECEDENTS

1 Jephson Family Papers at Mallow Castle. Casement to Louisa Jephson-Norreys, 1 June 1895.
2 Nephew of Dr Henry Jephson, a Leamington GP.
3 Jephson papers. A.J. Mounteney Jephson: diary of the Emin Pasha Relief Expedition (1887–9).
4 *Ibid.*, 19 April 1887. See p. 21 for the other meetings between Casement and A.J. Mounteney Jephson.
5 Widow of Captain John Casement, RN, member, when a Commander, of Captain Hall's Naval Intelligence Division.
6 Private letter, Mrs Anne B. Casement to R.M.S., 28 October 1971.
7 Jephson Papers. The Hon. Emily G. Ward of Castle Ward, Downpatrick to Louisa Jephson-Norreys, 22 November 1894.
8 Jephson Papers. Casement to Louisa Jephson-Norreys, 10 June 1895.
9 Private letter, Brigadier Maurice Denham Jephson to R.M.S., 20 October 1967.
10 Inconsistent spelling of one's own name was not rare at this time, as is evident in many Jephson records.
11 Brigadier Jephson acknowledged the help of Basil O'Connell, genealogist, in unravelling this part of the genealogy.
12 Jephson Papers. Casement to Louisa Jephson-Norreys, 1 June 1895.
13 Private letter, Lord Dunalley to R.M.S., 22 April 1972.
14 L.G. Redmond-Howard, *Sir Roger Casement: A Character Sketch Without Prejudice*, p. 9.
15 This has since been rectified in Burke's *Irish Family Records*.
16 PRO HO 161. Casement, Letts's Pocket Diary for 1903, fly-leaf: 'Name for Novel: The Far from Maddening Crowd, by R Mc. Asmundr Serene Enclosings of a mightier Self'.
17 NLI 8602. Casement to Mrs A.W. Hutton, 26 November 1904.

18 E. Hambloch, *British Consul: Memories of Thirty Years' Service in Europe and Brazil*, p. 75.
19 Notable Casement examples are in the churchyard of Middle Church (Church of Ireland), Ballinderry, Co. Antrim and Kensal Green, London, which has the grave of Major-General Sir William Casement, KCB, of the Bengal Army, member of the Supreme Council of India.
20 Private letter, Charlotte Casement to R.M.S., 15 May 1967.
21 PRO WO 31. Commander-in-Chief Memoranda Papers, Abstract 823, Hugh Casement to Lieutenant-General Fitzroy Somerset, September 1840.
22 Sir Denham Jephson-Norreys, Bart. was particularly active in this field.
23 Jephson Papers. Sir William Betham to Sir Denham Jephson-Norreys, Bart., 6 August 1838.
24 R.D. Casement, 'Kossuth's Irish Courier', *United Irishman*, 25 February 1905, p. 3, (signed 'X').
25 *Ibid*.
26 L. Kossuth, *Meine Schriften aus der Emigration*, vol. 3, pp. 342–6.
27 *Ibid*.
28 P. Singleton-Gates, 'Casement: A Summing-Up', unpublished typescript, p. 19.
29 NLI 13077.
30 Casement, *op. cit.*, p. 3.

CHAPTER 2 EARLY LIFE

 1 D. Gwynn, *The Life and Death of Roger Casement*, p. 428: a priest had 'splashed water over him'.
 2 NLI 13074. Parry Papers.
 3 '1868 Die 5 Augusti sub conditione baptizati sunt Carolus Gulielmus, Thomas Hugo, et Rogerius David, filii Rogerii et Anna Casement (olim Jephson)
a me
Felice Poole S.J.
Miss Ap.'
 4 NLI 13080. Casement to McVeagh, 20 May 1911.
 5 *Nation*, 29 July 1911.
 6 R.D. Casement, *Some Poems of Roger Casement*, Introduction by Gertrude Parry (née Bannister), p. xi.
 7 *New York Times*, 25 April 1916.
 8 British Library of Political and Economic Science (London School of Economics) – Morel F8, Casement to E.D. Morel, 27 June 1904.
 9 Jephson Papers. A.J. Mounteney Jephson: diary of the Emin Pasha Relief Expedition, 14 April 1887.
10 *Ibid*., 17 April 1887.
11 Conrad to R.B. Cunninghame Graham, 26 December 1903, quoted in G. Jean-Aubry, *Joseph Conrad: Life and Letters*, vol. 1, p. 324.
12 e.g. H. Ward, *A Voice from the Congo*, pp. 206–7 and F. Puleston, *African Drums*, pp. 278–9.
13 British Library of Political and Economic Science (London School of Economics) – Morel F8, Casement to E.D. Morel, 27 June 1904.
14 PRO FO 128/324. Casement to Milne Cheetham, 11 May 1908.
15 *Ibid*.
16 NLI 10464. Green Papers. Casement to Alice Stopford Green, 20 April 1907.

17 A. Newman, 'Life of Roger Casement, Martyr in Ireland's Cause', *The Irish Press*, weekly instalments: 13 December 1919–13 March 1920.
18 NLI 13088. Memoir of Gertrude Parry.
19 Tape recorded interview with R.M.S., 24 March 1972.
20 *Minutes of Evidence, Fifth Report of the Royal Commission on the Civil Service*, PP 1914–16 (Cd 7749) XI Q 38,489.
21 *Ibid.*
22 *Report on the Administration of the Niger Coast Protectorate*, August 1891 to August 1894, PP 1895 (Cd 7596) LXXI.
23 *Ibid.*
24 *Ibid.*, Inclosure 17. Mr Casement to Sir C. MacDonald, Opobo, 10 April 1894.
25 *Ibid.*
26 *Ibid.*
27 *Ibid.*
28 *Ibid.*
29 *Ibid.*
30 *Ibid.*
31 *Ibid.*
32 *Report on the Administration of the Niger Coast Protectorate*, 1894–5, PP 1895 (Cd 7916) LXXI.
33 PRO FO 2/64. Casement to Sir Claude MacDonald, 4 July 1894.
34 PRO FO 2/64. Casement to Sir Claude MacDonald, 24 November 1894.
35 Jephson Papers. Casement to Louisa Jephson-Norreys, 10 June 1895.
36 *Report on the Administration of the Niger Coast Protectorate*, August 1891 to August 1894, PP 1895 (Cd 7596) LXXI.
37 Jephson Papers. Casement to Louisa Jephson-Norreys, 10 June 1895.
38 *Ibid.*, Casement to Louisa Jephson-Norreys, 29 June 1895.
39 *Minutes of Evidence, Fifth Report of the Royal Commission on the Civil Service*, PP 1914–16 (Cd 7749) XI Q 38,489.

CHAPTER 3 BRITISH CONSUL

1 *Minutes of Evidence, Fifth Report of the Royal Commission on the Civil Service*, PP 1914–16 (Cd 7749) XI Q 38,555.
2 *Ibid.*, Q 38,560.
3 *Portugal, Report for the Year 1896 on the Trade and Commerce of Lorenzo Marques*. (Foreign Office Annual Series No. 1904. Diplomatic and Consular Reports on Trade and Finance.) 1897. (C. 8277–122) XCII.
4 *Minutes of Evidence, Fifth Report of the Royal Commission on the Civil Service*, PP 1914–16 (Cd 7749) XI Q 38,494.
5 *Ibid.*, Q 38,495.
6 *Ibid.*
7 *Bulletin Officiel*, 7 November 1905.
8 M. Lane, *Edgar Wallace: The Biography of a Phenomenon*, p. 214.
9 PRO HO 161. Casement, Letts's Pocket Diary for 1903.
10 *Ibid.*, 17 April 1903.
11 PRO HO 161. Casement, Dollard's Diary for 1910 and Letts's Desk Diary for 1911. The coincidence of the years spanned by the only extant diaries in British Government hands (the other two 'diaries' in the Public Record Office are not diaries at all, but a note book containing a few disconnected jottings and an accounts ledger) with those of parallel official reports covering the

same times and places is believed by the forgery school of thought to be highly significant.

12 PRO HO 161. Casement, Letts's Pocket Diary for 1903, 28 February.
13 *Ibid.*, 2 March.
14 *Ibid.*, 12 March. Lady Edgcumbe, the second wife of Sir Robert Edgcumbe.
15 *Ibid.*, 17 March. This was the fifth Duke of Montrose, who was then fifty-one (not his twenty-five year old heir, as wrongly supposed by P. Singleton-Gates and M. Girodias, *The Black Diaries*, p. 111 (footnote), which misled Professor Reid on this point: *The Lives of Roger Casement*, p. 37).
16 *Ibid.*, 18 March.
17 *Ibid.*, 23 March. Sir John Macdonell.
18 *Ibid.*, 21 September.
19 *Ibid.*, 20 May.
20 *Ibid.*, 28 May.
21 *Ibid.*, 11 July.
22 *Ibid.*, 21 July.
23 *Ibid.*, 3 August.
24 *Ibid.*, 5 August.
25 *Ibid.*, 13 August.
26 *Ibid.*, 14 August.
27 *Ibid.*, 16 September.
28 *Ibid.*, 5 June.
29 *Ibid.*, 25 July.
30 *Ibid.*, 22 June.
31 *Ibid.*, 29 July.
32 *Ibid.*, 30 August.
33 *Ibid.*, 6 September.
34 A Belgian, *The Truth about the Civilisation in Congoland.*
35 *Correspondence and Report from His Majesty's Consul at Boma respecting the Administration of the Independent State of the Congo*, PP 1904 (Cd 1933) LXII.
36 *Further Correspondence respecting the Administration of the Independent State of the Congo*, PP 1904 (Cd 2097) LXII.
37 H.W. Wack, *The Story of the Congo Free State: Social, Political, and Economic Aspects of the Belgian System of Government in Central Africa.*

CHAPTER 4 CONSUL ON LEAVE

1 PRO HO 161. Casement, Letts's Pocket Diary for 1903.
2 *Ibid.*, 24 December.
3 *Ibid.*, 25 December.
4 *Ibid.*, 26 December.
5 NLI 13074. Parry Papers. Note of a message recorded by Gertrude Bannister.
6 S.J. O'Grady, *History of Ireland: The Heroic Period.*
7 E. Boyd, *Ireland's Literary Renaissance* (3rd ed., 1968), p. 59.
8 R.D. Casement, *The Crime Against Europe: The Writings and Poetry of Roger Casement*, collected and edited by H.O. Mackey, p. 203 (from the third stanza of 'Portglenone').
9 Casement, *Some Poems of Roger Casement*, edited by Gertrude Parry (née Bannister), p. 15 (opening lines of 'Benburb').
10 *Ibid.*, p. 12 (opening lines of 'The Irish Language').

11 A.S. Green, *The Making of Ireland and its Undoing*, p. 345.
12 NLI 10464 (2). Green Papers. Casement to Alice Stopford Green, 24 April 1904.
13 J.R. Green, *The Making of England*.
14 J.R. Green, *The Conquest of England*, edited by A.S. Green.
15 A.S. Green, with subsequent additions by Casement and Bulmer Hobson: published anonymously, *Irishmen and the English Army*. This was circulated by the Dungannon Clubs which, founded by Hobson and Denis McCullough, sought to bring about a regeneration of Irish traditions by intellectual, material and physical means and thus attract support from a wider spectrum of society than might be found in the country houses of Antrim.
16 Alfred Noyes Papers at Lisle Combe, St Lawrence, Isle of Wight; quoted by Desmond Berry in letter to Noyes, 14 May 1957, p. 3.
17 Alfred Noyes Papers. Correspondence of May 1957, between Noyes, Roger McHugh, Herbert Mackey and a member of the Berry family about Casement's letters to R.G.J.J. Berry.
18 NLI 13088. Casement, Brief to counsel.
19 H. Montgomery Hyde (ed.), *Trial of Sir Roger Casement*, Notable British Trials Series (new ed.), p. 15; from the concluding remarks of the opening speech for the prosecution.
20 The First Earl of Birkenhead, *Famous Trials*, undated edition, p. 240. In the second edition of *F.E. The Life of F.E. Smith First Earl of Birkenhead*, by his son, The Second Earl of Birkenhead, it is stated on p. 295: 'F.E. Smith was wrongly briefed when he said that Casement's hatred of Britain was "sudden in origin". He had been an Irish separatist as early as 1905–06.'

CHAPTER 5 CONSUL OF GREAT BRITAIN AND IRELAND

1 PRO FO 366/781. Reports (majority and minority) of the Departmental Committee on the Consular Service, January 1939. Sir Hughe Knatchbull-Hugessen to Sir Alexander Cadogan, 20 January 1939.
2 *Brazil, Report for the Year 1879 on the Trade and Commerce of Santos*. Commercial. No. 42 (1880) (Trade Reports). Reports from Her Majesty's Consuls on the Manufactures, Commerce, etc., of their Consular Districts. Pt. VI, 1880 (C.2701). LXXIV.
3 E. Bradford Burns, *The Unwritten Alliance: Rio-Branco and Brazilian–American Relations*, pp. 2–4.
4 *Brazil, Report for the Year 1884 on the Trade and Commerce of Santos*. Commercial. No. 17 (1885) (Trade Reports). Reports from Her Majesty's Consuls on the Manufactures, Commerce, etc. of their Consular Districts. Pt. V, 1884–5 (C.4444). LXXVIII.
5 *Brazil, Report for the Year 1888 on the Trade of Santos*. (Foreign Office Annual Series No. 498. Diplomatic and Consular Reports on Trade and Finance). 1889. (C.5618–51). LXXVIII. (The exact number of slaves was 107,329).
6 PRO FO 369/5. Thornton to Secretary of State, 22 May 1906.
7 PRO FO 369/5. Thornton to Secretary of State, 10 October 1906.
8 PRO FO 369/5. Casement to Rowland Sperling, 13 October 1906.
9 *Minutes of Evidence, Special Report from Select Committee on Putumayo*. 1913 (H. of C. Paper 148) XIV Q 8466.
10 *Minutes of Evidence, Fifth Report of the Royal Commission on the Civil Service*, PP 1914–16 (Cd 7749) XI Q 38,555.

11 PRO FO 369/63.
12 *General Instructions for Her Majesty's Consular Officers*, 1893 edition.
13 PRO FO 369/63.
14 PRO FO 128/308.
15 PRO FO 369/64.
16 See Appendix B.
17 *Report of the Committee appointed to inquire into the Constitution of the Consular Service*, PP 1903 (Cd 1634) LV.
18 PRO FO 128/308.
19 PRO FO 369/63. Casement to Secretary of State, 15 December 1906.
20 PRO FO 128/315. Casement to William Haggard, 29 April 1907.
21 *Brazil, Report for the Years 1905–06 on the Trade of Santos*. (Annual Series No. 3952. Diplomatic and Consular Reports) 1908 (C.3727–35). CIX.
22 Shortly after the report appeared, Guinness was condemned by the municipal authorities in Rio de Janeiro. There was a scandal and the analyst was later committed for trial.
23 G. de C. Parmiter, *Roger Casement*, p. 220.
24 PRO FO 369/5. Casement to Sperling, 20 October 1906. The letter to Sperling bound within this despatch is dated 6 November 1906.
25 NLI 13081. Casement to Sir Edward Grey, 4 March 1907.
26 NLI 13074. Parry Papers. Casement to Gertrude Bannister, 1 April 1907.
27 PRO FO 369/63. 4 March 1907.
28 Private letter, Consuelo Keevil to R.M.S., 18 April 1972.
29 E. Hambloch, *British Consul: Memories of Thirty Years' Service in Europe and Brazil*, p. 74.
30 Private letter, Consuelo Keevil to R.M.S., 18 April 1972. An interesting aspect of this information is that its source was quite unaware of the possible sexual significance of the incident. Without Hambloch's account, and benefit of hindsight, sinister conclusions would not spring to mind and the anecdote would serve to show Casement's refusal to accept conventions of class.
31 PRO FO 369/64.
32 NLI 13074. Parry Papers. Casement to Gertrude Bannister, August 1907.

CHAPTER 6 FROM CONSUL TO CONSUL–GENERAL

1 PRO FO 369/199. Transferred to Santos, as from 29 February 1908, Charles B. Rhind only lived until 17 August. A despatch (519 of 5 January 1909) from Acting Consul Sandall, gave details of assets and claims against his estate, which revealed solvency. Rhind had bequeathed all property to his housekeeper, Mme Cecile Marion. The minutes sum up the situation: 'Funeral expenses came to £96.3.9.! We have only about £80 in hand which could go towards these expenses. The circumstances are discreditable. . .' and No. 35060 refers to 'his disreputable style of living'.
2 *Minutes of Evidence, Fifth Report of the Royal Commission on the Civil Service*, PP 1914–16 (Cd 7749) XI Q 38,633.
3 *Ibid*.
4 *Ibid*.
5 PRO FO 743/22.
6 PRO FO 128/324.
7 PRO FO 128/324. Casement to Milne Cheetham, 11 May 1908.
8 PRO FO 128/324.
9 *Brazil, Report for the Year 1907 on the Trade of Pará*. (Annual Series No.

4111. Diplomatic and Consular Reports) 1908 (C.3727–194). CIX.

10 *Minutes of Evidence, Fifth Report of the Royal Commission on the Civil Service*, PP. 1914–16 (Cd 7749) XI Q 42,565.

11 Subsequently described in M. Booth and G.M. Booth, *An Amazon Andes Tour*.

12 PRO FO 128/324. Casement to Milne Cheetham, 24 November 1908, a farewell letter, marked 'Private'.

13 *Ibid*.

14 PRO FO 128/324. Casement to Milne Cheetham, 4 June 1908.

15 NLI 13080. Casement to Lord Dufferin, 4 March 1908.

16 E. da Cunha, *Os Sertoes* ('Rebellion in the Backlands'). See especially p.xxlx.

17 PRO FO 128/324. Casement to Milne Cheetham.

18 NLI 13080. Casement to Lord Dufferin, 4 March 1908.

19 NLI 13074. Parry Papers. Casement to Gertrude Bannister, 6 March 1908.

20 PRO FO 369/198. Cheetham to Sir Edward Grey, 12 March 1909, Report on consulate-general at Rio de Janeiro.

21 *General Instructions for Her Majesty's Consular Officers*, 1893 edition, p. 15.

22 PRO FO 369/198. Cheetham to Sir Edward Grey, 12 March 1909: 'there has been no one at the Consulate in the last two years who knows the Portuguese language thoroughly.'

23 PRO FO 369/198. Casement to Sir Edward Grey, 2 November 1909.

24 PRO FO 369/196. Casement to Secretary of State, 7 September 1909.

25 PRO FO 369/196. Casement to Lord Dufferin, 2 August 1909.

26 PRO FO 369/196.

27 PRO FO 369/196.

28 PRO FO 369/196. Casement to Marine Department, London, 13 August 1909; Marine Department to Casement, 29 September 1909.

29 PRO FO 369/196.

30 PRO FO 369/196. Casement to Secretary of State, 20 September 1909.

31 NLI 13074. Parry Papers. Casement to Gertrude Bannister, 15 May 1908.

32 E. Hambloch, *British Consul: Memories of Thirty Years' Service in Europe and Brazil*, p. 72.

33 PRO FO 369/198.

34 Sir Roger Casement, *Ireland, Germany and the Next War*, Part 1.

35 G. de C. Parmiter, *Roger Casement*, pp. 93–6, from a letter of Casement's quoted in full. The headmaster, Mr W.A. Fullerton, wrote to the school's most famous old boy in May 1912, to ask him for a subscription. Casement, who was receiving an impressive amount of hospitality in Germany when the letter eventually reached him, replied in hostile vein. It was a school of the Protestant Ascendancy and was unaware that it had nurtured, as his closing words proclaimed, a 'very pronounced Irish Nationalist'.

36 PRO HO 161. Casement, Dollard's Diary for 1910, 12 March.

CHAPTER 7 THE PUTUMAYO: MISSION FOR A CONSUL-GENERAL EXTRAORDINARY

1 *Correspondence respecting the treatment of British Colonial Subjects and Native Indians employed in the collection of Rubber in the Putumayo District*. PP 1912–1913 (Cd 6266) LXVIII.

2 *Report and Special Report from the Select Committee on Putumayo, Proceedings, Minutes of Evidence*. 1913 (H. of C. Paper 148) XIV.

3 Lieutenant Maw, RN.

4 Lieutenant Herndon, United States Navy.

5 *Report and Special Report from the Select Committee on Putumayo, Proceedings, Minutes of Evidence*. 1913 (H. of C. Paper 148) XIV Q 11121.

6 *Ibid.*, Appendix No. 3.

7 R. Collier, *The River that God Forgot*, p. 49.

8 R. de Castro, *En El Putumayo y sus affluentes*, the diary of Eugenio Robuchon.

9 *Report and Special Report from the Select Committee on Putumayo, Proceedings, Minutes of Evidence*. 1913 (H. of C. Paper 148) XIV Q 12269.

10 W.E. Hardenburg, *The Putumayo: The Devil's Paradise*, an anthology of depositions and narratives, edited by Reginald Enock, with additional material from Casement's Putumayo Report.

11 Founded in 1877, initially *Truth* concentrated on society scandals and stock exchange irregularities. Encouraged by early successes it became recognized as 'the swindlers' scourge' and extended its range to include the most deserving causes.

12 *Report and Special Report from the Select Committee on Putumayo, Proceedings, Minutes of Evidence*. 1913 (H. of C. Paper 148) XIV Q 399.

13 PRO HO 161. Casement, Dollard's Diary for 1910, 22 May. (Date inserted by Casement as this diary did not provide for Sunday entries.)

14 *Ibid.*, 17 June.

15 *Ibid.*, 23 June.

16 PRO FO 371/722. Unsigned minute, 1 October 1909, dealt with by Rowland Sperling.

17 PRO FO 371/722, minute by Sperling, 7 October 1909.

18 PRO FO 369/198. George Pogson to Foreign Office, 9 June 1909.

19 PRO FO 369/198. War Office to Foreign Office, 30 July 1909, reference: 93871/23 (M.S.3.).

20 PRO HO 161. Casement, Dollard's Diary for 1910, 9 November.

21 What did not emerge in the Select Committee enquiry, but would have been powerful evidence for the existence of slavery in the Putumayo, was that Captain Whiffen purchased and took to Montserrat two girl slaves, Josephine and Theresea. They were baptized in St Anthony's Church, Montserrat on 19 December, 1909 (Baptismal Register, p. 48, nos. 378/9.) Josephine's granddaughter was working in the Cable and Wireless Office, Montserrat in 1976. Casement too, bought two Indians. (See page 93.)

22 PRO FO 371/722. Admiralty to Foreign Office, 12 November 1909.

23 *Morning Leader*, 27 September 1909.

24 Originally Colonel The Hon. R.H. Bertie, CB accepted leadership of the commission (despite Arana's protests that he might be unsuitable in the eyes of the Peruvian Government because of his official rank). He was taken ill on the voyage and had to return to England after reaching Manaos.

25 Some members of the Select Committee thought that the sudden transition from a basic salary of £150 pa to £1,000 pa might have sinister significance.

26 Peruvian Amazon Company to Under Secretary of State for Foreign Affairs, 8 June 1910.

27 *Minutes of Evidence, Fifth Report of the Royal Commission on the Civil Service*, PP 1914–16 (Cd 7749) XI Q 38,499.

28 PRO FO 369/198. Cheetham to Sir Edward Grey, 12 March 1909, Report on Consulate-General at Rio de Janeiro.

29 By 'Amazon' he meant 'Madeira'.

30 PRO FO 371/368. P.C. Knox, Department of State, Washington, to Secretary of State, 28 June 1910.
31 *Slavery in Peru*, House of Representatives Document.
32 PRO FO 161. Casement, Dollard's Diary for 1910, 23 July. Mrs G. was Alice S. Green; E.D.M. was Edmund D. Morel, Hon. Sec. of the Congo Reform Association.

CHAPTER 8 COMMISSION OF ENQUIRY

 1 Not only in the Dollard's Diary for 1910; Casement's Cash Ledger (PRO HO 161) has in its summary of January expenditure a brief list of gifts, including the entry: '4.7.0. Mrs Cazes'. 28 January has: '2 Photo Frames for Mrs Cazes 4.7.6.'
 2 PRO HO 161. Casement, Dollard's Diary for 1910, 3 September.
 3 *Ibid.*, 30 November.
 4 *Ibid.*, 1 September.
 5 PRO FO 371/968. Arthur Nicolson to Louis Mallet, 24 October 1910.
 6 A. Noyes, *The Accusing Ghost or Justice for Casement*.
 7 B. Hobson, *Ireland Yesterday and Tomorrow*, p. 82.
 8 Private letters, Florence Patterson to R.M.S., 1972–8.
 9 PRO HO 161. Casement, Dollard's Diary for 1910, 28 October.
10 NLI 13085–86. Casement, Putumayo Diary, 28 October 1910.
11 The other friend of Casement who remembered Casement's verbal reference to a perverted diary was P.S. O'Hegarty, quoted by W.J. Maloney, *The Forged Casement Diaries*, p. 198.
12 NLI 13085–86. Casement, Putumayo Diary, 5 October 1910.
13 *Ibid.*, 25 November 1910.
14 Private letter, Captain Roger Hicks, RN to R.M.S., 4 September 1978.
15 PRO HO 161. Casement, Cash Ledger for 1911, fly-leaf. This page was not reproduced in the Scotland Yard typed edition of the diaries and, consequently, has never been published.
16 PRO HO 161. Casement, Dollard's Diary for 1910, on blotter facing 16 and 17 September. This (pencilled) passage very nearly provides proof of the genuineness of this diary. Casement was in the habit of scribbling rough drafts of letters on the blotting pages (the diary has interleaved blotting pages throughout) and, according to René MacColl, *Roger Casement, A New Judgment*, p. 85, some of these sentences formed part of a letter dated 17 September 1910, received by Mrs Green (an unlikely accessory to forgery). Unfortunately the letter in question is missing from the Green Papers in the National Library of Ireland and, when approached, neither René MacColl nor Mrs Green's nephew and executor, Robert J. Stopford, was able to throw any light on its whereabouts.
17 'Quechua' is the term used in C.R. Enock, *The Andes and the Amazon*, p.138, which Casement had read not more than two months previously.
18 NLI 13073. Note by Casement on letter to him from Charles Roberts, chairman of the Select Committee on the Putumayo, dated 6 June 1913.
19 PRO HO 161. Casement, Dollard's Diary for 1910, 12 November.
20 NLI 13085–86. Casement, Putumayo Diary, 31 October 1910.
21 J. Rothenstein, *Summer's Lease*, p. 16.
22 *La Prensa*, 10 February 1911.
23 PRO FO 371/1201. Enclosure no. 2 in Lucien J. Jerome's no. 41 of 29 March 1911. The London agents of the Inambari Pará Rubber Company were

Messrs Harrison and Crossfield of 49, Eastcheap, London, EC.

24 *The Times*, 17 February 1911.
25 PRO FO 371/1201. The Tambopata Rubber Syndicate had its London office with Messrs Anthony Gibbs and Sons, 22, Bishopsgate Street Within, London, EC.
26 PRO FO 371/1201. Casement to Spicer, 12 July 1911.
27 PRO FO 371/1201. Jerome to Casement, 9 June 1911.
28 Aguero, Fonseca, Jiminez, Montt, Normand, Aristides Rodriguez and Aurelio Rodriguez.
29 Alfredo Montt had, in addition to committing other crimes, murdered Aredomi's brother.
30 For example, those of E. Hambloch, *British Consul: Memories of Thirty Years' Service in Europe and Brazil*, p. 147 and B. Thomson, *Queer People*, pp. 91–2. Thomson was Assistant Commissioner of Metropolitan Police at the time of the Easter Rising and, with his friend Captain Hall, Director of Naval Intelligence, interrogated Casement on his arrival at Scotland Yard in April 1916.
31 Twenty-four million acres of Putumayo territory were ceded to Colombia during the second term of office of President Augusto Leguia.
32 NLI 13085–86. Tizon to Casement, 29 September 1910.
33 Alapno Lopes, Aurelio Rodriguez, Homero Rodriguez and Pablo Zumaeta. The latter, far from being in disgrace, was at this time made acting mayor of Iquitos; as late as 4 June 1914, a despatch from Ernest Rennie, British Minister in Lima (PRO FO 371/2082) refers to Arana's brother-in-law as 'Mayor Senor Zumaeta of Iquitos'.
34 PRO FO 95/776. Casement to Sir Edward Grey, 19 June 1911.
35 R. MacColl, *Roger Casement, A New Judgment*, p. 96.

CHAPTER 9 THE PUTUMAYO REPORT

1 *Report and Special Report from the Select Committee on Putumayo, Proceedings, Minutes of Evidence*. 1913 (H. of C. Paper 148) XIV Q 6294: Dickey to Gubbins, 8 January 1910.
2 *Report by His Majesty's Consul at Iquitos on his Tour in the Putumayo District*. Miscellaneous No. 6. 1913 (Cd 6678).
3 NLI 13074. Parry Papers. Casement to Gertrude Bannister, 1 September 1909.
4 J. Bryce, *South America, Observations and Impressions*, Chapter XI, Brazil.
5 Private letters, John Cadbury (William Cadbury's son) to R.M.S., April 1972.
6 The preacher was Canon Hensley Henson.
7 *Report from Select Committee on Putumayo, Minutes of Evidence*. 1913 (H. of C. Paper 148) XIV Q 4.
8 *Ibid.*, Q 399.
9 'David Serrano had been working for 8 years in his estate La Reserva. He had domesticated [civilised] the Jabayena indians, who have now become slaves to the terrible Peruvian syndicate.' *Provincia do Pará*, 4 June 1908.
10 The contents of what became known as 'The Black Box' (it was actually a tin trunk). Dr H.O. Mackey, author of several books on Casement, including *Roger Casement. The Secret History of the Forged Diaries*, told R.M.S. that the box was a malicious invention of John Horgan, who spoke of it to René MacColl (*Roger Casement, A New Judgment*, p. 284). However, a telegram

from the German Foreign Office to the German Embassy, Washington, signed by Zimmermann, contained a message over the signature 'Roger', which included the words 'tell Bigger, solicitor, Belfast (? to) conceal everything belonging to me' (6 November 1914, quoted in *Documents Relative to the Sinn Fein Movement*, 1921 (Cd 1108) XXIX). Francis Bigger was an old friend of Casement and did as requested, not knowing that the telegram had been intercepted and decoded by Room 40 O.B. (Naval Intelligence). Later the trunk was opened, when there was a need to find a suit of clothes for Casement to wear at his trial (the one he was wearing had been ruined when his boat capsized between the U.19 and the Irish coast) and, if Horgan's statement is to be believed, all was discovered and destroyed there and then. Among the papers, said to include many love letters, was at least one diary and it is unthinkable that others were not written during the years 1904–9.

11 Rocca was said to have demanded a loan to set up a printing business, Hardenburg to have demanded £7,000. Whiffen, when drunk in a London club, was persuaded to write an incriminating note in Spanish (a language which he did not properly understand) in which his price was £1,000; he became suspicious and tore it up, but Arana was able to produce it, carefully repaired, and enter it as evidence before the committee. In addition, Casement, though this was not put before the committee, was also supposed to have requested £1,000 when he first arrived in Iquitos. This allegation is alluded to in the *Minutes of Evidence, Report from Select Committee on Putumayo*, 1913 (H. of C. Paper 148) XIV Q 12324.

12 *Ibid.*, Q 1606.

13 *Ibid.*, Q 211.

14 *Ibid.*, Q 2919.

15 *Ibid.*, Q 2937.

16 Rhodes House Library, MS B.Emp. S22. G344. Casement to Charles Roberts, 4 January 1913.

17 PRO HO 161. Casement, Dollard's Diary for 1910, 12 August: 'Pogson *is* an ass!' and again later on the same day, 'He *is* an ass.'

18 *Report and Special Report from Select Committee on Putumayo, Proceedings, Minutes of Evidence*. 1913 (H. of C. Paper 148) XIV Q 13405.

19 *Ibid.*

20 *Ibid.*, Q 390.

21 *Ibid.*, Q 393.

22 *Ibid.*, Q 627.

23 One director, Sir John Lister Kaye, had been a friend of Sir Francis Bertie for forty years. In 1914 he asked Bertie (ambassador in Paris at the time) for a reference. Bertie declined, as diplomatic etiquette demanded, and added that the Putumayo was another reason which made it impossible for him to oblige. Related in PRO FO 800 (Series B) 1914, Bertie to Tyrrell, 26 January 1914.

24 *The Anti-Slavery Reporter*, series VI, vol. 12, pp. 8–9, November 1976.

25 Notably *The West Coast Leader* of 11 November 1913 on the subject of Normand.

26 *Fifth Report of the Royal Commission on the Civil Service*, PP 1914–16 (Cd 7748) XI (p. 40).

27 *Report of the Committee appointed to inquire into the Constitution of the Consular Service*, PP (Cd 1634) LV.

28 *Fifth Report of the Royal Commission on the Civil Service*, PP 1914–16 (Cd 7748) XI (Part II, Chapter V. vi).

29 *Fourth Report of the Royal Commission on Civil Establishments*, PP 1890 (Cd 6172) XXVII.
30 *Report from the Select Committee on Putumayo*, 1913 (H. of C. Paper 148) XIV Appendix No. 5, Memorandum on the Slave Trade Acts by Guy Stephenson, Assistant Public Prosecutor.
31 *Ibid.*, Q 2845 (part of Casement's answer to a question put to him by Sir Thomas Esmonde).

CHAPTER 10 IRELAND AND GERMANY

1 Alfred Noyes Papers. Casement to John H. Morgan, 18 December 1912.
2 Alfred Noyes Papers. Casement to Morgan, 26 May 1913.
3 Alfred Noyes Papers. Casement to Morgan, 13 May 1913.
4 Sidney Parry: a Roman Catholic friend of Gertrude Bannister who married her after her cousin's execution. He had rubber interests in the City.
5 Alfred Noyes Papers. Casement to Morgan, 20 May 1913.
6 Alfred Noyes Papers. Casement to Morgan, 26 May 1913.
7 Morgan was by this time Professor of Constitutional Law at the University of London. His *The New Irish Constitution* had been published in London in 1912; he was editor and principal contributor.
8 Alfred Noyes Papers. Casement to Morgan, 3 June 1913.
9 Alfred Noyes Papers. Casement to Morgan, 4 June 1913 (delivered by hand by Casement on 4 June). Morgan was trying to help Ireland in his own, constitutional, way and this letter from Casement bears an interesting pencilled note on the back page in Morgan's hand:
'The amendment
"That the Assembly receives the memorial, & with regard to the question of H. Rule the Assly reaffirms the unanimous decision of last year – namely, the Assly considers that the views of the vast majority of the Presbyterians of Ireland received suffict expression at the Presbyterian Convention held in Belfast on 1st Feb. 1912 & does not consider it necy to make any pronouncement on the subject at present" '.
10 At this stage in his development, Casement frequently places Ulster in quotation marks, as though seeking to deny its existence as a genuine entity.
11 Alfred Noyes Papers. Casement to Morgan, 21 August 1913.
12 Alfred Noyes Papers. Casement to Morgan, 29 August 1913.
13 Alfred Noyes Papers. Casement to Morgan, no date.
14 E. Hambloch, *British Consul: Memories of Thirty Years' Service in Europe and Brazil*, p. 145.
15 John Cadbury Papers. W.A. Cadbury, 'A Personal Statement', p. 2.
16 R.D. Casement, 'Ulster and Ireland', *Fortnightly Review*, November 1913.
17 Klein Papers. Casement to Father Nicholson, 16 March 1915 (from a copy). Major-General Julius Klein stated that his collection of Casement material, including MS letters to Father Nicholson, disappeared from his office while he was away on active service.
18 Winifred Myers (formerly the property of J.H. Morgan), purchased at Sotheby's on 15 July 1957. Casement to Richard Morten, 1 May 1914.
19 Casement, 'The Elsewhere Empire', *Irish Freedom*, February 1914.
20 *Irish Independent*, 5 October 1914.
21 *Documents Relative to the Sinn Fein Movement*, 1921 (Cd 1108). XXXIX.
22 Later Sir Francis Lindley, a diplomat who enjoyed a distinguished career. His

reminiscences, published as *A Diplomat off Duty* (1928), naturally made no mention of Casement.

23 PRO FO 95/776. Findlay to Sir Edward Grey, 31 October 1914. This particular group of records is simply a loose collection of letters, mainly handwritten. It came to light in December 1967.

24 PRO FO 95/776. Kitchener to Sir Edward Grey, merely dated '28th'.

30 *Documents Relative to the Sinn Fein Movement*. 1921 (Cd 1108) XXXIX.

26 *The Irish Soldier*, 16 October 1918, p. 2. Anonymous.

27 Klein Papers (from a copy). Father Nicholson to Julius Klein, no date.

28 *The Irish Soldier*, 16 October 1918, p. 2. Anonymous.

29 Klein Papers (from a copy). Casement to Father Nicholson, 8 February 1915.

30 *Documents Relative to the Sinn Fein Movement*. 1921 (Cd 1108) XXXIX.

31 Klein Papers (from a copy). Father Nicholson to Julius Klein, no date.

32 Klein Papers (from a copy). Casement to Father Nicholson, 25 February 1915.

CHAPTER 11 IMPRISONMENT AND TRIAL

1 Klein Papers (from a copy). Casement to Father Nicholson, 25 February 1915.

2 Klein Papers (from a copy). Casement to Father Nicholson, 14 March 1915.

3 Klein Papers (from a copy). Casement to Father Nicholson, 16 March 1915.

4 *Ibid*.

5 R. Monteith, *Casement's Last Adventure*, pp. 101–10.

6 Klein Papers (from a copy). Casement to Father Nicholson, 3 June 1915.

7 Daniel Julian Bailey. He had joined the Irish Brigade under the name 'Beverley'.

8 NLI 13088. Notes to Counsel.

9 The likeliest dates of arrival are 3 or 4 July 1895. Casement had intended to visit the Jephsons if he had a week or ten days to spare before his next Foreign Office posting; in fact he had a month.

10 Alfred Noyes Papers. Hegarty to Alfred Noyes, 28 May 1957.

11 H.O. Mackey, *Roger Casement, The Secret History of the Forged Diaries*, pp. 12–13.

12 Nevertheless, it should be added that when the prisoner was transferred to Brixton lice were found on him, as a result of his having worn his water-logged suit for so long.

13 Tape recorded interview with R.M.S., 20 February 1972.

14 A. Noyes, *The Accusing Ghost or Justice for Casement*, p. 91.

15 Klein Papers. Shaw to Julius Klein, 19 December 1934. The statement is reproduced in full as Appendix C.

16 G.B. Shaw, *A Discarded Defence of Roger Casement. With an introduction by Clement Shorter and an Appendix by Roger Casement*. A privately printed limited edition of twenty-five numbered copies. Copy no. 22, signed by Clement Shorter, is in the British Museum.

17 Casement thought this a good point; he noted that the sympathy for Germany expressed by his German friend, Kuno Meyer, was disapproved of by the English press because Meyer had been a professor in England.

18 Klein Papers. Shaw to Julius Klein, 19 December 1934.

CHAPTER 12 DIARIES AND DEATH

1 W.J. Maloney, *The Forged Casement Diaries*.
2 A. Noyes, *The Accusing Ghost or Justice for Casement*.
3 B. Thomson, *The Scene Changes*, p. 329.
4 H.O. Mackey, *Roger Casement: The Truth about the Forged Diaries*, p. 61.
5 D. Rudkin, 'Postface to "Casement" ', *The Listener*, vol. 89, no. 2289, pp. 171–2.
6 Thomson, op. cit., p. 276.
7 Tape recorded interview with R.M.S., 20 April 1972. This information also appears in the typescript of Singleton-Gates's unpublished work, 'Casement: A Summing-Up'.
8 *Ibid*.
9 Noel Harris Papers. The Archbishop of Canterbury (Dr Davidson) to The Rev. John Harris, 14 July 1916.
10 E.F. Baldwin, 'Herbert Ward, Explorer, Sculptor, War Worker', *Outlook*, CXXX, 8 February 1922, p. 227. Cited by B.L. Reid, *The Lives of Roger Casement*, p. 417.
11 Florence Patterson Papers. A copy in the hand of John Irvine. Casement to Elizabeth and Gertrude Bannister, 30 June 1916.
12 Father E.F. Murnane, priest of Holy Trinity, Bermondsey. Casement had known him before the mission to Germany.
13 D. Rudkin, *Cries from Casement as his Bones are Brought to Dublin*, p. 26.

APPENDIX A CONSULAR FUNCTIONS IN CASEMENT'S DAY

1 *Report from the Select Committee on Consular Service and Appointments*, PP 1857–8 (482) VIII.
2 *Fifth Report of the Royal Commission on the Civil Service*, PP 1914–16 (Cd 7748) XI.
3 Quoted in D.C.M. Platt, *The Cinderella Service: British Consuls since 1825*, p. 5.
4 *Minutes of Evidence, Fifth Report of the Royal Commission on the Civil Service*, PP 1914–16 (Cd 7749) XI Q 38,547.
5 *Ibid*., Q 38,546.
6 PRO FO 369/64. William Davidson to Sir Eric Barrington, 25 May 1907.
7 E. Hambloch, *British Consul: Memories of Thirty Years' Service in Europe and Brazil*, p. 79.
8 *Ibid*., Preface.
9 *Minutes of Evidence, Fifth Report of the Royal Commission on the Civil Service*, PP. 1914–16 (Cd 7749) XI Q 38,547.
10 *Ibid*., Q 38,240.
11 *Ibid*., Q 38,548.
12 *Ibid*., Q 38,576.
13 *Instructions to Consuls, Merchant Shipping and Seamen*, 1905 edition.
14 *Minutes of Evidence, Fifth Report of the Royal Commission on the Civil Service*, PP 1914–16 (Cd 7749) XI Q 38,602.

APPENDIX C G.B. SHAW TO JULIUS KLEIN

1 G.B. Shaw, *A Discarded Defence of Roger Casement. With an introduction by Clement Shorter and an Appendix by Roger Casement.*.

BIBLIOGRAPHY

❦

Abbreviations are the same as those used in the notes and references.

UNPRINTED SOURCES

(a) *Public Repositories*

Rio Legation Records containing correspondence with consuls:
  PRO FO 128/308
  PRO FO 128/315
  PRO FO 128/324
  PRO FO 128/334
  PRO FO 128/343
General Correspondence, Consular of the Foreign Office:
  PRO FO 2/64
  PRO FO 366/781
  PRO FO 369/4–5
  PRO FO 369/51
  PRO FO 369/63–4
  PRO FO 369/123–5
  PRO FO 369/196–9
  PRO FO 369/276–8
  PRO FO 369/355–6
  PRO FO 369/446–8
  PRO FO 629/9–12
  PRO FO 743/22
General Correspondence, Political:
  PRO FO 371/367–8
  PRO FO 371/722
  PRO FO 371/967–8
  PRO FO 371/1200–3
  PRO FO 371/1451–4
  PRO FO 371/1732–4
  PRO FO 371/2081–2
Correspondence, Christiania Legation:
  PRO FO 95/776

Correspondence, Paris Embassy:
  PRO FO 800 Series B 1914 188
The Casement Diaries:
  PRO HO 161 1901 War Office Army Book 153
                1911 Letts's Desk Diary
It was also found necessary to consult the MSS of the other three Casement
'Diaries', although they were published by Singleton-Gates in 1959 (See Published
Works, below). Singleton-Gates was working from a faulty typescript and the
published work contains many errors.
                1903 Letts's Pocket Diary
                1910 Dollard's Diary
                1911 Cash Ledger
Commander-in-Chief Memoranda Papers (India):
  PRO WO 31/823
Maloney Papers:
  NLI 5588
Cadbury Papers:
  NLI 8358
Hutton Papers:
  NLI 8602
Green Papers:
  NLI 10464 (2)
Casement (Misc.) Papers:
  NLI 13073
  NLI 13077
  NLI 13080–13081
Parry Papers:
  NLI 13074
Putumayo Diary, 1910:
  NLI 13085–13086
Brief and Notes to Counsel:
  NLI 13088
Hobson Papers:
  NLI 13158
Correspondence at Rhodes House:
  MS B.Emp.S22 G 344 Casement to Charles Roberts
Correspondence at British Library of Political and Economic Science (London
School of Economics):
  Morel F8 Casement Correspondence

(b) *Private Papers*

John Cadbury Papers, Birmingham:
  Cadbury, W.A., 'A Personal Statement', January 1916.
  'Further Note by W.A.C. on Roger Casement', March 1956.
Jephson Family Papers at Mallow Castle, Co. Cork:
  Miscellaneous correspondence.
Julius Klein Papers, Chicago:
  G.B. Shaw on Casement.
  Letters, Casement to Father Nicholson; only known copies (MSS believed
destroyed).
Alfred Noyes Papers, Lisle Combe, Isle of Wight (in possession of Hugh Noyes):

BIBLIOGRAPHY

MS letters and post cards, Casement to J.H. Morgan.
Letters from other researchers in the field, and Casement friends and relations.
Florence Patterson Papers at Crawfordsburn, Northern Ireland:
Correspondence, copies of, including Casement to Gertrude Bannister.

MATERIAL IN POSSESSION OF THE AUTHOR

Transcripts of tape recorded interviews:
with Allison, W.C., 24 March 1972
with King, A.E., 20 February 1972
with Klein, J., 10 June 1972
with Singleton-Gates, P., 20 April 1972
Typescripts:
Singleton-Gates, P., 'Casement: A Summing-Up'; it was the author's intention to
have it published in London in 1966.
O'Donoghue, F., 'Kerry in the Easter Rising, 1916', possibly to be published in
Tralee.
The following correspondents provided information, much of it hitherto
unknown:

Africa	Oliver G. Morel, Mrs R.C. Morel
South America	Consuelo Keevil
Ireland	Anne B. Casement, Charlotte Casement, Nuala Creagh, Brigadier Maurice Denham Jephson, Florence Patterson.
USA	William H. Allen
Germany	Major-General Julius Klein
England	John Cadbury, Noel Harris (son of the Rev. John Harris, Secretary of The Anti-Slavery Society), Captain Roger Hicks, RN, Sir John Rothenstein, Peter Singleton-Gates.

UNPUBLISHED FOREIGN OFFICE SOURCES MADE AVAILABLE BY THE FOREIGN OFFICE

Her Majesty's Protectorate Niger Coast. Major Sir Claude M. MacDonald, HBM
Commissioner and Consul-General, *Rules Governing the Employment of
Officers in the Protectorate Service*. No. 1, 1894.
General Instructions for H.M.'s Consular Officers, printed for the Foreign Office,
1893.
General Instructions for H.M.'s Consular Officers, printed for the Foreign Office,
1907.
*Instructions to Consuls relating to matters affecting the British Mercantile
Marine, under 'The Merchant Shipping Acts'*, printed for the Board of Trade,
1888. (The main Acts to which this referred were: Merchant Shipping Act, 1854,
Merchant Shipping Amendment Acts, 1855 and 1862, Merchant Shipping
(Colonial) Act, 1869, and Merchant Shipping Act, 1873.)
Instructions to Consuls, Merchant Shipping and Seamen, printed for the Board of
Trade, 1905.
Instructions relating to Naval Courts, issued by the Board of Trade, 1878, 1885,
1893, 1896, 1904 and 1912.
*Instructions for Guidance of Naval Officers employed in the Suppression of the
Slave Trade*, 1892.

BIBLIOGRAPHY

GOVERNMENT PUBLICATIONS

Report from the Select Committee on Consular Service and Appointments, PP 1857–8 (482) VIII.

Fourth Report of the Royal Commission on Civil Establishments, PP 1890 (Cd 6172) XXVII.

Report on the Administration of the Niger Coast Protectorate, August 1891 to August 1894, PP 1895 (Cd 7596) LXXI.

Report on the Administration of the Niger Coast Protectorate, 1894–95, PP 1895 (Cd 7916) LXXI.

Report of the Committee appointed to inquire into the Constitution of the Consular Service, PP 1903 (Cd 1634) LV.

Correspondence and Report from His Majesty's Consul at Boma respecting the Administration of the Independent State of the Congo, PP 1904 (Cd 1933) LXII.

Further Correspondence respecting the Administration of the Independent State of the Congo, PP 1904 (Cd 2097) LXII.

Correspondence respecting the treatment of British Colonial Subjects and Native Indians employed in the collection of Rubber in the Putumayo District, PP 1912–13 (Cd 6266) LXVIII.

Report by His Majesty's Consul at Iquitos on his Tour in the Putumayo District. Miscellaneous No. 6, 1913 (Cd 6678) LI.

Report and Special Report from the Select Committee on Putumayo, Proceedings, Minutes of Evidence. 1913 (H. of C. Paper 148) XIV.

Fifth Report of the Royal Commission on the Civil Service, PP 1914–16 (Cd 7748) XI.

Minutes of Evidence, Fifth Report of the Royal Commission on the Civil Service, PP 1914–16 (Cd 7749) XI.

Documents Relative to the Sinn Fein Movement, 1921 (Cd 1108) XXIX.

OTHER OFFICIAL PUBLICATIONS

Belgium: *Congo Free State*, Bulletin Officiel, November 1905.
USA: *Slavery in Peru*, House of Representatives Document, Washington 1913.

ANNUAL REPORTS, CONSULAR

By Consul Cowper:
Brazil, Report for the Year 1879 on the Trade and Commerce of Santos. Commercial No. 42 (1880) (Trade Reports). Reports from Her Majesty's Consuls on the Manufactures, Commerce, etc., of their Consular Districts. Pt. VI. 1880 (C. 2701). LXXIV.

Brazil, Report for the Year 1888 on the Trade of Santos. (Foreign Office Annual Series No. 498. Diplomatic and Consular Reports on Trade and Finance). 1889. (C.5618–51). LXXVIII.

By Acting-Consul Hampshire:
Brazil, Report for the Year 1884 on the Trade and Commerce of Santos. Commercial. No. 17 (1885) (Trade Reports). Reports from Her Majesty's Consuls on the Manufactures, Commerce, etc., of their Consular Districts. Pt. V. 1884–5 (C.4444). LXXVIII.

BIBLIOGRAPHY

By Consul Casement:

Portugal, Report for the Year 1896 on the Trade and Commerce of Lorenzo Marques. (Foreign Office Annual Series No. 1904. Diplomatic and Consular Reports on Trade and Finance) 1897. (C.8277–122) XCII.
Brazil, Report for the Years 1905–06 on the Trade of Santos. (Annual Series No. 3952. Diplomatic and Consular Reports) 1908 (C.3727–35) CIX.
Brazil, Report for the Year 1907 on the Trade of Pará. (Annual Series No. 4111. Diplomatic and Consular Reports) 1908 (C.3727–194). CIX.

NEWSPAPERS AND PERIODICALS

(Only journals cited in the text, or containing articles or letters having a direct bearing on the argument, are listed).
With contributions by Casement (see also bound anthologies of his political articles, below):
United Irishman, Dublin, 25 February 1905, 'Kossuth's Irish Courier', signed 'X': about Roger Casement, Senior.
Nation, Dublin, 29 July 1911, a letter, signed 'A Catholic Reader'.
Irish Review, Dublin, July 1913, 'Ireland, Germany and the Next War'.
Fortnightly Review, London, 1 November 1913, 'Ulster and Ireland'.
Irish Freedom, Dublin, March 1914, 'The Elsewhere Empire'.
Irish Independent, Dublin, 5 October 1914, letter urging support for Germany rather than Great Britain in European War.
Other periodicals, cited or of general relevance:
Anti-Slavery Reporter, The, London, November 1976; report of 1974 attempt by Survival International to buy remaining 120 Andoke rubber-gatherers out of debt-bondage.
Catholic Bulletin, Dublin, January–December 1928; narrative of experiences of member of Casement's Irish Brigade, McKeogh.
Express, Daily, London, 10 June 1916; Casement described as 'extremely degenerate traitor'.
Irish Press, The, Philadelphia, 13 December 1919 – 13 March 1920 (weekly instalments): Agnes Newman (Casement's sister), 'Life of Roger Casement, Martyr in Ireland's Cause'.
Irish Soldier, The, Dublin, 16 October 1918, anonymous, 'Further Disclosures about Casement's Irish Brigade'.
Irish Times, Dublin, 21 February 1937; assessment of Casement by Sir Basil Thomson.
La Prensa, Lima, 10 February 1911; allegations of abuse of natives by Inambari Pará Rubber Company.
La Sanción ('Sensation'), Iquitos, 1907: an irregularly published news-sheet, largely a collection of testimonies alleging atrocities committed by employees of what became the Peruvian Amazon Company. (*La Felpa* ('A Drubbing'), Iquitos, 1907–8: *La Sanción* under a new name.)
Listener, The, London, 8 February 1973, David Rudkin, 'Postface to "Casement" ': the authenticity of the Casement Diaries discussed.
Mirror, Daily, London, 7 December 1903; Casement praised.
Morning Leader, London, 27 September 1909; account of Peruvian Amazon Company's secretary's attempt to bribe reporter, Horace Thorogood.
New York Times, New York, 25 April 1916; report of interview with Captain H.G. Harrison, for whom Casement had been purser.

BIBLIOGRAPHY

O Jornal do Commercio, Manaos, 2 June 1908; account of alleged Peruvian atrocities.

Provincia do Pará, Pará, 4 June 1908; account of alleged Peruvian atrocities.

Threshold, Belfast, Spring–Summer, 1960, Roger McHugh, 'Casement: The Public Record Office Manuscripts'.

Times, Sunday, London, 6 December 1908, Peruvian Amazon Company advertisement (cited in Minutes of Select Committee on Putumayo, Q 1477).

Truth, London: 22 September 1909, pp. 663–6

29 September 1909, pp. 719–26

6 October 1909, pp. 781–3

13 October 1909, pp.846–7

27 October 1909, pp.971–4

3 November 1909, pp.1034–9

10 November 1909, pp.1103–4

Allegations of atrocities in the Putumayo.

In addition use was made of a traditional source of consular trade statistics, the *Brazilian Review*, Rio de Janeiro, and the mouthpiece of English interests in Brazil, *South American Journal*, London.

BOOKS

1 Collections of articles by Casement which appeared as books. Slight adjustments occurred in the selection of material, but in the main the books were combinations of the following titles:

'The Causes of War and the Foundation of Peace'

'The Keeper of the Seas'

'The Balance of Power'

'The Enemy of Peace'

'The Problem of the Near East'

'The Duty of Christendom'

'The Freedom of the Seas'

'Ireland, Germany and the Next War'

'The Elsewhere Empire'

The anthologies consulted were:

The Crime against Ireland and How the War may right it, no place, publisher or date given, but it was in fact published in Berlin by the German Foreign Office in 1915.

Ireland, Deutschland und die Freiheit der Meere und andere Aufsatze, Diessen, Jos. C. Huber, 1916.

The Crime Against Europe (collected and edited by H.O. Mackey), Dublin, C.J. Fallon, 1958.

2 Poetry by Casement:

Some Poems of Roger Casement (with an introduction by Gertrude Parry), Dublin and London, Talbot and T. Fisher Unwin, 1918: sixteen poems. The largest collection of Casement's poems (fifty-one) forms Part IV of Mackey's *The Crime Against Europe*, above.

3 Biographies of Casement:

Gwynn, D., *The Life and Death of Roger Casement*, London, Jonathan Cape, 1930.

Hyde, M.H., Introduction to *Trial of Sir Roger Casement*, London, William
   Hodge, 1960. This was intended to replace the earlier edition in the Notable

British Trial series (G.H. Knott, 1917) which, apart from being out of print, had suffered much from strict application of the Official Secrets Act.

Inglis, B., *Roger Casement*, London, Hodder & Stoughton, 1973.

MacColl, R., *Roger Casement, A New Judgment*, London, Hamish Hamilton, 1956.

Mackey, H.O., *The Life and Times of Roger Casement*, Dublin, C.J. Fallon, 1954.

Parmiter, G. de C., *Roger Casement*, London, Arthur Barker, 1936.

Reid, B.L., *The Lives of Roger Casement*, New Haven and London, Yale University, 1976.

4 Other published works, broadly grouped in accordance with their geographical relevance:

Africa

Anonymous ('A Belgian'), *The Truth about the Civilisation in Congoland*, London, Sampson Low, Marston, 1903.

Bentley, W.H., *Life on the Congo*, London, The Religious Tract Society, n.d.

Bentley, W.H., *Pioneering on the Congo*, London, The Religious Tract Society, 1900.

Glave, E.J.G., *Six Years of Adventure in Congo-Land*, London, R.H. Russell, 1893.

Jean-Aubry, G., *Joseph Conrad: Life and Letters*, London, Heinemann, 1927.

Lane, M., *Edgar Wallace: The Biography of a Phenomenon*, London, William Heinemann, 1938.

Middleton, D., *The Diary of A.J. Mounteney Jephson, Emin Pasha Relief Expedition, 1887–1889*, Cambridge University Press, 1969.

Puleston, F., *African Drums*, London, Victor Gollancz, 1930.

Wack, H.W., *The Story of the Congo Free State: Social, Political, and Economic Aspects of the Belgian System of Government in Central Africa*, New York, Putnam's Sons, 1905.

Ward, H., *A Voice from the Congo*, London, William Heinemann, 1910.

Ward, S., *A Valiant Gentleman*, London, Chapman & Hall, 1927.

South America

Bates, H.W., *Naturalist on the River Amazona*, London, John Murray, 1863.

Bello, J.M., *A History of Modern Brazil, 1889–1964*, Stanford University Press, California, 1966.

Bennett, F., *Forty Years in Brazil*, London, Mills & Boon, 1914.

Bernstein, H., *Modern and Contemporary Latin America*, New York, Lippincott, 1952.

Booth, M., and Booth, G.M., *An Amazon Andes Tour*, London, printed for the authors by Edward Arnold, 1910.

Bryce, James, *South America, Observations and Impressions*, London, Macmillan, 1912.

Burnes, E.B., *The Unwritten Alliance: Rio-Branco and Brazilian–American Relations*, New York and London, Columbia University, 1966.

Burton, I., *The Life of Captain Sir Richard Burton* (2 vols), London, Chapman & Hall, 1893.

Collier, R., *The River that God Forgot*, London, Collins, 1968.

da Cunha, E., *Os Sertoes* ('Rebellion in the Backlands'), Rio de Janeiro, F. Alves, 1902.

de Castro, R. (ed.), *En El Putumayo y sus affluentes* (the diary of Eugenio

Robuchon), Lima, publication made at the cost of the Peruvian Government, 1907.

Enock, C.R., *The Andes and the Amazon – Life and Travel in Peru*, London, T. Fisher Unwin, 1907.

Hambloch, E., *British Consul: Memories of Thirty Years' Service in Europe and Brazil*, London, George G. Harrap, 1938.

Hardenburg, W.E. (ed. C.R. Enock), *The Putumayo: The Devil's Paradise*, London, T. Fisher Unwin, 1912.

Kettle, Sir Russell, *Deloitte and Co., 1845–1956*, Oxford, printed privately at the Oxford University Press, 1958.

Maxwell, K.R., *Conflicts and Conspiracies, Brazil and Portugal 1750–1808*, Cambridge University Press, 1973.

Ireland

Biggs-Davison, J., *The Hand is Red*, London, Johnson, 1973.

Blanshard, P., *The Irish and Catholic Power*, London, Derek Verschoyle, 1954.

Boyd, E., *Ireland's Literary Renaissance*, Dublin, Figgis, 1916. (Revised, 3rd ed., 1968).

Dangerfield, G., *The Damnable Question: A Study in Anglo–Irish Relations*, London, Constable, 1977.

Eglinton, J., *Irish Literary Portraits*, London, Macmillan, 1935.

Green, Alice Stopford, *The Making of Ireland and its Undoing*, London, Macmillan, 1908.

Hobson, B., *Ireland Yesterday and Tomorrow*, Tralee, Anvil, 1968.

Jephson, M.D., *An Anglo-Irish Miscellany*, Dublin, Allen Figgis, 1964.

Lynch, F.M., *The Mystery Man of Banna Strand*, New York, Vantage, 1959.

Lyons, F.S., *Ireland Since the Famine*, London, Weidenfeld & Nicolson, 1971 (revised edition, 1973).

MacBride, M.G., *A Servant of the Queen*, London, Victor Gollancz, 1938.

McNeill, R., *Ulster's Stand for Union*, London, John Murray, 1922.

Marreco, A., *The Rebel Countess: The Life and Times of Constance Markievicz*, Philadelphia and New York, Chilton, 1967.

Miller, D.W., *Church, State and Nation in Ireland, 1898–1921*, Dublin, Gill and Macmillan, 1973.

Morgan, J.H. (editor and contributor), *The New Irish Constitution: An Exposition and Some Arguments*, London, Hodder & Stoughton, 1912. The introduction and Chapter I, 'The Constitution: A Commentary', are by Morgan. (Alice S. Green contributed Chapter VIII, 'Irish Nationality'.)

Norman, E.R., *The Catholic Church and Ireland in the Age of Rebellion, 1859–1873*, London, Longman, 1965.

O'Broin, L., *Dublin Castle and the 1916 Rising*, London, Sidgwick & Jackson, 1970.

O'Faolain, S., *The Irish: A Character Study*, New York, Devin-Adair, 1949.

O'Grady, S.J., *History of Ireland: The Heroic Period*, London, Sampson Low, Searle, Marston & Rivington and Dublin, E. Ponsonby, 1878 (Vol. 1 of 2 vols).

O'Hegarty, P.S., *The Victory of Sinn Fein*, Dublin, Talbot, 1924.

Redmond-Howard, L.G., *Sir Roger Casement: A Character Sketch Without Prejudice*, Dublin, Hodges Figgis, 1916 (published between Casement's arrest and execution).

Rudkin, D., *Cries from Casement as his Bones are Brought to Dublin*, London, BBC, 1974.

Sullivan, A.M., *The Last Serjeant*, London, Macdonald, 1952.
Yeats, W.B., *The Collected Poems*, London, Macmillan, 1950.

Germany
Blücher, Princess Evelyn, *An English Wife in Berlin*, London, Constable, 1920.
Blücher, Prince Gebhard Lebrecht, (ed. by his widow, Evelyn, Princess Blücher),
    Memoirs, London, John Murray, 1932.
Brownrigg, Sir Douglas, *Indiscretions of the Naval Censor*, London, Cassell,
    1920.
Corbett, Sir Julian, *History of the Great War, Naval Operations*, Vol. 1 to the
    Battle of the Falklands, December 1914, London, Longmans, Green, 1920.
Curry, C.E. (ed.), *Sir Roger Casement's Diaries, 'His Mission to Germany and
    the Findlay Affair'*, Munich, Arche, 1922.
Hoy, H.C., *40 O.B. or How the War was Won* (foreword by Sir Basil Thomson),
    London, Hutchinson, 1932.
James, Sir William, *The Eyes of the Navy*, London, Methuen, 1955.
Kahn, D., *The Codebreakers*, London, Weidenfeld & Nicolson, 1966.
Monteith, R., *Casement's Last Adventure*, Chicago, published by the author
    under the auspices of The Irish People Monthly, 1932. (Revised and enlarged
    edition, with foreword by Franz von Papen, Dublin, Michael F. Moynihan,
    1953.)
Prill, F., *Ireland, Britain and Germany: Problems of Nationalism and Religion in
    19th century Europe*, London, Macmillan, 1975.
Spindler, K., *Gun Running for Casement in the Easter Rebellion, 1916*, Berlin,
    August Scherl, 1920 (English translation, London, W. Collins, 1921).
Spindler, K., *The Mystery of the Casement Ship*, Berlin, Kribe-Verlag, 1931.
Stuart, F., *Der Fall Casement: Das Leben Sir Roger Casements und der
    Verleumdungsfeldzug des Secret Service*, Hamburg, Hanseatische, 1940.
Tuchman, B.W., *The Zimmermann Telegram*, London, Constable, 1959.

The Times History of the War, especially Vol. VIII (1916), London, 1914–21.

5 Books with direct or indirect bearing on Casement's diaries:
Howgrave-Graham, H.M., *Light and Shade at Scotland Yard*, London, John
    Murray, 1947.
Lasswell, H.D., *Propaganda Technique in the World War*, London and New
    York, Kegan Paul, Trench, Trubner, 1927.
Mackey, H.O., *Roger Casement: The Secret History of the Forged Diaries*,
    Dublin, Apollo, 1962.
Mackey, H.O., *Roger Casement: The Truth about the Forged Diaries*, Dublin,
    C.J. Fallon, 1966.
Maloney, W.J., *The Forged Casement Diaries*, Dublin, Talbot, 1936.
Noyes, A., *The Accusing Ghost or Justice for Casement*, London, Victor
    Gollancz, 1957.
Ponsonby, A., *Falsehood in War-Time*, London, Allen & Unwin, 1928.
Singleton-Gates, P., and Girodias, M., *The Black Diaries* (limited edition
    containing 1911 Cash Ledger, in addition to 1903 and 1910 Diaries), Paris,
    Olympia, 1959.
Stuart, Sir Campbell, *Secrets of Crewe House*, London, Hodder & Stoughton,
    1920.
Thomson, Sir Basil, *Queer People*, London, Hodder & Stoughton, 1922.
Thomson, Sir Basil, *The Scene Changes*, London, Collins, 1939.

BIBLIOGRAPHY

6 General:

Birkenhead, The First Earl of, *Famous Trials of History*, London, Hutchinson, 1926.

Birkenhead, The Second Earl of, *F.E., The Life of F.E. Smith, First Earl of Birkenhead*, London, Eyre & Spottiswoode, 1959. (A fuller treatment than the author's first biography of his father, published, 2 vols, in 1933 and 1935.)

Devoy, J., *Recollections of an Irish Rebel*, New York, Chas. P. Young, 1929.

Ewing, A.W., *Man of Room 40: The Life of Sir Edward Ewing*, London, Hutchinson, 1939.

Gill, W.W., *A Third Manx Scrapbook*, London, Arrowsmith, 1963.

Green, J.R., *The Making of England*, London, Macmillan, 1882.

Green, J.R. (ed. A.S. Green), *The Conquest of England*, London, Macmillan, 1883.

Henrick, B.J., *The Life and Letters of Walter H. Page*, London, William Heinemann, 1930.

Higham, C., *The Adventures of Conan Doyle*, London, Hamish Hamilton, 1976.

Hyde, M.H., *The Other Love*, London, Heinemann, 1970.

Jenkins, R., *Asquith*, London, Collins, 1964.

Kneen, J.J., *The Personal Names of the Isle of Man*, London, Oxford University Press, 1937.

Kossuth, L., *Meine Schriften aus der Emigration*, (3 vols) Pressburg and Leipzig, C. Stampfel, 1880–2. (Volume 3 contains the references to Casement's father.)

Monger, G.W., *The End of Isolation: British Foreign Policy, 1900–1907*, London, Nelson, 1963.

Nevinson, H.W., *Last Changes, Last Chances*, London, Nisbet, 1928.

Platt, D.C.M., *The Cinderella Service: British Consuls since 1825*, London, Longman, 1971.

Reading, The Second Marquess of, *Rufus Isaacs, First Marquess of Reading* (vol. 2, 1914–35), London, Hutchinson, 1945.

Rothenstein, Sir John, *Summer's Lease*, London, Hamish Hamilton, 1965.

Rothenstein, W., *Men and Memories*, vol. 2, London, Faber & Faber, 1932.

Seely, J.E.B., *Adventure*, London, William Heinemann, 1930.

Shaw, G.B., *A Discarded Defence of Roger Casement. With an Introduction by Clement Shorter and an Appendix by Roger Casement*, London, limited edition of twenty-five copies privately printed for Clement Shorter, 1922.

Steiner, Z., *The Foreign Office and Foreign Policy, 1894–1914*, Cambridge University Press, 1969.

7 The following works of reference were also useful:

The Colonial Office List
Directory of Dublin
The Foreign Office List and Diplomatic and Consular Year Book
The Girls' School Year Book
The Navy List
Who's Who
Who Was Who

INDEX

Aberdeen, Seventh Earl of, and Countess Aberdeen, 24
Acré Territory, 69
Advance (boat), 22
Afghans, 12
African International Association, later International Association, eventually Congo International Association, 21
Aguero, 94
Akpania, Chief of, 27, 28
Alarco, Abel, 79, 80, 82
Aldred, Thomas, 60
Aldred, William, 60
Allen, Ben, 136, 140
Allison, William Charles, 24
Allison, W. J. and Company Ltd, 24
Amazonas, 68
Amazon river basin, 59, 60, 67, 69, 70, 77–97, 98, 101, 107, 113
Amerindians, 69, 73, 74, 77, 78, 79, 80–1, 82, 88–9, 91–2, 93, 95, 96, 100, 103, 106–7, 146
Anang, King of, 26
Andes, 69, 79, 96
Andes and The Amazon, The (Reginald Enock), 86
Andoke Indians, 78, 107
Anglo-Irish literature, 44–6
Anti-Slavery Society, 82, 84, 86, 89, 94, 101, 106, 140, 147
Antrim, Glens of, 42–7, 111, 113, 119, 145
Arana, J.C. and Hermanos (company), 79, 101
Arana, Julio César, 69, 78–9, 80, 81, 83, 86, 87, 88, 89, 96, 100, 101, 102, 103, 106, 107
Arana, Lizardo, 79, 80
Arbour Hill Military Barracks, 126
Ardrigh (Francis J. Bigger's house), 112
Aredomi (or Pedro, or Ricudo), 93
Argentina, 85
Atahualpa (river steamer), 92
Atkin, Mr Justice, 134
Atkinson, L.H., 73
Attorney-General, The, *see* Sir Frederick E. Smith
Aud (ship), 125
Australia, 144
Avory, Sir Horace, 132

Bachelor's Walk, 115
Bailey, Daniel Julian, 123, 125, 128
Bailey, The Hon. A., 37
Baldwin, Stanley, 140
Ballinderry, 10
Ballycastle, 42, 82
Ballýmena, 43
Ballymena Academy (formerly Church of Ireland Diocesan School, Ballymena), 17, 73, 75
Ballymoney, 113–14
Banco do Brazil, 74
Bannister, Edward (Gertrude's father), 18, 19, 35
Bannister, Edward (Gertrude's brother), 18
Bannister, Elizabeth (or 'Eily', Gertrude's sister), 18, 142, 143
Bannister, Gertrude (C's cousin, later married Sidney Parry), 18, 24, 25,

62, 64, 127, 129, 140, 142, 143

Bannister, Grace (née Jephson, Gertrude's mother), 18, 142

Barbadians, 82, 84, 88, 89, 90, 92, 100, 103, 104, 106

Barbados, 70, 82, 93, 98, 99, 101

Barclay, Colville, 60

Barnes, Louis H., 84, 87

Barrington, Sir Eric, 41

Barry, Brian, 73, 75, 86, 105

Bates, Henry Walter, 68

Belem, see Pará

Belfast, 42, 64, 111, 112, 113, 139

Belgian Commission of Enquiry (Congo), 36, 40; preliminary reply to C's report, 40; Report on Congo Free State, 49, 50

Belgium, 20, 21, 36, 37, 121, 124

Bell, E.S., 83

Benburb (poem by C.), 45

Benedetti, Antonio, 40–1

Bentley, Reverend W. Holman, 23, 39

Berlin, 117, 118, 120, 125; Conference of, 36

Bernstorff, Count Johann Heinrich von, 115, 118

Berry, Desmond, 49

Berry, Colonel R.G.J.J., and Mrs Berry, 48–9, 70

Betham, Sir William, Ulster King-at-Arms, 12

Bethmann-Hollweg, Theobald von, 117

Bigger, Francis Joseph, 47, 48, 139

Bishop, Frederick, 90

Black Box, 139

Blackwell, Sir Ernley, 139, 141

blancos, 82, 88

Blaney Castle, County Monaghan, 73

Blücher, Count (later Prince) Gebhard von, 117

Blücher, Countess (later Princess), née Evelyn Stapleton-Bretherton, 117, 125

Bluebell, HMS, 125

Board of Trade, 68, 74, 106

Bodkin, Archibald H., 132

Boer War, see South African War

Boma, 35, 41

Bompoli, 39

Bonny, SS, 20

Booth, George, 69

Booth, Margaret, 69

Booth Steamship Company, 69

Boras Indians, 78

Bororo Indians, 73

Botocudo Indians, 74

Bourchier, Arthur, 27

Bourne, Francis Alphonsus, Roman Catholic Archbishop of Westminster (later Cardinal), 97, 143, 144

Bow Street Magistrates Court, 128

Branson, G.A.H., 132

Brazil, 23, 49, 55, 56, 66, 68, 70, 74, 75, 77, 85, 105

Brazilians, 62, 67, 70, 74

Brazilian Review, 61

British Association, 29

British South Africa Company, 30

Brixton Prison, 126, 128, 142

Brown, John, 83

Brussels, 35–6

Bryce, James, 99

Buckingham Palace, 49

Buenos Aires, 75, 82

Burrows, Captain Guy, 39

Burton, Richard, 62

Butler, Richard Austen (Home Secretary), 139

Buxton, Travers, 94, 101

buy-Irish campaigns, 24

Byward Tower, 127

Cadbury, William, 99, 114

Cadogan, Sir Alexander, 54

Calabar District, 25–8

Cambridge Apostles, 135

Campbell, Vice-Consul, 71

Canisius, E., 39

cannibalism, 26, 99

Canning, George, 54

Canterbury, Archbishop of, see Randall Thomas Davidson

Cape Colony, 30

Cape Gazette, 32

Cape Town, 34

Caqueta river, 77

Carabaya Region, 94

Cara-Paraná river, 77, 78, 79, 88

Carson, Sir Edward, 44, 112

Carsonism, 113

Cartwright, Chauncey W., 57, 58

Casemates (Number 2A), The Tower of London, 127

Casement, Agnes (C's sister, known as
'Nina'), 8, 14, 18, 24, 42, 143, 144
Casement, Anne (C's mother, née
Jephson); genealogy, 4–8; marriage,
1, 8, 14, 55; Roman Catholic
baptism (secret) of children, 17;
impact on C. of religious and social
background, 1–4; death, 15, 16, 17;
remembered by C. in death cell, 142
Casement, Anne Beatrice, 6
Casement, Charles William Jephson (a
brother of C.), 8, 15, 18, 99, 144
Casement, Charlotte, 10
Casement, George, 10
Casement, Hugh (son of George), 10,
20
Casement, John, 14, 17, 18, 20
Casement, Roger (C.'s father): Grand
Tour, 12; India: cornetcy in Third
Dragoon Guards, 12, temporary
orthodoxy in imperial service, 12;
Kossuth helped by, contribution to
Hungarian independence, 13–14;
marriage, 1, 8, 14, 55; North Antrim
Militia, commission in, 14;
self-effacement, 14; spiritualist
leanings, 15; death, 15
Casement, Roger David: antecedents:
ancient origins of family, 9; early
forms of family name, 9, 10;
genealogy (and C.'s interest in),
4–16; mixed marriage of parents, 1,
8, 14, 55; Roman Catholic relatives,
8–9; Ulster influences, 2, 42–52;
Unionist background, 2, 12
anti-slavery activities, 38–41,
77–92; see also Slavery
awards: Queen's South African
Medal, 35; Companion of the
Order of St Michael and St George,
49; knighthood, 97, 131, 132;
repudiates and returns; insignia,
117; degraded from, 134
childhood and early career: born
near Kingstown, County Dublin,
1; secret Roman Catholic baptism,
17–18; orphaned, 15, 17; ward in
Chancery, 17; schooling, 17;
school holidays, 18–19; moves
into Bannister household,
Liverpool, 18; Anglican
confirmation, 19; Elder Dempster

Line, shipping clerk, 20; three
journeys to Africa as purser, 20;
employee of International
Association (Congo), 20–1;
member of Sanford Expedition,
21–3; directs survey of
Matadi-Stanley Pool railway line,
23; temporary lay missionary, 23;
directs construction of
Matadi-Stanley Pool railway line,
23
Civil Service in Nigeria (Oil Rivers
Protectorate): surveyor, 25;
Assistant Director-General of
Customs, 25; General Service
Officer, 28; First Nigerian
expedition, 26–7; Second
Nigerian expedition, 27–8; Third
Nigerian expedition, 28
consular service: Lorenzo Marques,
30–3; South African War service,
34–5; St Paul de Loanda, 34;
Kinchasa/Boma, 35–9; Santos,
56–63; Pará, 65–70; promoted to
Consul-General, Rio de Janeiro,
70; on special service in Putumayo
Territory, 77–92, 98–9; attitude
to honorary consuls, 60, 66, 98,
103, 105, 106, 107; considers
resignation, 41, 64, 70; resigns,
112; see also Congo, Consular
Service, Foreign Office, Putumayo
Territory (river basin)
German venture: visits United States
of America to arrange, 115;
'Findlay Affair, The', 116,
119–20; Irish-German 'Treaty',
117, 134; attempts to recruit Irish
Brigade, 61, 115, 117–24;
embarks for Ireland in submarine,
125
Irish Separatism: seen as Ireland in
microcosm, 1–4; development of
commitment to Separatism, 19,
24, 42–52, 75, 76, 90–2, 109–25,
130–1, 135, 146–7; language and
other cultural revival movements,
42–9, 64, 119; leaves (consular),
influences and activities during,
42–9, 64, 75, see also Antrim,
Glens of; first separatist speech, at
Ballymoney, 113–14; arrested, 125

Norwegian experiences: British Minister attempts to capture, 116; Christensen, Adler, seen as double agent, 116; Open Letter to Sir Edward Grey, 115

personal attributes: derived from family difficulties, *see* Magherintemple (and for destruction of personal papers); generosity/meanness, 60, 126; and Santos Charitable Appeal (Appendix B), 156; interest in archives and clerical matters, 32, 57–9, 62, 65–6, 71, 76; religious attitudes and reconciliation, 17–19, 143–4; sexual proclivities, 1–2, 4, 30, 37, 75, 86, 102, 116, 137, 145; social insecurity, 1–4, 37, 43, 55–6, 146; sudden fame, effect of, 41, 50; travel, belief in, 66–7, 69, 85

physical ailments, 30, 33, 42, 70, 71, 109, 122, 123, 125

reports (published): despatches to The Commissioner, Oil Rivers Protectorate: account of first Nigerian expedition, 26–7; account of second Nigerian expedition, 27–8; Foreign Office, Annual Consular Reports: Lorenzo Marques, 32–3; Santos, 61, 69; Pará, 68–9; Congo Report (White Paper), 23, 36, 39–40, 49–50; Putumayo Report (Blue Book), 93, 95–6, 98–100, 102, 106

reports (unpublished): Madeira-Mamoré Railway, 67; Pará Health, 67–8

suicidal intent and attempts, 117, 125–6, 127–8, 129–30

trial and execution: Tower of London, 44, 126–8, 140; Brixton Prison, 126, 128, 142; Pentonville Prison, 18, 134, 142; magisterial enquiry, 128; trial, 132–4; speech from dock, 134; appeal, 134; petitions for reprieve, 134 and Appendix D, 161; execution, 144

writings: articles, 13–14, 52, 114–15; consular reports, 23, 32–3, 39–41, 49–50, 61, 67–9, 93, 95–6, 98–100, 102, 106; letters, 4–6, 9, 23, 28, 30, 47, 60, 61, 62, 64, 67, 69, 70, 74, 75, 89, 94, 99, 104, 109–15, 118–24, 142–3; literary aspirations, 32; poetry, 45–6

Casement, Mrs Thomas (Blanche), 144
Casement, Thomas Hugh (a brother of C.), 8, 15, 18, 99, 109, 144
Casement, General Sir William, 11
Cathleen-ni-Houlihan (W.B. Yeats), 52
Catholic emancipation, 12
Cauca Valley Railroad, 81
Caucheros (rubber-gatherers), 78
Cave, Sir George, 132
Cazes, David, 82, 83, 87, 92, 93, 98, 101, 103
Cazes, Mrs David, 93
Centenary of 1798 rebellion, 46
Chaplin, Cornet, 13
Chapman, Arthur, 71–2, 102
Cheetham, Milne, 67, 71, 72, 85, 101; report on Rio de Janeiro Consulate-General, 71, 72, 85
Childers, Erskine, 114
Chinese labour, 67
Christensen, Adler, 116, 117, 118, 119, 120, 145
Christian (Franciscan) mission, 96–7, 99, 100, 117
Christiania (now Oslo), 116, 118
Church of Ireland Diocesan School, *see* Ballymena Academy
Clark, Stephen, 142
Clan-na-Gael, 115, 116, 119
Cloghaneely Irish College, 64
Collins, Michael, 43, 144
Colombia, 69, 77, 78, 79, 81, 96, 100, 106
Colonial Office, 100–1, 103
Companion of the Order of St Michael and St George, 49
Companies Act, 100, 103, 106
Congo: allegations of atrocities in, 35, 36, 38, 41; C.'s expeditions in, 5, 21–3, 38–40, consular responsibility for, 35, investigations and achievement, 35, 38–41, 105–6, 146; *see also* Casement, Roger David; Foreign Office
Congo Free State, 36
Congo, French, 34, 35

Congo International Association, *see* African International Association

Congo Railway, 23, 67

Congo Reform Association, 41, 47, 50, 82, 84, 114

Congo Report (White Paper), 23, 36, 39–40, 49, 67; international repercussions of, 40, 106, 108

Connacht (Connaught), 112

Connemara, 'white Indians' of, 92, 110

Conrad, Joseph, 22, 51

Consular Instructions (General Instructions for H.M.'s Consular Officers), 31, 55, 58–9, 65, 72, 74, 101–2, 146, 147

Consular Service: attempted definition of functions of consul, 50, 61, 74 and Appendix A, 149; distinct from Diplomatic Service, 31, 53–4, 144; effect on C., 76, 144; emoluments, 54; possible extension of obligations into international humanitarian field, 103, 105–6, 147; problems of climate and language, 31, 54–5, 72; rights in Portuguese dominions, 65; social obligations of consuls, 54, 72, 76; *see also* Casement, Roger David; Foreign Office

Consular Service, Departmental Committee, 54

Consular Service, Royal Commission on the Civil Service (and C.'s testimony), 107–8 and Appendix A, 149

Consulate-Legation records, 76

Consulate of Great Britain and Ireland, 52, 61

consuls, honorary, 60, 66, 98, 103, 105, 106, 107

Coquilhatville, 40

Cork, 126

Correrias, 78

Corumba, 73

Costa, Carlos Augusta, 86

Counsel, Brief to, 51; Notes to, 126

Cowper, Francis, 54–5, 56

Cox, Miss, 64

Craig, A.W., Captain, R.N., 83

Craig, James (Lord Craigavon), 43

Criminal Appeal Act, 134

Cross river, 26, 28

Crossman, Richard, 137

Crotty, Father, 117–18, 124

Cuba, 67

Curragh incident, 114

Curran, John Philpot, 142

Cushendun, 43, 46, 47

Cuyubá, 73

da Cunha, Euclides, 70

Darling, Mr Justice, 134

Davidson, The Most Reverend Randall Thomas, Archbishop of Canterbury, 97, 140–1

Dawn (ship), 61

debt-bondage, *see* peonage

de Castro, Rey, 80

Delagoa Bay, 30, 34

Deloittes, 84

Denham, *see* The Savoy, Denham

Dennett, Richard Edward, 47

Devil's Paradise, The (Walter Hardenburg), 82

Devoy, John, 115, 119, 124, 129

Diaries, Black, 1, 9, 24, 30, 37–9, 42, 57, 75, 82, 83, 86, 87, 89, 90, 91, 92, 93, 102, 126, 132, 134–41; *see also* Casement, Roger David (under personal attributes, sexual proclivities)

diary of Sir Basil Thomson, extracts from (published in his autobiography, *The Scene Changes*), 137

Dickey, Dr Herbert Spencer, 98

Dickinson, Willoughby, 101–2, 105

Dilke, Charles, 82

Dobbs, Margaret (of Castle Dobbs), 44, 47, 143

Don Pedro, Emperor, 75

Dormer, Cecil Francis, 57

Doyle, Sir Arthur Conan, 140

Doyle, Michael Francis, 129

Dryhurst, Sylvia, 44

Dual Monarchy, 13, 62

Dublin, 42, 46, 82, 90, 109–11, 114, 123, 125, 126, 132, 144

Dufferin, Lord Terence, 70

Duffy, George Gavan, 128, 129

Duggan, Eamon, 144

Easter Rising, 124–5, 129, 131, 141

Eberhardt, Charles C., 81

Ebury Street, London, 109

Ecuador, 69, 77, 78, 85
Edgcumbe, Lady, 37
Edinburgh Castle (ship), 86
Edward VII, King, 49
Egypt, 131, 134
Eisteddfod, 46, 51
El Comercio (newspaper), 78
Elder Dempster Line, 20, 35
El Encanto, 81, 88, 92, 98
Elsewhere Empire, The (Roger David Casement), 114
Emin Pasha (Relief Expedition), 5
Enock, Reginald, 78, 86
Epondo Case, 39, 40
Esene, 27
Estado de São Paulo (newspaper), 56

Farquharson, The Hon. Louisa Elizabeth (of Invercauld Castle), 51
Feis (Irish Cultural Festival), 46–7, 49, 51, 119, 142
Feis-Ceoil (Irish Folk Music Festival), 46
Figgis, Darrell, 114
Findlay, Mansfeldt de Cardonnel (and 'The Findlay Affair'), *see* Casement, Roger David
Fletcher, Vice-Consul, 68
Fonseca, Innocente, 94
Foreign Office (British): administration of Oil Rivers Protectorate (Nigeria), 25; attitude to consuls, 31–2, 53–4, 72, 108; clerical inefficiency, 57–9, 62; Congo, atrocity file, 41, report (White Paper), 23, 36, 39–40, 41, 49–50; mishandling of C.'s Haiti and San Domingo appointment, 64, 76; Norwegian incident ('The Findlay Affair'), *see* Casement, Roger David; Putumayo Report (Blue Book), 93, 95–6, 98–100, 102, 106; response to allegations about British registered rubber companies other than the Peruvian Amazon, 94; retrospective alteration of C.'s terms of reference, 104; toning down of despatches and reports, 39, 50, 69; *see also* Casement, Roger David; Congo, Consular Service
Foreign Office (German), 115, 116–17
Foreign Office Instructions, 72
forgery department, alleged, 137

Fox, W., 84, 87, 91
France, 105, 125
Funchal, 37

Gaelic League, 46
Gaelic Revival, 44; *see also* Irish dramatic movement; Irish language movement; Irish literary renaissance
Gaelic Society of London, 51
Gallipoli Campaign, 131
Garibaldi, Giuseppe, 130
genealogy, *see* Casement, Roger David (under antecedents)
Germany, 32–3, 48, 51, 75, 113–17, 122–5, 130, 131, 133, 135; declaration in favour of Irish independence, 118; Irish-German 'Treaty', 117, 134; *see also* Casement, Roger David
Ghost of Roger Casement, The (W.B. Yeats), 11
Gielgud, H.L., 84, 87, 88, 91
Gladstone, William Ewart, 29
Glave, Edward, 23, 35
Gomes, Senhor (Vice-Consul), 60–1
Gosselin, Sir Martin, 35
Grand Central Hotel, Belfast, 139
Grand Pará, 68
Great Britain: extension of responsibility for colonial peoples, 103; C.'s lack of genuine *pied à terre* in, 42
Greaves, Thomas, 66
Green, Alice Stopford, 47–8, 50, 62, 86, 110, 114, 119, 129, 139, 142, 146
Green, John Richard, 47, 114
Grey, Sir Edward, 49, 62, 82, 83, 84, 93–4, 95, 96, 97, 100, 117, 118
Griffith, Arthur, 13, 62
Guarujá, 63, 74
Gubbins, John Russell, 98
Guinness (the product), 61, 69

Haggard, Sir William, 14, 59, 60, 61, 67, 71, 72, 102
Haiti and San Domingo consul-generalship, 64, 76
Hambloch, Ernest, 63, 71, 74, 75, 108, 113
Hall, Captain Reginald (Director of

Naval Intelligence), 126, 136, 137, 140, 141
Hampshire, Acting Consul, 56
Humurummy, *see* Omarino
Hardenburg, Walter, 81–2, 83, 84, 85, 88, 102
Harmsworth, Alfred, 36
Harris, Noel, 140–41
Harris, Reverend (later Sir) John, 82, 86, 103, 140–41
Harrison, Captain H.G., 20
Hart-Davies, Thomas, 83
Hawksworth, Reverend Alan S., 58
Hegarty, D.J. ('Senex'), 126
Henry VIII, King, 6
Hewitt, James Albert, 74
Hibernia HMS, 116
Hicks, Lieutenant-Colonel F.R., 91
Hicks, Roger B.N., Captian R.N., 91, 139
Hilary (ship), 86
Hislop, James, 66
Hislop, Mary, 66
Hobson, Bulmer, 43, 45, 46, 47, 49, 62, 90, 115, 139
Holt, John, 35
Home Rule, 29, 45, 46, 49, 111, 112–13, 115, 118, 122, 133, 144
Home Rule Bill, 29
Horridge, Sir Thomas, 132
Howth, 114
Huayna (river steamer), 87
Hughes, Emrys, 137
Huitoto Indians, 78, 93, 106
Humphreys, Travers, 132
Hungarian independence, 13–14
Hyde, Douglas, 46
Hyde, Montgomery, 139

Ibiaku, 26
'Ide', *see* McNeill, Ada
Igara-Paraná river, 78, 79, 88
Ikoko, 39
Ikorasan, 27
Inambari Para Rubber Company, 94
India, 10, 11, 12–13, 37, 131
Indostan, 88
Inokun people, 26–7
International Association, *see* African International Association
In the Putumayo and its Tributaries (Eugenio Robuchon), 80

Iquitos, 80, 81, 82, 87, 89, 91, 92, 93, 96, 98, 99, 100, 105
IRB, *see* Irish Republican Brotherhood
Ireland: centenary of 1798 rebellion, 46; C.'s growing obsession with, 42–52, 109–25, 146–7; in C.'s consular reports, 33, 61–2, 69; seen by C. as link between Europe and America, 114–15
Irish agricultural co-operative movement, 47
Irish Brigade (in Germany), 61, 113, 115–25, 133–4
Irish Brigade (in South Africa), 34, 111
Irish dramatic movement, 46
Irish exports: lace, linen, poplin, whisky, 69
Irish flag, 91, 121–2
Irish language movement, 44–6, 64, 119
Irish Language, The (poem by C.), 45–6
Irish literary renaissance, 44, 64, 119
Irish Nationalists, 75, 114, 133, 148
'Irish Putumayo', 92
Irish Republic, 144
Irish Republican Brotherhood, 13, 122, 125; IRB Military Council, 125
Irish stowaways, 63
Irish Volunteers, 114, 115, 124, 125, 126, 133
Irish World (newspaper), 123
Italy: and Congo Free State, 36, 40; and Garibaldi, 130
Itu, 26

Jabayena Indians, 102
Jamaica, Governor of, 67, 68
James II, King, 5
Japanese Minister to Brazil, 73
Japura river (Brazilian name for Caquetá river), 77
Jephson, Anne, and Jephson genealogy, *see* Casement, Anne
Jephson, Grace, *see* Grace Bannister, wife of Edward
Jephson, Brigadier Maurice Denham, 6, 126
Jephson, Mounteney, A.J., 5, 21, 22
Jephson-Norreys, Louisa, 4, 6, 9, 29, 30, 126
Jephsons of Carrick-on-Suir, 6–8, 16

Jephsons of Mallow, 5–6, 7, 8, 11–12, 16, 29, 30, 37, 56; and treason, 5; ignorance about C.'s mother, 16; links with Plantagenets and Strongbow, 12
Jerome, Lucien J., 94, 96
John (pet dog), 37–8
John Bull, SS, 12
Johnston, Sir Harry, 39, 105–6, 147
Jones, Alfred, 20
Jones, Artemus, 128, 133
Joynson-Hicks, William, 104, 139

Keevil, Consuelo, 63
Keevil, John, 60, 63
Kerry, County, 125, 128
Kilcoole, 114
Kimberley, First Earl of, 25
Kinchasa, 35
King, A.E. (Corporal), 127–8
King, Guy T., 81–2
Kitchener, First Earl of Khartoum and of Broome, 116, 124
Klein, Julius, 120, 122
knighthood (C.'s), 97, 131, 132
Knatchbull-Hugessen, Sir Hughe, 54
Knox Little, H., 75
Kossuth, Lajos, 13–14
Krooboys, 27, 28
Kruger, President, 34
Kwo Ibo, 27
Kwo Ibo river, 27

La Chorrera, 79, 88, 89, 92
La Felpa (news-sheet, formerly *La Sanción*), 80–1, 102
Lamothe family, 9
Lansdowne, Fifth Marquess of, 37, 40
La Prensa (newspaper), 80, 94
La Reserva, 102
Larranaga Ramires, 79
La Sanción (news-sheet, later *La Felpa*), 80, 102
Las Palmas, 4, 37, 109
Laxey Wheel, 10
Lebensraum, 75
Lecocq, Madamoiselle, 72–3
Lecocq, Robert, 72–3
Le Cosmopolite Hotel, Iquitos, 87
Leinster, 33
Leopold II, King, 20, 21, 23, 35–6, 39 40, 49, 96, 110, 112

Leopoldina Railway, 75; Syndicate, 74
Lex Loci marriages, 58–9
Liberal (river steamer), 88, 91, 92
Lima, 69, 78, 80, 82, 94, 95, 96, 99, 101, 107
Limburg, 117, 118, 120, 122
Limerick Volunteers, 114
Lindley, Francis O., 116
Linthorpe (ship), 28
Lisbon, 34, 41, 49, 53, 55, 64, 70
Liverpool, 18, 70, 82
London and Brazilian Bank, 65
London and River Plate Bank, 60, 63
London University, 51
Lords, House of, 134
Lorenzo Marques, 30, 32–3, 34, 35, 56; C.'s annual consular report from 32–3
Loreto, 78, 89, 101
Lupton, Percy, 58
Lynd, Robert, 44, 142

MacBride, Major John, 34, 111
MacDonald, Sir Claude, 25, 27, 28–9
Macdonald, Sir Hector, 37, 138–9
Macdonell, Sir John, 37
MacDonnell Commission, 68
McGarrity, Joe, 115, 124
Mackey, Dr Herbert O., 139, 140
McLachlan, Donald, 137
McNeill, Ada ('Ide'), 43–4, 47, 143
MacNeill, Eoin, 46, 119
McNeill, Ronald (later First Baron Cushendun), 43–4
MacNeill, Swift, 80, 103
McNeills of Cushendun, 43
Madeira, 86
Madeira-Mamoré Railway, 23, 67, 81
Madeira river, 67, 68
Magherintemple, 6, 9, 14, 15, 17, 19, 20, 21, 22, 29, 30, 34, 35, 42, 43, 47, 64, 82, 126, 142, 143, 145, 146
Making of Ireland and its Undoing, The (Alice Stopford Green), 48
Malayan rubber plantations, 107
Mallet, Louis, 58, 94
Mallow Castle, *see* Jephsons of Mallow
Mallow Station, 126
Man, Isle of, 9, 10
Manaos, 68, 70, 80, 81, 86, 87, 93
Maranhaõ, 68
Mark, Francis, 56–7, 58

Matadi, 23
Mboye, 39
Meath, Church of Ireland Archdeacon of (Alice Green's father), 47
Michell, George B., 98, 99
Millar, 139
Milligan, Alice, 45, 47, 52, 142
Milner, Sir Alfred, 34
missionaries, 36, 94
Monroe Doctrine, 84, 99
Monteith, Robert, 124, 125
Montrose, Fifth Duke of, 37
Montserrat (British West Indies), 83
Montt, Alfredo, 94
Morel, Edmund D., 35, 41, 47, 50, 86, 96, 106, 109, 110
Morgan, John Hartman, 51, 109, 110, 111, 112, 113, 119, 128, 129, 134, 142
Morning Leader (newspaper), 84
Morrisson, Reverend, 39
Morten, May, 50, 51, 113
Morten, Richard, 50, 51, 91, 110, 113, 114, 142
Moses Room, 50–1, 112
Mounteney Jephsons, *see* Jephsons of Mallow
Mozambique, 30; Company, 70
muchachos, 82
Müller (spy), 137
Munich, 125
Munster, 33
Murnane, Father E.F., 143
Murphy, John B., 39
Murphy, Sergeant, 118

Napo river, 78
National African Company (later Royal Niger Company), 29
Netherlands Railway Line (South Africa), 34
New York, 122, 125
Nicholson, Father John T., 117–18, 119–20, 121, 122–3, 124
Nicolson, Sir Arthur, 89, 116
Nigeria, 4, 25–9, 30, 31, 32
Nordenflycht, Baron von, 75
Normand, Armando, 94; diary theory, 90, 136, 140
Norway, 116, 120
Noyes, Alfred, 24, 51, 90, 126, 136, 137, 140

Nuremberg, American War Crimes Commission at, 51

Ocaina Indians, 78
O'Donnell, 90–1, 98
O'Gorman, Father, 117–18
O'Grady, Standish, 44
O'Hegarty, P.S., 62
Oil Rivers Protectorate, *see* Nigeria
Oiritu, 30
Old Calabar, 25, 26, 27, 28
Oldham, Constance, 46
Olivier, Sir Sydney, 67
Omarīno (later Hamurummy), 93
O'Meara, Thomas, 74
O'Neill, 45
'O Paiz', special correspondent of Rio, 73
Opobo, 28
Opobo river, 26, 27
Oskar II (ship), 116
Oslo *see* Christiania

Palmerston, Third Viscount, 13
Pará, 55, 58, 64, 65–70, 76, 78, 83, 93, 99, 105; C.'s annual consular report from, 68–9, 85, 91; health and sanitation of, 67–8
Paraguay, 69
Paranagua, 60
Pardo, José, 80
Paredes, Dr Romulo, 90, 96, 98–9
Paris, 35, 74, 93, 94, 98, 139
Parisians, 62
Parminter, Alfred, 23, 35, 39
Parminter, W.G., 23
Parnell, Charles Stewart, 1, 142
Parry, Mrs Sidney, *see* Bannister, Gertrude
Parry, Sidney 110, 142
Patterson, Florence (Bulmer Hobson's sister), 46, 90
Peace Preservation Act, 113
Pedro *see* Aredomi
Pentonville Prison, 18, 134, 142
peonage, 77, 78, 79, 81, 107
Percy, Lord, 37
Perkins, W.B., 81, 85
Peru, 38, 69–70, 77, 78, 79, 80, 81, 85, 87–93, 94, 95, 96, 97, 99, 104, 107
Peruvian Amazon (Rubber) Company, 78–9, 80, 81, 82, 83, 84, 85, 88, 92,

94, 96, 98, 100, 101, 102–3; *see also*
Putumayo Territory (river basin)
Peruvian Commission to investigate
Putumayo, 90, 92, 96, 107
Peruvian Society for the Protection of
Indians, 94
Petropolis, 55, 58, 59, 67, 72, 73, 74,
75, 76, 102, 146
Philadelphia, 115
Phipps, Constantine, 35
Pickerell, American consul, 86, 105
Pickersgill, HM Consul, 39
Pisango (Pizarro), Simon, 91
Pius X, Pope, 80
Plunkett, Joseph, 122–3, 128
Plunkett, Sir Horace, 24, 47
Pogson, George, 83, 86, 105
Poole, Father, 18
Portglenone House, 45
Portglenone (poem by C.), 45
Portrush, 42
Portugal, 33–4, 35, 53; dominions of,
65, 93
Portuguese East Africa, 30–3
Portuguese language, 72
Portuguese West Africa, 34–5
Pretoria, 30, 34
Protestants, 'Black', 8, 12, 25, 55, 91;
Nationalist, 19, 42–4, 46, 114
Provincia do Pará (newspaper), 81
Public Prosecutor, 106
Puleston, Frederick, 23
Pullen, C.G., 71, 73
Putumayo Report (Blue Book), *see*
Casement, Roger David
Putumayo Territory (river basin), 14,
21, 77–93, 95–7, 98–9, 100, 106–7,
108, 140, 146, 147; allegations of
slavery in, 69, 76, 80–3, 84, 94,
100–2; investigation by Commission
of Enquiry, 84, 85, 86, 87–93; Select
Committee, House of Commons,
proceedings and report, 57, 77, 78,
79, 80, 84, 85, 87, 100–7, 147; *see
also* Casement, Roger David;
Peruvian Amazon (Rubber)
Company; Slavery

Queen Anne's School, Caversham, 143
Queen's South African Medal, 35

racionales, 82, 88

Rathlin islanders, 47
Reading, First Marquess of (Rufus
Isaacs), 132, 133
Redmond (family of John), 9, 115, 117,
118, 144; Redmondite, 118
Redmond-Howard, L.G. (nephew of
John Redmond), 8
Rennie, Ernest, 107
Republic, The, 44
Rhind, Charles B., 65, 146
Rhondda, 51
Rhyl, 17, 18
RIC, *see* Royal Irish Constabulary
Richhill Castle, 48–9, 70
Ricudo, *see* Aredomi
Rio-Branco, 85
Rio de Janeiro, 55, 60, 63, 65, 70,
71–6, 82, 99, 144
Rioja, 78–9
Roberts, Charles, 78, 100, 103, 104,
105, 147
Robuchon, Eugenio, 80, 83
Rocca, Benjamin Saldana, 80; his son,
81, 84
Rodriguez, Aurelio, 98
Roger Casement (W.B. Yeats), 136
Room 40 OB, 115, 119
Rothenstein, Sir John, 93
Rothenstein, William, 93
Royal Anthropological Institute, 74
Royal Commission on the Civil Service,
107; report of, 107–8
Royal Irish Constabulary, 126, 128
Royal Niger Company, *see* National
African Company
Rubber, *see* sernambi
Ryan, Father F.M., 126

St Anne's, Stanley (Anglican Church),
19
St Asaph, 18
St Helena, 110
St James's Club, 53
St Mary's, Rhyl (Roman Catholic
Church), 18
St Paul de Loanda, 34, 35
Sanchez, Ramon, 101
Sanford, 'General' Henry Shelton, and
expedition, 5, 21, 22, 23, 35
Santo Amaro, 63
Santo Antonio, 67
Santos, 54–63, 66, 70, 74, 76, 99; C.'s

annual consular report from, 61, 69
São Paulo, 56, 58, 59, 60, 70
Savoy, The (Denham,
  Buckinghamshire), 50–1, 110, 112
Scotland Yard, 126, 130, 132, 137, 139
Scottish Nationalism, 51
Select Committee, House of Commons,
  on Putumayo, see Putumayo
  Territory (river basin)
sernambi (type of rubber), 77
Serrano, David, 102
Shanahan, Dr Michael, 125
Shan Van Vocht, 'The Poor Old
  Woman' (Ireland), 52
Shaw, Charlotte, 129
Shaw, George Bernard, 129, 130–2,
  135
Sheppard, 39
Shorter, Clement, 140
Sikhs, 12, 13
Singleton-Gates, Peter, 140
Sinn Fein, 13, 43, 45, 49, 62, 111
Sjöblom, Reverend E., 39
Slavery, 28–9, 35, 36, 40, 56, 69,
  77–82, 85, 88–9, 91, 95–6, 103,
  105–7
Slave Trade Acts, 106, 108
Smith, Sir Frederick Edwin,
  Attorney-General, 51, 97, 128, 131,
  132, 133, 134, 141
social problems of consuls, 53–4; see
  also Consular Service
Society of Friends, 43
Soldan, Dr Paz, 92
Some Recollections of an Irish R.M.
  (Somerville and Ross), 63
Somerset House, 103
Somerset, Lieutenant-General Fitzroy,
  11
Sotheby's, 51
South Africa, 34, 35, 37, 109, 144
South African War, 25, 34–5, 64, 83,
  111, 121
South America, 48, 50, 55, 71, 76, 81,
  85, 98, 103, 104
Southampton, 86
Spain, 93
Sperling, Rowland, 57, 58, 83
Sphere, The, 140
Spicer, Gerald, 87, 94, 95, 101, 102
spiritualism, 15
Stack, Austin, 125

Stanley Pool, 23
Stanley, Sir Henry Morton, 20, 22, 39
Stapleton-Bretherton, Evelyn, see
  Blücher, Countess (later Princess)
Story of the Congo Free State, The
  (Henry Wellington Wack), 40
suicidal intent and attempts of C., see
  Casement, Roger David
Sullivan, Alexander Martin, 129, 130,
  132, 133, 134, 141
Survival International, 107

Taft, William Howard, President, 99
Tambopata Rubber Syndicate, 94
Tara, 46, 82
Teneriffe, 110
Thomson, Sir Basil, 126, 136, 137, 138,
  139, 140, 141
Thornton, Thomas, 56–7
Thorogood, Horace, 84
Timanis, 27
Times, The, 94, 105, 124
Tizon, Juan, 88, 92, 93, 96
Tocantins river, 67
Tone, Wolfe, 48
Tower of London, 44, 126, 140; C.'s
  accommodation within, 127–8
Tralee, 125
Transvaal, 30, 32, 34
Treaty, Anglo-Irish (1921), 42
'Treaty', Irish-German (1914), devised
  by C., 117, 134
Truth (magazine), 69, 82, 83, 84, 89,
  100
Truth about the Civilisation in
  Congoland, The ('A Belgian'), 39
Tupi-Guarani language, 69, 91
typhus, 92, 112

U-19 submarine, 125, 129
U-20 submarine, 125
Uganda, 29, 30
Uitlanders, 34
Ulster, 42, 43, 49, 55, 63, 70, 111, 112,
  113, 122, 133, 142; Volunteer Force,
  113, 114, 133
Ulster and Ireland (Roger David
  Casement), 114
ultra-violet ray machine, 137, 140
Underwood, Vice-Consul, 41
United States of America, 36, 40, 81–2,
  85, 94, 99, 100, 105, 114, 115, 122,

124, 132, 136, 141, 143
Unionism, 43, 44, 46, 50, 118
United Irishman, 13
United Nations, 147; Economic and
Social Council, 147
Urofia, King of the Inokun people, 26

Valcarcel, Judge, 96, 98
Vatan, M., acting French consular
agent, 88, 92
Vatican, 118
Vega, John B., 79
Victoria (Brazil), 73, 75, 86

Wack, Henry Wellington, 40
Walcott, Captain, 141
Wall, T.A., 25
Wallace, Edgar, 36
Walrond Committee, 60, 107
Ward, The Hon. Emily, 6, 7
Ward, Herbert, 23, 142
Ward, Rodney Sanford (formerly
Roger Casement Ward), 142
War Office, 83
Warrenpoint, 139
Washington, 81, 99, 115, 117, 118,
141
Waugh, Joseph, 60
Wedel, Count George von, 117

Weekly Freeman, 19
Wedgwood, Josiah, 82
Weisbach, Captain Raimund, 129
Westminster Abbey, 100
Westminster, Roman Catholic
Archbishop of, *see* Bourne, Francis
Alphonsus
Wethli, Felix, 51
Whiffen, Captain Thomas, 83, 84, 89
Whitehouse, John Howard, 141
Who's Who, 141–2; *Who Was Who*,
141–2
Widdin, 13–14
William of Orange, Prince, 5
Wilton, Lady, 37

Yeats, William Butler, 11, 45, 52, 136
Yerbury, Major, 12
Youle, Vice-Consul, 73
Youngs of Galgorm Castle, 43;
Charlotte, 43; Rose, 42, 43
Yurumaguas (launch), 87

Zaire, *see* Congo
Zimmermann, Count Artur von, 117;
telegram, 141
Zossen, 124
Zumaeta, Pablo, 79, 92, 98, 99